ANSWERING THE OBJECTIONS OF Atheists, Agnostics, & Skeptics

RON RHODES

HARVEST HOUSE PUBLISHERS

EUGENE, OREGON

Cover by Terry Dugan Design, Minneapolis, Minnesota

Cover Photos © DBIMAGE / Brand X Pictures / Getty Images; Imagine That / Alamy; JupiterImages / Comstock

ANSWERING THE OBJECTIONS OF ATHEISTS, AGNOSTICS, AND SKEPTICS

Copyright © 2006 by Ron Rhodes
Published by Harvest House Publishers
Eugene, Oregon 97402
www.harvesthousepublishers.com

Library of Congress Cataloging-in-Publication Data

Rhodes, Ron.
 Answering the objections of atheists, agnostics, and skeptics / Ron Rhodes
    p. cm.
 Includes bibliographical references.
 ISBN-13: 978-0-7369-1288-4 (pbk.)
 ISBN-10: 0-7369-1288-6
 1. Apologetics. 2. Atheism. 3. Agnosticism. 4. Skepticism. I. Title.
 BT1212.R46 2006
 239'.7—dc22   2005019226

Printed in the United States of America

06 07 08 09 10 11 12 13 14 / DP-MS / 10 9 8 7 6 5 4 3 2

For David and Kylie

ACKNOWLEDGMENTS

This book is the result of countless hours of research and study. It would have been impossible to complete without the unending support of my wife, Kerri, and my two children, David and Kylie. I never tire of thanking them.

I do not know how many thousands of e-mails I have received over the past decade, but the number is substantial—and a good number of them have been from Christians asking for help on answering various objections or arguments raised by atheists, agnostics, and skeptics. This extended process of interacting with people on hard issues via e-mail has, I believe, helped prepare me to write the present volume. To each of you, I offer thanks!

I have also received a healthy share of e-mails from atheists, agnostics, and skeptics. Some wrote merely to belittle my Christian beliefs. Others wrote in an attempt to bait me into an argument, which, from the tone of the e-mails, they seemed quite sure they would win. Still others wrote because they were sincerely seeking after the truth. It is this latter group that I enjoyed interacting with the most. To each of you, I offer not only my thanks for your willingness to listen, but also my prayers, with the hope that our exchange of ideas caused a change in your heart regarding belief in God. I hope to see each of you in heaven one day.

CONTENTS

WHAT YOU
BELIEVE MATTERS

I still wince in pain when I think about it. My back went out right around the turn of the new millennium, and I experienced pain as I have never experienced it before. We are talking *apocalyptic* pain—a "great tribulation" pain right in my lower back.

What an absolute horror it was! I was in my house in Southern California. Suddenly, without warning, I was flat on my back. Every movement hurt. Meanwhile, my wife and two children were in Texas, visiting relatives. Fortunately, I had my cell phone with me and was able to contact my wife. Up until the time she arrived back in California to help me, members of my church, who had keys to my house, brought me meals and served me in bed. I felt utterly helpless and dependent, but I knew God was in charge. I had to keep reminding myself of this as I remained unable to walk for the next two months.

Aside from taking an arsenal of medications, my doctor—toward the end of the two-month period—put me into 12 sessions of physical therapy. By this time, I was barely able to walk—and only then by leaning against the wall with my hands.

It turned out that my physical therapist was an atheist who had just read Lee Strobel's excellent book *The Case for Christ*. Though my therapist said the book was well written and had many good arguments, it was not quite enough to persuade him. At the time, Lee was a member of my church. In fact, I had met Lee for lunch just a short time prior to my back going out. After my first therapy session, I e-mailed Lee to let him know about my atheistic therapist. He wrote back, saying, "Sounds like you have a kingdom assignment."

Lee, of course, was right. I do not believe it was an accident that I was paired with an atheistic physical therapist. God was providentially behind what happened. During each of the physical therapy sessions that followed, I took every opportunity to provide further substantive evidence for Christianity. By the time the 12 sessions were complete, my therapist was open to the reality of God, started attending church, and agreed to read a number of my books. Lee planted the seed; I watered it. Together, we answered the objections of this resistant atheist. Many of the arguments I used in dialogues with this atheist are found in the book you are holding in your hands.

By the way, my back is much better these days, though it still flares up from time to time. As I look back in hindsight, the entire episode reminds me of another book I recently wrote, entitled *Why Do Bad Things Happen If God Is Good?* I am convinced that our good God allowed this bad thing to happen to me so that the objections of an atheist could be answered. I remember telling him, with a smile on my face, "God must care a lot about you! Why else would He have gone to such drastic measures to arrange twelve meetings between us?"

WHY IT MATTERS

I cannot think of a more crucial component of our belief system than the question as to whether or not God exists. Whether a person believes he was specially created by God or was just a cosmic accident that evolved out of primordial slime in primeval times will play a large role in molding who he is for the rest of his life. Whether or not a person believes in God will certainly have a profound impact on his sense of morality, and will influence the way he views and treats other people. In short, whether or not a person believes in God will affect his entire worldview and philosophy of life.

Let us go a bit further with this line of thought. If there is no God who created us, and we are just the chance product of evolutionary processes, as atheists believe, then there is no genuine uniqueness for humanity. We are no more important than a barnyard animal. There is no God to whom we are responsible, and no divine commandments to obey. All this talk about "sin" and "repentance" is just a lot of hot air. There is no need for a Savior and no need to "trust in Christ." Man is the master of his own destiny. He is his own god. Ethical principles are determined in accordance with humanistic goals and a relativistic view of truth.

In this scenario, there can be no ultimate purpose to life or living. Man is adrift in a purposeless universe. This life is all there is, with no afterlife to look forward to. There will be no future judgment. As Cornell biologist William Provine put it, there is "no life after death; no ultimate foundation for ethics; no ultimate meaning for life."[1] Whatever meaning and purpose exists for atheists is something they must manufacture for themselves. Ultimately, one's destiny is to be buried in the ground and that is the end of it.

Certainly belief or disbelief in God can have a dramatic influence on the decisions one makes, and the positions one takes on various social issues. Christian philosopher William Lane Craig explains:

> Beliefs about God often influence positions on important and controversial issues, such as sexual behavior, abortion, medical research using stem cells, and, of course, prayer in public schools and government support for religious schools and charities. Many decisions in daily life—not just on Sunday—also depend on belief or disbelief in God. Social action has often been motivated by belief in God. Friendships, communities, and political alliances frequently form or break down because of common or conflicting beliefs about God.[2]

Moreover, as Christian apologists Norman Geisler and Frank Turek note, whether or not God exists will cause one to come up with radically different answers on the ultimate questions of life:

Origin: Where did we come from?

Identity: Who are we?

Meaning: Why are we here?

Morality: How should we live?

Destiny: Where are we going?[3]

Consider the different answers that come from atheists and Christians in response to these questions:

	Atheist	Christian
Origin	Evolution	Created by God
Identity	A random accident from chance mutations	Purposefully created in the image of God
Meaning	Self-made	Serve and follow God
Morality	Whatever works for you	God's holy law
Destiny	The dust	Eternal life in heaven

In view of such factors, I suggest that it matters a great deal that we *believe rightly in the present lifetime*. Once we pass through death's door, one's eternal destiny is forever sealed. Let us not forget that ideas have consequences: "Good ideas have good consequences, and bad ideas have bad consequences."[4] *What you believe matters!*

IS THERE SUCH A THING AS ABSOLUTE TRUTH?

One cannot discuss the importance of "believing rightly" without addressing contemporary attitudes toward the issue of truth. Today, relativism is rampant. As one thinker put it, "It is the height of presumption to think that one knows the key truth for all people. On the other hand, it is the apex of love to 'allow' others to have their own 'truth.'"[5]

The idea that truth is relative has long been taught to our children in public school curriculums such as "values clarification." This curriculum has sought to help students discover their own values. The idea is that values are not to be imposed from without, such as from Scripture or from parents, but must be discovered within. The underlying assumption is that there are no absolute truths or values. What works *for you* is "true."

The problem is, if all truth is relative, then one person's "truth" is just as good as another person's "truth." This ultimately means that any religion's "truth"—including the religion of atheistic humanism—is as good as Christianity's truth. Any "truth"—including the atheistic "truth" of there being no God—is as good as Christianity's truth that there is a God. The reality is, however, that the claims "there is a God" and "there is no God" cannot *both* be true. If one is absolutely true, the other is absolutely false. There is no third alternative. (This is an illustration of what philosophers call the Law of the Excluded Middle.) As well, one cannot argue that the claims of *theism* (there is one true personal God), *pantheism* ("all is God"), *panentheism* ("all is in god and god is in all"), and *polytheism* (there are many gods) are all true, because they contradict each other. If one of them is true (theism), then the others are necessarily false. (This is an illustration of what philosophers call the Law of Non-contradiction.) Try as you may, you cannot get around these laws. They will relentlessly force you to think logically.

The fact is, there are numerous logical problems in the thinking of atheists. Some atheists in the past, for example, have held to the "principle of empirical verifiability." This principle affirms that a statement is meaningful *only* if it is true by definition (such as 2+2=4) or if it is empirically verifiable (provable by observation). The big problem here is that the principle of empirical verifiability *is itself* not true by definition, nor is it empirically verifiable, and hence it cannot be classified as a meaningful statement.[6]

Others may throw up their hands and resolve that truth just

cannot be known. The problem with this perspective, however, is that *it itself* claims to be a truth that is known, and hence the claim philosophically self-destructs. Logic has a thorny way of thwarting false views about truth. (This will become further evident as we progress through the book.)

Christians, of course, believe in absolute truth. Absolute truth is that which is true for all people, at all times, in all places. If certain things are absolutely true, then certain things are also absolutely false. Two contrary claims cannot be true at the same time. Such claims are mutually exclusive.

It is interesting to observe that all of us—Christians and non-Christians alike—expect our interactions with other people to be characterized by truth, not relativism. If we are sick, we expect the doctor to truthfully tell us what is wrong, and to give us an honest opinion on the right treatment for our ailment. We expect our bankers to handle our money with truth and honesty. We expect pilots to land at the right airport in the right city. We expect our spouses to be true and faithful to us. We expect our president's words to be characterized by truth and integrity, and we get angry at the slightest suspicion of falsehood. We all prefer to be told the truth accurately when we listen to the evening news instead of having it "spun" by people with obvious biases.[7]

Why is it, then, that so many people take a relativistic approach when it comes to religious beliefs? They are not being consistent. This leads me to conclude that many people are *selective relativists,* especially regarding religion. The reason they are selective is that life is easier and more comfortable when one doesn't have to worry about obeying moral absolutes, such as "You shall not commit adultery" (Exodus 20:14). Such absolutes, they say, take the joy out of living. (More on this later in the book.)

The problem is, the view that all truth is relative is not logically satisfying. One might understand the statement "all truth is relative" to mean that it is an *absolute* truth that all truth is relative. Of course, such a statement is self-defeating, since there are supposedly no absolute truths, and is therefore false. Second, one could understand this as saying that it is a *relative* truth that all truth is relative. But such a statement is ultimately meaningless.

Christianity, by contrast, rests on a *foundation* of absolute truth (1 Kings 17:24; Psalm 25:5; 43:3; 100:5; 119:30; John 1:17; 8:44; 14:17; 17:17; 2 Corinthians 6:7; Ephesians 4:15; 6:14; 2 Timothy 2:15; 1 John 3:19; 3 John 4,8). This absolute truth clearly delineates for us moral North and South. By contrast, in moral relativism, there is no means of telling which way is North and which way is South when it comes to right and wrong. As people accelerate down the road where moral relativity takes us, there is no absolute truth, no center stripe down the highway of life. There are many casualties along this highway.

Christians believe that absolute morals are grounded in the absolutely moral God of the Bible. Scripture tells us, "Be perfect, therefore, holy as the Father in heaven is perfect" (Matthew 5:48). Moral law flows from the moral Lawgiver of the universe. God stands against the moral relativist whose behavior is based on "whatever is right in his own eyes" (Deuteronomy 12:8 NASB; Judges 17:6; 21:25; Proverbs 21:2).

Of course, claiming that there are absolute truths is a risky business today. After all, we live in an age of tolerance. One risks being accused of *in*tolerance if one should say anything negative about someone else's beliefs. The apostle Paul once asked, "Have I now become your enemy by telling you the truth?" (Galatians 4:16). Speaking the truth can get you in trouble!

More often than not, however, those making accusations of intolerance are the *true* intolerant ones in our midst. They claim to be tolerant of the beliefs of all people, but they are unbendingly intolerant of Christians who believe in God and who love Jesus. As one thinker recently put it, "The fundamentalism of tolerance is just as dogmatic as any other fundamentalism, only it is deceptive in its profession of tolerance....It may actually prove to be less tolerant, since it does not seem to recognize the right of others to reject its relativistic view."[8]

THE APOLOGETIC CHALLENGE

The word *apologetics* comes from the Greek word *apologia,* which means "defense." Apologetics focuses on the defense of Christianity. There are many positive benefits of apologetics:

- Apologetics provides well-reasoned evidences to the atheist, agnostic, and skeptic as to why he ought to choose Christianity rather than remain in unbelief.

- Apologetics can remove the mental roadblocks that prevent atheists and nonbelievers from responding to the gospel.

- Apologetics can be used to show the unbeliever that all the other options in the smorgasbord of world religions are not really options at all, since they are false.

- Apologetics provides not only a defense for the faith, it also provides security to Christians who need to be sure their faith is not a blind leap into a dark chasm, but rather, faith founded on fact.

- Apologetics does not *replace* our faith, it *grounds* our faith.

- Apologetics demonstrates *why* we believe *what* we believe.

God calls each of us to "contend earnestly for the faith which was once for all handed down to the saints" (Jude 3 NASB). We are called to contend for the faith by *telling it like it is.* We are to "always be prepared to give an answer to everyone who asks you to give the reason for the hope that you have. But do this with gentleness and respect" (1 Peter 3:15). We must become equipped with apologetic answers so that when an opportunity arises, we will have an arsenal of information that can be used to intelligently defend Christianity. It is my hope and prayer that this book will serve to beef up your apologetic arsenal so that you will be equipped to speak about Christianity to atheists, agnostics, and skeptics. In short, my goal is to help you succeed if God gives you a kingdom assignment.

1

UNDERSTANDING ATHEISM, AGNOSTICISM, AND SKEPTICISM

There have been quite a number of famous atheists throughout history. These include such luminaries as English poets Percy Shelley and Lord Byron, French philosophers Voltaire and Jean-Paul Sartre, German philosophers Karl Marx and Friedrich Nietzsche, Austrian psychoanalyst Sigmund Freud, and American writers Mark Twain and Upton Sinclair.[1] Many other people, in turn, have become atheists as a result of the influence of such luminaries.

Atheism received a significant shot in the arm during the eighteenth-century Enlightenment. During this time, a thoroughly secularized worldview emerged. Empirical knowledge (knowledge that comes only through the five senses), reason, and the scientific method became the *modus operandi* of the day. There developed a widespread faith in rationality. Many people came to believe in and trust only that which could be tested and studied. Eventually this methodology was applied to religious matters, including the foundational issue of God's existence. Many concluded that the evidence for a divine Creator-God was insufficient, and hence many became skeptics and atheists. Many of those who did not become skeptics or atheists became deists, embracing the idea that God initially created the world but has since been uninvolved in it.

Atheists have always constituted a relatively small percentage of the population. In 1994, 240 million people worldwide claimed to be atheists. That is roughly four percent of the world's population. A recent Gallup poll indicates that less than two-fifths of one percent of Americans (a little over 900,000) say, or were willing to admit to pollsters, that they are atheists.[2] Agnosticism, the view that one cannot be certain about the existence of God, is more widespread, comprising about 16 percent of the world's population.

As of this writing (2005), a number of respected scholars have suggested that atheism is on the decline. In March 2005, noted theologian Wolfhart Pannenberg told United Press International that "atheism as a theoretical position is in decline worldwide." Oxford scholar Alister McGrath agrees, suggesting that atheism's "future seems increasingly to lie in the private beliefs of individuals rather than in the great public domain it once regarded as its habitat." The Reverend Paul M. Zulehner, dean of Vienna University's divinity school, commented that "true atheists in Europe have become an infinitesimally small group. There are not enough of them to be used for sociological research."[3]

One reason suggested for the decline of atheism is that modern science seems to be pointing away from atheism. Professor Antony Flew is cited as one example of a long-time atheist who has now come to believe in the existence of a deistic God as a result of evidence from the intelligent design movement.[4] (We will examine intelligent design in detail in chapter 6.)

For now, my goal is simply to define atheism and differentiate it from agnosticism and skepticism. I think you will come to agree with me that the three are quite closely related.

WHAT IS ATHEISM?

The word *atheism* comes from two Greek words: the prefix *a*, meaning "no" or "without," and *theos*, meaning "God" or "deity." An atheist is a person who does not believe in God or any deity.

I find it interesting that the term *atheism* was once used among the Greeks and Romans in regard to Christians, who denied the gods of pagan religions. It was only much later that the term *atheist* came to be used in regard to a denial of the personal Creator-God of the Christian Bible.[5] As scholar Michael Martin said, "In Western society the term atheism has been used more narrowly to refer to the denial of theism, in particular Judeo-Christian theism, which asserts the existence of an all-powerful, all-knowing, all-good personal being."[6]

There have been various kinds of atheists throughout history. Some have argued that the idea of God is mythological, and there is no need for such mythology in modern times. Others say there once was a God but He died. Others have argued that because of the finitude and limitations of "God-talk" (that is, language about God), we really cannot know anything about such a being. Still others come right out and dogmatically assert that there never has been and never will be a God.[7]

Some atheists argue that atheism is the default position of all human beings. David Eller, in his book *Natural Atheism*, wrote:

I was born an atheist. All humans are born atheists. No baby born into the world arrives with specific religious beliefs or knowledge. Such beliefs and knowledge must be acquired, which means that they must first exist before and apart from the new life and that they must be presented to and impressed on the new suggestible mind—one that has no critical apparatus and no alternative views of its own. Human infants are like sponges, soaking up (not completely uncritically, but eagerly and effectively) whatever is there to be soaked up from their social environment. Small children in particular instinctively imitate the models that they observe in their childhood, but I was not compelled to attend or practice any particular religion, and as I grew I never saw any reason to "convert" to any particular religion. I have thus been an atheist all my life. I am a natural atheist.[8]

Eller is aware that Christian critics challenge the idea that one can be a "natural atheist." He says his critics

claim that atheism requires an active rejection of religious belief, which cannot occur without prior exposure or even commitment to religion. So, a newborn is not yet an "atheist" but something other than atheist or theist, they maintain—a "pre-theist" maybe. Atheism must be a choice. I see this argument as spurious and actually negatively motivated. Theists do not want to admit that they were once atheists too and that they gave it up not by any choice they made but by the forces imposed on them by a religious world.[9]

Reacting against the claim by Christian apologists that atheism itself constitutes a religious belief, prominent atheist George Smith argues that atheism, in its most basic form, is not a belief, but rather is the *absence* of a belief.[10] Atheism is said to be "no more a religion than bald is a hair color or health is a disease."[11] "The definition for atheism that we use, put simply, says that atheism is the lack of a god-belief, the absence of theism, to whatever degree and for whatever reason."[12]

The problem with this line of argumentation, Christian theists point out, is that once you say "I lack a belief in God," you have in fact affirmed a religious "belief." Further, this line of argumentation fails to recognize that atheism is in fact a faith system. After all, atheists cannot offer definitive proofs that God does not exist, and hence there must be an element of faith in their viewpoint. The late science fiction writer Isaac Asimov, one of the more prominent signers of the Humanist Manifesto II, was being intellectually honest when he stated, "Emotionally I am an atheist. I don't have the evidence to prove that God doesn't exist, but I so strongly suspect he doesn't that I don't want to waste my time."[13] The lack of evidence to prove God does not exist—to merely suspect that God does not exist—is a position that quite obviously involves a level of faith. Atheism is a *faith system*.

TYPICAL ATHEISTIC BELIEFS

Atheism Is Man-centered. The American Atheists creed affirms:

> An atheist loves himself and his fellow man instead of a god. An atheist accepts that heaven is something for which we should work now—here on earth—for all men together to enjoy. An atheist accepts that he can get no help through prayer, but that he must find

in himself the inner conviction and strength to meet life, to grapple with it, to subdue it and to enjoy it. An atheist accepts that only in a knowledge of himself and a knowledge of his fellow man can he find the understanding that will help to a life of fulfillment.[14]

Atheism Denies the Existence of God. God did not create human beings. Rather, human beings created God. God is a myth. While Christians argue that all things need a cause, and therefore the universe must have been caused by God, one must logically proceed to ask, "Who caused God?" While Christians point to the entire Bible as a revelation from God, atheists claim that the God of Old Testament "revelation" is vicious and cruel, ordering His people to murder women and children. While Christians argue for the love of God, the Bible portrays God as sending people to hell to suffer for all eternity. In view of such problems, it is more reasonable, atheists say, to believe that God does not exist.

Atheism Affirms that the Universe Is Eternal. God is not the creator of the universe. The universe can be explained in terms of the philosophy of naturalism. The universe is eternal. The late famous scientist Carl Sagan, in his popular PBS television show *Cosmos,* said that "the cosmos is all that is or ever was or ever will be."[15] More than one scholar has noted that Sagan's comment seems to be a purposeful substitution for the *Gloria Patri:* "Glory be to the Father and to the Son and to the Holy Ghost. As it was in the beginning, is now, and ever shall be, world without end." Of course, Sagan did not believe in the existence of God or a Creator. To him, the universe is infinitely old and self-existing. The universe alone gave birth to life on this planet. We are literally children of the cosmos.[16]

Atheism Espouses Human Evolution. We need not appeal to the existence of a Creator-God to account for human beings. Rather, human beings evolved via Darwinistic natural selection. "Once we accept the theory of evolution by natural selection, the traditional idea of God really does go out of the window."[17] We are told that "living creatures on earth are a direct product of the earth. There is every reason to believe that living things owe their origin entirely to certain physical and chemical properties of the ancient earth." Indeed, "nothing supernatural appeared to be involved—only time and natural physical and chemical laws operating within the peculiarly suitable environment."[18]

Atheism Affirms the Reality of Evil. Evil truly exists, and it constitutes a powerful argument against the existence of God. As scholar Alvin Plantinga stated, "Many believe that the existence of evil (or at least the amount and kinds of evil we actually find) makes belief in God unreasonable or rationally unacceptable."[19] Theologians William Hamilton and Thomas Altizer have flat-out concluded that God is dead. British empiricist David Hume asked in regard to God, "Is he willing to prevent evil, but not able? Then he is impotent. Is he able, but not willing? Then he is malevolent. Is he both able and willing: whence then is evil?"[20] If there *is* a God—and He is all-good and all-powerful—then, atheists argue, such atrocities as Hitler's murder of six million Jews should never have happened. It is more reasonable to conclude that such evil disproves the existence of God.

Atheism Denies an Afterlife. Human beings do not have an immortal soul. Most atheists consider humans to be strictly material beings. "There is no mind apart from brain. Nor is there a soul independent of body."[21] Hence, when a human dies, that is the end of him.

Atheism Denies Moral Absolutes. Ethical guidelines emerge in human societies by trial and error—much in the way traffic laws emerged after the invention of the car. "Right" actions are those that bring the greatest good in the long run.[22] Changing situations bring about the need for new or adjusted ethical guidelines.

Atheism Is Anti-religion. Atheists can be quite vitriolic in their condemnation of organized religion. Scholar Alister McGrath comments, "What propels people toward atheism is above all a sense of revulsion against the excesses and failures of organized religion. Atheism is ultimately a worldview of fear—a fear, often merited, of what might happen if religious maniacs were to take over the world."[23]

WHAT IS AGNOSTICISM?

The word *agnosticism* comes from two Greek words: *a,* meaning "no" or "without," and *gnosis,* meaning "knowledge." Agnosticism literally means "no knowledge" or "without knowledge." More specifically, an agnostic is a person who claims he is unsure (having "no knowledge") about the existence of God. One scholar suggests that an agnostic is "a person who believes that something is inherently unknowable by the human mind. When applied to the sphere of theistic belief, an agnostic is one who maintains that some aspect of the supernatural is forever closed to human knowledge."[24]

There are two forms of agnosticism. "Soft agnosticism," also called "weak agnosticism," says we *do not* know if God exists. "Hard agnosticism," also called "strong agnosticism," says we *cannot* know if God exists.[25] Soft agnosticism says the existence and nature of God are not known, while hard agnosticism says that God is unknowable, that He cannot be known.[26]

Logically, agnosticism is a self-defeating belief system. To say "one cannot know about reality" is a statement that presumes knowledge about reality. Hence, the statement is self-falsifying. The statement amounts to saying, "One knows enough about reality to affirm that nothing can be known about reality."[27] One must *possess* knowledge of reality in order to *deny* knowledge of reality. As Christian scholar J. Budziszewski put it, "To say that we cannot know anything about God is to say something about God; it is to say that if there is a God, he is unknowable. But in that case, he is not entirely unknowable, for the agnostic certainly thinks that we can know one thing about him: That nothing else can be known about him."[28] In the end, then, agnosticism is an illogical position to hold to.

WHAT IS SKEPTICISM?

The word *skepticism* comes from the Latin word *scepticus,* which means "inquiring," "reflective," or "doubting." This Latin word, in turn, comes from the Greek word *scepsis,* which means "inquiry," "hesitation," or "doubt."[29] A skeptic is a person who is tentative in his or her beliefs, neither denying nor affirming God's existence. He or she is hesitant, doubtful, and unsure as to whether there is a God. Even if there is a God, a skeptic is unsure as to whether a person can really know Him.

An obvious philosophical problem with this viewpoint is that the skeptic is certainly not skeptical that his worldview of skepticism is correct. He is certainly not doubtful that his worldview of doubt is correct. In fact, the skeptic is quite sure that his viewpoint must be correct.

FREEDOM AND RESPONSIBILITY

Every American is guaranteed the free exercise of religion. This right is one of the things that makes America so great. The First Amendment, ratified in 1791, affirmed that "Congress shall make no law respecting an establishment of religion or prohibiting the free exercise thereof."[30]

In keeping with this, James Madison, the fourth president of the United States (1809–17), wrote, "The religion...of every man must be left to the conviction and conscience of every man....We maintain, therefore, that in matters of religion no man's right is [to be] abridged by the institution of civil society."[31] Such religious freedom is cherished by every American.

U.S. Supreme Court Justice Hugo Black expressed the majority opinion of the court in saying that the "establishment of religion" clause of the First Amendment includes the fact that neither a state nor the federal government "can force nor influence a person to go to or remain away from church against his will or force him to profess a belief or disbelief in any religion." As well, "No person can be punished for entertaining or professing religious beliefs or disbeliefs, for church attendance or nonattendance."[32]

What this means for atheists, agnostics, and skeptics is that they have the full support of the U.S. Constitution to believe as they do. Human judges at the highest court in the land say they are safe. A person cannot be forced to attend a church or to profess belief in any religion.

My greater concern is with the divine Judge who, understandably, is much less sympathetic to the cause of atheism. Indeed, the one who denies God's existence is labeled a "fool" (Psalm 14:1; 53:1). The Hebrew word for "fool," *nabal*, literally means "stupid," "wicked (especially impious)," and "vile person." Interestingly, Psalm 14:1 ties atheism to immoral behavior: "The fool says in his heart, 'There is no God.' They are corrupt, their deeds are vile; there is no one who does good." Theologian Charles Ryrie thus comments that the fool "is described as to his belief (*no God*) and behavior (*no one...good*)."[33]

This highlights a point we will examine later in the book—that is, many people become atheists because doing so relieves them from having to pay attention to the moral commandments made by a holy God. The problem is, though human beings are absolutely free to believe as they wish during their short mortal lives, *all* will face God at a future judgment, and *all* will be held responsible. Those who enter eternity without Christ will spend eternity apart from Christ. That is why I have a sense of urgency in my heart in seeking to answer the objections of atheists, agnostics, and skeptics.

ANSWERING THE OBJECTIONS OF ATHEISTS, AGNOSTICS, AND SKEPTICS

We have seen that atheists believe there is no God; agnostics claim to be unsure about the existence of God; skeptics neither deny nor affirm God's existence but express great doubt. Practically speaking, many of the arguments raised by these three groups are similar if not entirely the same. It therefore makes great sense to deal with their primary objections collectively in a single book.

This book is divided into topical chapters. In each, I list common objections raised by atheists, agnostics, and skeptics, and then provide answers to each of these objections. This question-answer format makes it easy for you to obtain the information you are looking for.

Because of space limitations, I had to be selective regarding which objections to answer. Based on many years of experience in dealing with atheists, agnostics, and skeptics, I chose those topics most likely to surface in the course of a typical dialogue. The bibliography at the end of the book lists recommended resources that will further benefit you.

2

WHY ISN'T
THE EVIDENCE
OVERTLY CLEAR?

During my first year in college, I befriended a young college student named Hal. He was very personable, very talkative, and very rational. He was also a hardcore atheist.

I was a young Christian at the time, and I admit that my apologetic skills were minimal at best. I remember that the primary objection Hal raised against belief in God was that there was no overt evidence that He was really there. Surely if God existed, He would provide abundantly clear evidence for it. But there is none. Hence, God must not exist. Hal could not understand why I, a college student seeking higher learning, would do something so foolish as to believe in a God that had not overtly proved His existence. He thought my faith was groundless.

I did not do a good job of defending Christianity that year. I wish I had known then what I know now. If there is any good that came out of that experience, it is that God used it to build a hunger in my heart for stronger apologetic answers.

In this chapter, we will consider objections that relate to the evidence for God's existence.

Objection: God does not exist. Some atheists categorically state that there is no God, and all atheists, by definition, believe it.

Answering the Objection: From a logical standpoint, this assertion is indefensible. A person would have to be omniscient and omnipresent to be able to say from his or her own pool of knowledge that there is no God. Only someone who is capable of being in all places at the same time—with a perfect knowledge of all that is in the universe—can make such a statement based on the facts. Christian apologists Bob and Gretchen Passantino put it this way:

> In order to prove with complete certainty that there are no white crows anywhere in the universe, we would have to search every portion of the universe thoroughly and simultaneously (in case the white one flies away as we approach). By analogy, to prove with complete certainty that God does not exist would require virtually infinite knowledge of the material world and the immaterial world and anything hypothetically "beyond" both states of existence.[1]

In like manner, Ravi Zacharias observes that in "postulating the nonexistence of God, atheism immediately commits the blunder of an absolute negation, which is self-contradictory. For, to sustain the belief that there is no God, it has to demonstrate infinite knowledge, which is tantamount to saying, 'I have infinite knowledge that there is no being in existence with infinite knowledge.'"[2] To put it another way, a person would have to *be* God in order to *say* there is no God.

Robert Morey suggests this point can be forcefully made by asking the atheist if he has ever visited the Library of Congress in Washington, D.C. Mention that the library presently contains over 70 million items—books, magazines, journals, and so forth. Point out that hundreds of thousands of these were written by scholars and specialists in the various academic fields. Then ask, "What percentage of the collective knowledge recorded in the volumes in this library would you say is within your own pool of knowledge and experience?" The atheist will likely respond, "I don't know. I guess a fraction of one percent." You can then ask, "Do you think it is logically possible that God may exist in the 99.9 percent that is outside your pool of knowledge and experience?" Even if the atheist refuses to admit the possibility, Morey says, you have made your point.[3]

Some atheists have wised up and recognized there is no way to prove God does not exist from their own pool of knowledge. Hence, some now refrain from arguing *against* the existence of God. They have turned the tables and hold that the burden of proof is on Christians to prove that God *does* exist. Atheist George Smith thus writes, "When the atheist is seen as a person who lacks belief in a god, it becomes clear that he is not obligated to 'prove' anything."[4] Of course, the fatal flaw with this line of argumentation is that once you say "I lack a belief in God," you have in fact *affirmed* a religious "belief," and are therefore now required to prove it.

Objection: Belief in God ought to be rejected because it is based on faith, not reason. Atheists will not accept the existence of God, or any doctrine, on faith because they reject faith as "a valid cognitive procedure."[5]

Answering the Objection: What atheists often seem to forget is that virtually any worldview requires a certain amount of faith. Humanist and atheist Carl Sagan is a good example of this point. As I noted earlier, Sagan, at the beginning of his famous TV show *Cosmos*, commented, "The cosmos is all that is or ever was or ever will be." The problem is, Sagan is a finite being with limited knowledge, and he is confined to being in one place at a time (he is not omnipresent). How can he make a sweeping, all-encompassing statement such as "the cosmos is all that is or ever was or ever will be"? My friends Norman Geisler and Frank Turek point out that "Sagan was operating in the realm of probability just like Christians are when they say God exists. The question is, who has more evidence for their conclusion? Which conclusion is more reasonable?"[6] Christians believe atheism requires *more* faith than Christianity does because there is more evidence that Christianity is true. The less evidence one has for a position (such as the atheistic position), the more faith one must muster up to believe it.[7] (Throughout this book, I will provide substantive evidence in favor of Christianity.)

Objection: If there really is a God, why isn't His existence more overtly clear to people? Why doesn't God make it so obvious to everyone that they all immediately repent and turn to Him for salvation? Why doesn't God shower us with "hard proof," such as continuous miracles that attest to His reality?

In voicing this objection, atheists often appeal to the maxim of nineteenth-century scholar W.K. Clifford: "It is wrong always, everywhere, and for everyone, to believe anything upon insufficient evidence."[8] In keeping with this, a modern atheist asserts, "We can remind believers that the theistic position consists entirely of claims, controversial and untestable claims; that the theist is obligated to prove those claims; that the listener (the atheist) is not obligated to prove anything."[9]

Atheists believe the universe is fully explainable in terms of the philosophy of naturalism, which espouses the idea that all phenomena in the universe can be explained wholly in terms of natural causes and laws.[10] They conclude there is no empirical evidence—no "hard proof"—of supernatural intervention by a deity.

Answering the Objection: Empirical observation is a necessity for scientific endeavors. Science would be impossible without it. Empirical observation, however, is not the all-determining factor as to what is real and what is not real.

Reflect for a moment on the movie *Contact,* in which Jodie Foster plays Dr. Ellie Arroway, a radio astronomer seeking to fulfill a lifelong quest to discover life on other worlds. Her rejection of God and atheistic worldview were rooted in the death of her parents, especially the death of her father, when she was young. Throughout the movie, her love interest is religious scholar Palmer Joss, played by Matthew McConaughey.

At a social event, Ellie challenged Joss, "Is there an all-powerful, mysterious God that created the universe, but left us no proof of his existence? Or, is there simply no God, and we created him so we wouldn't feel so alone?"

Joss responded, "Did you love your father?"

Ellie said, "Yes, very much."

"Prove it!" Joss exclaimed. Before Ellie could respond, they were suddenly interrupted and the question was never answered. But the point was made. Empirical observation is not the all-determining factor as to what is real and what is not.

Later in the movie, after radio telescopes picked up signals from deep space, aliens sent blueprints for the construction of a transport machine. Toward the end of the movie, Ellie was chosen to go to wherever this transport machine would take her. She traveled a great distance, being transported through a wormhole, a tunnel through space and time. Completely mesmerized by what she was witnessing, she suddenly found herself on a beach where an alien appeared to her in the likeness of her own father. This was done to make her feel more comfortable. The alien told Ellie that though human beings were not yet ready to join alien civilizations, they had now taken their first small step.

Following this brief encounter, Ellie was quickly transported back to earth via the transport machine. In real time, however, those at mission control and on earth did not perceive that she had gone anywhere. Bottom line: Ellie had no "hard proof" for her experience with the alien being. A member of an international review panel asked her, "Should we take all this on faith?"

Now it was Ellie's turn to explain why it was indeed necessary to have faith:

> I had an experience I can't prove. I can't even explain it, but everything that I know as a human being, everything that I am tells me that it was real. I was part of something wonderful, something that changed me forever, a vision of the universe that tells us undeniably how tiny and insignificant, and how rare and precious we all are. A vision that tells us we belong to something that is greater than ourselves. That we are not—that none of us are alone. I wish I could share that. I wish that everyone, if even for one moment, could feel that awe, and humility, and hope.[11]

Granted, this is just a fictional story, but the point it illustrates is right on target. As this fictional character discovered, philosophers have pointed out that there are plenty of things in the world that are real and are rational to accept but cannot be scientifically proven. The love one has for another human being is just one example. Love is so real that, under certain circumstances, it might motivate a person to give up his very life on behalf of another person. Another example relates to rendering a judgment as to what is beautiful and what is ugly. The scientific method is irrelevant when it comes to aesthetic judgments. Such methodology cannot tell us whether one painting is more beautiful than another.[12] Yet another example involves the character trait of loyalty. This is an intangible but real trait.

I can think of another example: human relationships. Sometimes it is necessary to *believe* in a friend even though there is *no good evidence* as to why one should do so. Clifford's maxim (stated earlier), if applied to human relationships, would render them virtually impossible to maintain.

In view of such factors, the atheist ought to consider the possibility that he has a limited worldview—a worldview that excludes God—because he is utilizing a limited, insufficient methodology. Wrong methodology will *always* yield wrong conclusions.

The basic methodology of atheists is, "I believe only in that which can be observed empirically." Aside from what I have demonstrated earlier (that is, there are plenty of things in the world that are real—things that are rational to accept but cannot be scientifically proven), there is a further fatal flaw in atheistic methodology. The problem is that the statement "I believe only in that which can be observed empirically" is self-defeating because it cannot itself be derived from empirical observation.[13] Hence, this methodology self-destructs before it ever gets off the ground.

As for an atheist's insistence on continual miracles that attest to God's reality (Sagan suggests that throwing a glowing cross up in the sky might do the trick), one must note that it was never God's purpose to provide one attesting miracle after another throughout human history to overtly demonstrate or prove His existence. Rather, God has chosen to manifest His attesting miracles during certain revelatory times in human history. In biblical history, there have been perhaps four primary periods during which miracles were concentrated or clustered. (I realize these miracle accounts are based on the Bible, which atheists reject. I will deal with the reliability of the Bible in chapters 8 and 9.) These miraculous periods took place during the lifetimes of...

- *Moses and Joshua* (including the ten plagues inflicted on Egypt, the crossing of the Red Sea, the provision of manna in the wilderness, and the collapse of the walls of Jericho);

- *Elijah and Elisha* (including the resurrection of a widow's son, curing leprosy, the fire from heaven that consumed Elijah's sacrifice and destroyed the prophets of Baal, the miraculous falling of rain, and the multiplication of 20 loaves of new barley into a supply sufficient for 100 men);

- *Daniel* (including God's miraculous preservation of Shadrach, Meshach, and Abednego in the fiery furnace, and God's preservation of Daniel in the lion's den); and

- *Christ and the apostles* (including mighty healings, the casting out of demons, feeding 5,000 people, walking on water, turning water into wine, calming storms, and resurrecting people from the dead—especially Christ's resurrection *of Himself* from the dead).

These miracles served to authenticate God's prophets and apostles and the messages they brought from God to humankind.

For example, the New Testament reveals that the biblical apostles were all authenticated by miraculous signs. In 2 Corinthians 12:12 Paul affirmed, "The things that mark an apostle—signs, wonders and miracles—were done among you with great perseverance." In Acts 2:43 we read that "everyone was filled with awe, and many wonders and miraculous signs were done by [literally, *through*] the apostles" (insert added, see also Acts 5:12). It would seem clear from such verses that the mark of a true apostle of God was the God-sourced ability to perform signs, wonders, and miracles. The apostle Peter, for example, healed a number of people (Acts 3:16; 9:32-35) and raised a person from the dead (9:36-42). The apostle Paul also raised a person from the dead (20:6-12). These and other works performed by the apostles constitute "signs, wonders, and miracles," and distinguish the apostles from all pretend representatives of God. These miracles served to validate both the apostles and their message. (For an apologetic defense of the possibility of miracles, see chapter 4.)

It's important to observe that in between the historical periods in which miracles were clustered, miracles still occurred occasionally, at a rate much less frequent than during the four concentrated periods. As C.S. Lewis said, "God does not shake miracles into Nature at random as if from a pepper-caster. They come on great occasions: they are found at the great ganglions of history—not of political or social history, but of spiritual history which cannot be fully known by men."[14] It seems to be the case that the miracles occurred most frequently during periods of God's self-revelation to humankind.[15] The miracles that occurred during these periods were irrefutable signs from God designed to authenticate His revealed Word (the Old and New Testaments).[16]

Even as the apostles were aging, it seems that miracles began to taper off in number. There came a time when Paul could not heal Epaphroditus (Philippians 2:25-30) or Timothy (1 Timothy 5:23) or even himself (2 Corinthians 12:7-9). God's time of self-revelation was apparently coming to a close toward the end of the apostles' lives. Pastor Douglas Connelly notes, "The contrast is remarkable! At the beginning of the Book of Acts, multitudes are being healed; at the end of New Testament history, the companions of the apostles have to be left behind because of serious illness."[17]

Here is the point I am driving at: If it is true that even in biblical times there was not one miracle after another in rapid succession proving the existence of God, then certainly to a much greater extent people should not be expecting one miracle after another today.[18] From the divine perspective, overt "hard proof" was *already* provided during revelatory times, and with the reliable recording of this "hard proof" in the pages of the Bible, there is no need for God to continually throw a glowing cross up in the sky to prove His existence.

Objection: People would believe if they had some proof. "We are atheists because...there is no proof of the existence of God."[19]

Answering the Objection: As we noted, God provided overt proof of His existence in the past, and this proof was reliably recorded in Scripture for the benefit of future generations. What is very interesting to observe is that even in the periods of time when miracles were abundant, there were people who still refused to turn to God. For example, during the wilderness wanderings, the Israelites—after having witnessed mighty miracles by God in the land of Egypt—complained and rebelled against God. During the ministry of Jesus, which was permeated by many miracles, there were substantial numbers of people who still refused to turn to Him for salvation. This indicates that some people will not turn to God even if God's miraculous "hard proof" were to punch them in the nose on a daily basis. Such is the hardness of some people's hearts.

I believe God has a reason for not continually knocking us over the head with continuous miracles directly from heaven. One reason may be that God, in His sovereign plan, has chosen to work *through* human beings in an intermediary or representative fashion. In support of this, the Genesis account tells us that God created human beings in the image of God. The ancient Hebrew word for "image" was used in ancient times in a very interesting context. Whenever a king conquered a new territory, he would set up an image of himself in that territory to represent his sovereignty over it. When God created human beings, He created them in His "image" and then commanded them, "Fill the earth and *subdue* it. *Rule* over the fish of the sea and the birds of the air and over every living creature that moves on the ground" (Genesis 1:28, emphasis added). In other words, human beings were appointed to be God's vice regents on the earth. They were to *represent* God on earth, taking care of the earth and being good stewards.

Later God chose the Jews to be a "light unto the nations," their appointed task being to share the good news of God with all other people around the world (Isaiah 42:6). The Jews were to be God's *representatives* to the Gentiles. The Jews failed at this task, especially since they did not recognize Jesus as the divine Messiah.

Among the Jews themselves, the priests were called to represent human beings to God and to represent God to human beings (Exodus 30:10). God worked *through* the priests in an intermediary way to maintain His relationship with the Jewish people.

All the while, during Old Testament times, the prophets were on the scene, speaking forth the "Thus saith the Lord" revelations from God (for example, Exodus 4:22). They represented God's revelation to the people. God spoke *through* the prophets. These prophets were authenticated by miraculous signs and wonders.

Still later, Jesus was the perfect representative and revelation of God because He Himself was God in human flesh (John 1:1,14,18). God worked *through* Jesus to reach people.

Also in New Testament times, God continued to communicate His revelations to people *through* the apostles, who were authenticated by the same kinds of miracles as characterized the Old Testament prophets. Today, Christians are called by God to be His representatives in sharing the good news of the gospel with others (Matthew 28:19).

So in accordance with His sovereign plan, God has chosen to work *through* people in making Himself known to people. That is His chosen *modus operandi*. That is the way He normally carries out His business on earth. Granted, we sometimes fail miserably as God's representatives—a fact that shames us all. Nevertheless, throughout history, God has consistently worked *through* people in making Himself known *to* people.

God also continues to speak to us today in an intermediary way through the prophets and apostles inasmuch as their writings, inspired by God, have been preserved for us in the Bible. Through the Bible, God speaks to us today just as He spoke to people in ancient times when those words were first given. The Bible is to be received as God's words to us and revered and obeyed as such. When we submit to the Bible's authority, we place ourselves under the authority of the living God. The Scriptures "are God preaching, God talking, God telling, God instructing, God setting before us the right way to think and speak about him. The Scriptures are God showing us himself: God communicating to us who he is and what he has done so that in the response of faith we may truly know him and live our lives in fellowship with him."[20]

There is yet another possible reason that God does not continually shower humankind with overt supernatural manifestations. Some believe that such continuous interventions would interfere with His overall plan of sifting the true inner character of human beings over a prolonged time. In this line of thinking, each person has been given a stewardship of time on earth, and that person's allotment of time will serve to reveal his or her true nature, as well as reveal whether or not the person will repent and turn to God.

A passage that comes to mind is Revelation 2:20-21, where the sovereign and exalted Jesus in heaven said to the church at Thyatira, "I have this against you: You tolerate that woman Jezebel, who calls herself a prophetess. By her teaching she misleads my servants into sexual immorality and the eating of food sacrificed to idols. *I have given her time to repent of her immorality, but she is unwilling*" (emphasis added). Jesus here speaks of a period of time that has been allotted for this person to repent, to no avail. Had Jesus, or God the Father, suddenly showered miraculous "hard proofs" for His existence on her head, she likely would have externally hidden her true character and temporarily feigned obedience. (Even criminals behave rightly when a police officer is driving by. Lazy employees likewise feign hard work when the boss is walking by.) By allotting this woman a period of time, during which God patiently waited and watched from a distance, God sifted out her true character.

God does this with all of humanity. He gives each person an allotment of time on earth during which He sifts out their true character. If God on a daily basis threw a glowing cross up into the sky, many people would likely feign an obedience that is not genuine. God is interested in our true character. Hence, He watches from a distance, observing what we do in response to His Word and His invitation to salvation—*but only for a time*. Once our allotment of time is up, we must face God and give an account (Psalm 62:12; Matthew 16:27).

Objection: "I do not believe it!"

Answering the Objection: One of the greatest difficulties in dialoguing with atheists is that they often come across as having absolutely made up their minds, and will consider no further evidence on the issue. I like to challenge atheists to be open-minded. In fact, if I am dialoguing with an atheist who is closed to further discussion, I will say, "Before you make up your mind *for good,* allow me to suggest...," and then I provide further evidence on whatever issue we are discussing. The phrase "Before you make up your mind *for good"* is a subtle way of directing his or her thought to the reality that he or she has not finally and definitively made up his or her mind.

Some atheists have *intellectual* objections to Christianity, such as the problem of evil. Other atheists have *emotional* objections to Christianity, such as the hypocrisy they often witness in some Christians. Still other atheists have *volitional* objections to Christianity, primarily relating to their resistance to the moral commandments they would have to obey should they become Christians.[21] I will address each of these kinds of objections in this book. Yet no matter how persuasively we answer these objections, it will all be for naught unless the atheist is open-minded enough to consider the evidence. I therefore urge you to pray fervently for the person with whom you are dialoguing, specifically asking God to open his or her mind to the truth (see Acts 16:14).

3
WHY THERE IS
SOMETHING
RATHER THAN
NOTHING

Why is there *something* rather than *nothing?* Where did it all come from? What got it all started?

When I was a young boy, our family had a slide and a swing set in our hilly backyard in New Jersey. I often hung my legs on the horizontal bars that supported the slide, and as I hung upside-down, I would stare up into the sky and let my imagination run wild. *What would it feel like if there were no gravity and I suddenly fell upward into the sky?* The sky appeared so vast, so deep, and so high up that I imagined it would be an exhilarating experience. *What a magnificent thing the sky is,* I thought to myself.

One year for Christmas, my brothers and I received a big telescope. We set it up in the back lawn that night and aimed it straight at the glowing moon. We had seen pictures of the moon's craters in various school textbooks, but now, for the first time, we saw these craters in great detail through our telescope. We were excited.

We then aimed the telescope at various planets and stars, and were amazed at the vastness of all that we saw. More than once, we stayed up so late that our mother had to issue a rather stern order for us to go to bed. I am quite sure that had she not done that, we would have stayed up all night. We had a blast with that telescope.

It was years later before I began to get a better idea of the grandeur of the universe. Only about 4,000 stars are visible to the human eye without the help of a telescope. The universe's vastness becomes more evident with the help of the giant telescopes now available. Astronomers have statistically estimated that there are about 10^{25} stars (that is, 10 million billion billion stars) in the known universe. Some scientists have claimed that this is approximately the number of grains of sand in the world (I'm not sure how they figured that out). And who knows how many stars exist beyond the reach of our finite telescopes? There is no reason to think that our finite instruments have penetrated the outermost boundaries of interstellar space.

Theologian John MacArthur did some scientific digging and discovered some astonishing facts about the vastness of the universe:

> If you could bore a hole in the sun and somehow put in 1.2 million earths, you would still have room for 4.3 million moons. The sun is 865,000 miles in

diameter and 93 million miles away from earth. Our next nearest star is Alpha Centauri, and it is five times larger than our sun. The moon is only 211,453 miles away, and you could walk to it in twenty-seven years. A ray of light travels at 186,000 miles per second, so a beam of light would reach the moon in only one-and-a-half seconds. If we could travel at that speed, we would reach Venus in two minutes and eighteen seconds because it's only 26 million miles away. After four-and-one-half minutes we would have passed Mercury, which is 50 million miles away. We could travel to Mars in four minutes and twenty-one seconds because it's only 34 million miles away. The next stop would be Jupiter—367 million miles away—and it would take us thirty-five minutes. Saturn is twice as far as Jupiter—790 million miles—and it would take one hour and eleven seconds. Eventually we would pass Uranus, Neptune, and finally Pluto—2.7 billion miles away. Having gotten that far, we still haven't left our solar system, which moves in a multimillion-mile orbit through endless space. The nearest star is ten times further than the boundaries of our solar system—20 billion miles away. The North Star is 400 hundred billion miles away, but that still isn't very far compared with known space. The star called Betelgeuse is 880 quadrillion miles from us and has a diameter of 250 million miles, which is greater than the earth's orbit.[1]

I now return to where I began. Why is there *something* rather than *nothing?* Where did it all come from? What got it all started?

I believe there is something rather than nothing because God Himself brought the universe into being. He is the one who created all the planets, stars, and galaxies in all of their vastness (Genesis 1; Psalm 102:25; John 1:3; Colossians 1:16). Many believe the very existence of this universe constitutes a powerful argument for the existence of God.

This line of argumentation is known as the cosmological argument. Simply put, it says that every effect must have an adequate cause. The universe is an "effect." Reason demands that whatever caused the universe must be greater than the universe. That cause is God, who Himself is the uncaused First Cause. As Hebrews 3:4 says, "Every house is built by someone, but God is the builder of everything."

Objection: The universe is uncaused and is therefore eternal. Some atheists argue that the universe is uncaused and can be adequately explained in terms of natural laws alone.[2]

Answering the Objection: I once saw an interesting pencil sketch that portrayed a pencil-sketched hand coming up out of the pencil sketch, drawing itself into existence. It made a powerful point: *Something* does not come from *nothing*. As both scientists and philosophers agree, "from nothing, nothing comes." Something cannot be derived from absolute nothingness. As Christian scholar Kenneth Richard Samples notes, "To conclude otherwise is to violate one of the foundational principles of the scientific enterprise: causality."[3] It is thus absurd to claim that the universe is uncaused.

In keeping with this, it would likewise be absurd to claim that the universe is *self*-caused. The big problem is that if the universe created itself, it would have had to exist and *not* exist at the same time. As Christian apologist Dan Story explains, "In order for the universe to have caused itself to be, it could not have existed prior to itself. Yet, in order for it to have created itself, it must have had to have already existed. So, on this view, the universe existed and did not exist at the same time."[4]

Let us look at this another way: From a philosophical perspective, in an eternal universe, there would be an infinite series of causes and effects that would never lead to a first cause or starting point. This is known as an infinite regress, which is philosophically impossible. "You can't go on explaining how this finite thing causes this finite thing, which causes this other finite thing, and on and on, because that really just puts off the explanation indefinitely....No matter how many finite causes you line up, eventually you will have one that would be both causing its own existence and be an effect of that cause at the same moment. That is nonsense."[5]

If the universe is not *uncaused*, if it is not *self-caused*, if it is not *eternal*, the atheist is in a real dilemma to explain where the universe came from. Atheism cannot explain why there is *something* rather than *nothing*. Remember, out of nothing, nothing comes. But something exists. Where did it come from? Even skeptic David Hume commented, "Allow me to tell you that I never asserted so absurd a proposition as that anything might arise without a cause."[6]

As noted earlier, the law of causality is a fundamental principle of science, and, in fact, without it, science would be impossible.

> To deny the Law of Causality is to deny rationality. The very process of rational thinking requires us to put together thoughts (the causes) that result in conclusions (the effects). So if anyone ever tells you he doesn't believe in the Law of Causality, simply ask that person, "What caused you to come to that conclusion?"[7]

If you were watching television and the camera focused on some dominoes in the process of falling, but the camera did not show the *first* domino fall, what would your assumption be? You would assume that something—a person, perhaps a gust of wind, or maybe a mouse—had to start the process by pushing the first domino. Otherwise, the dominoes would still be standing. On a much grander scale, Christians believe the cause of the universe is a divine Creator. He is the One who started it all. He set cosmic things in motion. This divine Designer must be eternal and noncontingent. Scholar Jimmy Williams forces us to grapple with this fact:

> If something exists right now, it must have come from something else, come from nothing, or always existed. If it came from something else, then that something else must have come from nothing, always existed, or come from something else itself. Ultimately, either something has *always* existed, or at some point something came into being from nothing.[8]

Of course, Williams has come to the only logical conclusion, which is that the "something" that brought everything else into being was an eternal, infinite God (see Deuteronomy 33:27; Revelation 4:10). He realizes that no contingent being (one whose existence is dependent on another) can cause itself to exist, and hence the "first cause" must be uncaused or self-existent, transcending the contingent universe (see Exodus 3:14; John 5:26). All *contingent* beings (you and I) are dependent on this uncaused *noncontingent* "first cause" for our existence.

Objection: It is unreasonable to say the existence of the universe proves the existence of God.[9]

Answering the Objection: Many Christian philosophers believe this atheist objection is defeated by the kalam cosmological argument. The kalam (meaning "eternal") cosmological argument is summarized in the following syllogism, which has two premises and a conclusion:

1. Whatever had a beginning had a cause;
2. the universe had a beginning;
3. therefore, the universe had a cause.

If premises 1 and 2 are sound, then the conclusion is inescapable. No one questions premise 1. Obviously if something had a beginning, it must necessarily have had a cause. Premise 2 is supported by both philosophy and science. Philosophically, it is argued that there cannot be an infinite number of moments before today because an infinite number of moments cannot be traversed. A person can traverse only a finite number of days. If there were an infinite number of moments before today, then today would never have arrived. But *it has* arrived. Hence, there can only have been a finite number of days prior to today. Time and space must have had a beginning, and time has been ticking ever since that moment up to the present moment.[10] Below, we see that science supports this philosophical conclusion.

The Second Law of Thermodynamics. The first and second laws of thermodynamics are foundational to science and have never been contradicted in observable nature. The first law of thermodynamics is the law of energy conservation, and says that energy cannot be created nor destroyed; it can only change forms. The total amount of energy remains constant and unchanged. The late atheistic scientist Isaac Asimov said that in over 125 years, scientists have not witnessed a single violation of this fundamental law.[11]

The second law of thermodynamics says that in an isolated system (a system that neither loses nor gains energy from outside of itself, such as our universe), the natural course of things is to degenerate. The universe is running downward, not evolving upward. Although the total amount of energy remains constant and unchanged, there is always the tendency for it to become less available for usable work as time goes on.

Asimov noted that the second law basically means that the universe is getting increasingly disorderly. Clean a room, and it quickly becomes messy again. Clean a kitchen, and watch how fast it becomes disorderly again. "How difficult to maintain houses, and machinery, and our own bodies in perfect working order; how easy to let them deteriorate. In fact, all we have to do is nothing, and everything deteriorates, collapses, breaks down, wears out, all by itself—and that is what the second law is all about."[12]

This second law can be described in terms of *entropy*. An increase in entropy involves a transition from a more orderly state to a less orderly state—such as a cleaned-up bedroom becoming messy.

Based on the first and second laws of thermodynamics, we must conclude that our universe is headed toward an ultimate "heat death" in which there will be no more energy conversions.[13] The amount of usable energy will eventually deplete. Our universe is decaying. It is eroding.[14] It is moving from order to disorder. The universe—and everything in it, including the sun, our bodies, and the machines we build—is running down.

If the second law of thermodynamics is true, then the universe must not be eternal. Therefore, the universe must have had a beginning. Lincoln Barnett, in his book *The Universe and Dr. Einstein*, wrote, "If the universe is running down and nature's processes are proceeding in just one direction [entropy], the inescapable inference is that everything had a beginning; somehow and sometime the cosmic processes were started, the stellar fires ignited, and the whole vast pageant of the universe brought into being."[15] If you compare the universe to a clock, there had to be a time when the clock was fully wound up.[16] This implies the existence of a Creator who initiated things in the beginning.

In keeping with this, J.W.N. Sullivan, in *The Limitations of Science,* points to the fact that the universe must have had a beginning:

> The fact that the energy of the universe will be more disorganized tomorrow than it is today implies, of course, the fact that the energy of the universe is more highly organized today than it will be tomorrow, and that it was more highly organized yesterday than it is today. Following the process backwards we find a more and more highly organized universe. This backward tracing in time cannot be continued indefinitely. Organization cannot, as it were, mount up and up without limit. There is a definite maximum, and this definite maximum must have been in existence a finite time ago. And it is impossible that this state of perfect organization could have been evolved from some less perfect state. Nor is it possible that the universe could have persisted for eternity in that state of perfect organization and then suddenly, a finite time ago, have begun to pursue its present path. Thus the accepted laws of nature lead us to a definite beginning of the universe in time.[17]

The running down of the universe is well illustrated by the sun that illumines our earth. Scientists tell us that our sun is burning off its own mass at a rate of four million tons per second. Since the sun does not regenerate—since it does not produce any new mass—the mass that is burned off can never be regained once it is gone. It does not take a rocket scientist to realize that if four million tons of mass are burning away every second, then eventually, given enough time, the sun will simply run out of mass to burn. What is true of our sun is also true of the millions of stars in the universe. They are all burning away mass at a phenomenal pace. One day, the universe will experience a "heat death." *Show over!*

Here is the point to remember: If the sun is continually burning off its mass, and its available energy is continually being depleted, then there must have been a time when the sun (and all the other stars) were initially created and infused with all this energy. Since our universe is not yet dead, and since it will one day be dead (when all the energy runs out), it is obvious that the universe must have had a beginning.

The Big Bang Theory. Scientist Steven Hawking, in his book *The Nature of Space and Time* (1996), asserted that "almost everyone now believes that the universe, and time itself, had a beginning at the big bang."[18] The big bang theory holds that there was a massive cosmic explosion at a point in time, allegedly 13 to 15 billion years ago, that marked the beginning of the universe. We are told that the universe exploded into existence from a tiny volume smaller than the period at the end of this sentence.[19]

While some theologians and some in the scientific community[20] continue to reject the big bang theory, it remains true that a majority of astrophysicists and cosmologists today believe the big bang represents the beginning of the universe.[21] A key component of the big bang theory is the claim by astronomers that galaxies are moving away from the earth at a phenomenal speed. In his book *God and the Astronomers,* Robert Jastrow notes that astronomers Milton Humason and Edwin Hubble, using the 100-inch telescope on Mount Wilson, found that "the most distant galaxy they could observe was retreating from the earth at the extraordinary velocity of 100 million miles an hour."[22] Many have noted that there must have been quite a "big bang" to cause that kind of velocity. Jastrow believes we are presently witnessing the aftermath of a gigantic explosion.[23]

How long ago did this alleged explosion occur? Does this explosion give us a hint as to how old the universe is? Many believe so. Indeed, it is argued that by retracing the movements of the galaxies, accounting for their expansion speed, we can come to a point where all these galaxies were all packed together in a tiny "egg" that was very hot and very dense. "Putting an expanding universe in reverse leads us back to the point where the universe gets smaller and smaller until it vanishes into nothing."[24] Based on such measurements, it has been calculated that the universe may be 13 billion years old (some say 15 billion).[25] It is suggested that every star, every planet, every living creature is rooted in events set in motion at the moment of that cosmic explosion so long ago.[26]

Edwin Hubble, who postulated that the galaxies are moving away from each other, also postulated that the farther away the galaxies are, the faster they are receding. Scientists use the term "redshift" to describe the experimental finding that suggests this increase in speed. It is argued that as a galaxy moves farther away from earth, its color becomes redder, and the degree of color change is said to be directly proportional to the speed of the galaxy moving away from earth. Galaxies that are far away from earth manifest this "redshift."[27] This is allegedly due to the fact that "stars that move away from an observer emit light of a slightly longer wavelength—the faster they move, the greater the change in the wavelength."[28]

Some big bang advocates offer an analogy that makes the concept more understandable. If you are parked at an intersection in your car, and a train is about to pass by you, it will often blow its horn. As it passes by, the pitch of the horn goes from high to low. This change in pitch occurs because as the train is approaching you, the wavelength of the sound is compressed, whereas after it passes you and is moving away from you, the reverse happens, and the sound waves expand, thus lowering the pitch of the horn. In much the same way, it is argued, the "redshift" that is observed in distant galaxies implies they are moving away from us because red is the longest wavelength of visible light, and, as noted above, stars that move away from us emit light of a longer wavelength. The "degree of redness" is believed to indicate the speed at which the galaxies are moving away from us.[29]

When scientists began grappling with the implications of the big bang theory, many of them were disturbed—even repulsed— to find the theory pointing toward certain Christian themes, such as the idea that the universe had a beginning.[30] Albert Einstein, for example, developed a theory of general relativity which implied that the universe was expanding, and he was quite annoyed because this implied that the universe must have had a beginning (and hence the existence of a Beginner). This was unpalatable to Einstein's mind, so he came up with a "cosmological constant" to maintain a static universe, thus avoiding the idea that the universe was expanding and had a beginning. When other scientists proved to him that the universe was indeed expanding, he called his "cosmological constant" the biggest blunder of his career.[31] He eventually gave in to the idea that there must be a superior reasoning power responsible for bringing the universe into being—though the God he acknowledged is not the personal God of the Bible.

Robert Jastrow speaks of the evidence for the beginning of

the universe as a starting-point for faith for many people.[32] Astronomer Allan Sandage told one gathering at a conference that "contemplating the majesty of the big bang" helped make him "a believer in God, willing to accept that creation could only be explained as a 'miracle.'"[33] Hugh Ross likewise observes that "astronomers who do not draw theistic or deistic conclusions are becoming rare, and even the few dissenters hint that the tide is against them."[34]

Implications of Science for the Kalam Cosmological Argument. To review, the kalam cosmological argument states:

1. Whatever had a beginning had a cause;

2. the universe had a beginning;

3. therefore, the universe had a cause.

As noted earlier, no one doubts the validity of premise 1. In view of the scientific and philosophical theories discussed above, we can confidently say that premise 2 is soundly established. That being the case, the conclusion (point 3) is inescapable: *The universe had a cause.* That cause is the uncaused First Cause: God.

Objection: If everything that exists needs a cause, then God, too, must need a cause. Atheist George Smith asks: "If everything must have a cause, how did God become exempt?"[35]

Answering the Objection: The law of causality does not demand that *everything* must have a cause. Rather, it demands that *whatever had a beginning* had a cause. Only finite, contingent things need a cause. God did not have a beginning, and hence the atheistic objection is invalid. God is the First Cause that never came into being. While whatever *begins* to exist must have a cause, a being that exists *timelessly, eternally,* and *necessarily* is uncaused (Psalm 90:2).

Objection: Even if there were a first cause of the universe, the existence of the universe tells us nothing about the nature or character of this first cause.[36]

Answering the Objection: Contrary to the atheistic claim, Christian apologists such as William Lane Craig, J.P. Moreland, and Norman Geisler have more than ably demonstrated what we can know about the divine First Cause: For example:[37]

- Since the First Cause created the universe of space and time, He Himself must be *outside* of space and time. We can thus conclude that He is timeless and eternal. We can also conclude that He is immaterial since He transcends space.

- To have created the universe, in all of its incredible vastness, out of nothing, the First Cause must be incredibly powerful.

- To have created the universe with such intricate design, perfect for the existence of human life on earth, the First Cause must be incredibly intelligent.

- To have made an unending series of design choices requires that the First Cause be personal, for an inanimate, impersonal thing cannot make choices. God's personality is also evidenced in the fact that He created personal human beings.

All these characteristics are consistent with what the Bible reveals about God:

God Is Personal. The God of the Bible is a personal being with whom one can establish a relationship. God's personal nature is evident in that He hears (Exodus 2:24), sees (Genesis 1:4), knows (2 Timothy 2:19; Jeremiah 29:11), has a will (1 John 2:17), communicates (Exodus 3:13-14), plans (Ephesians 1:11), demonstrates emotion (Genesis 6:6), and demonstrates character (2 Peter 3:9). The God who bestowed personal characteristics on humankind is Himself personal. As Psalm 94 puts it, "Does he who implanted the ear not hear? Does he who formed the eye not see?" (verse 9).

God Is Eternal. Scripture teaches that God transcends time altogether. He is above the space-time universe. As an eternal being, He has always existed. God is the King eternal (1 Timothy 1:17), who alone is immortal (1 Timothy 6:16). God is the "Alpha and Omega" (Revelation 1:8) and is the "first and the last" (see Isaiah 44:6; 48:12). God exists "from eternity" (Isaiah 43:13), and "from everlasting to everlasting" (Psalm 90:2). He lives forever from eternal ages past (Psalm 41:13; 102:12,27; Isaiah 57:15).

God Is Spirit (Immaterial). The Scriptures tell us that God is Spirit (John 4:24). A spirit does not have flesh and bones (Luke 24:39). Hence, it is wrong to think of God as a physical being. Because God is a spirit, He is invisible. First Timothy 1:17 refers to God as "the King eternal, immortal, invisible, the only God." Colossians 1:15 speaks of "the invisible God" (see also John 1:18).

God Is Transcendent. The theological phrase "transcendence of God" refers to God's otherness or separateness from the created universe and from humanity. In 1 Kings 8:27, Solomon asserts of God that "the heavens, even the highest heaven, cannot contain you. How much less this temple I have built!" Psalm 113:5-6 asks, "Who is like the LORD our God, the One who sits enthroned on high, who stoops down to look on the heavens and the earth?"

God Is All-Powerful. God has the power to do all that He desires and wills. Some 56 times Scripture declares that God is almighty (for example, Revelation 19:6). God is abundant in strength (Psalm 147:5) and has incomparably great power

(2 Chronicles 20:6; Ephesians 1:19-21). No one can hold back God's hand (Daniel 4:35). No one can reverse God (Isaiah 43:13) and no one can thwart Him (Isaiah 14:27). Nothing is impossible with God (Matthew 19:26; Mark 10:27; Luke 1:37), and nothing is too difficult for Him (Genesis 18:14; Jeremiah 32:17,27). The Almighty reigns (Revelation 19:6).

God Is Omniscient. God knows all things, both actual and possible (Matthew 11:21-23). He knows all things past (Isaiah 41:22), present (Hebrews 4:13), and future (Isaiah 46:10). And because He knows all things, there can be no increase or decrease in His knowledge. Psalm 147:5 affirms that God's understanding "has no limit." God's knowledge is infinite (Psalm 33:13-15; 139:11-12; 147:5; Proverbs 15:3; Isaiah 40:14; 46:10; Acts 15:18; 1 John 3:20; Hebrews 4:13).

We conclude, then, that the evidence supports not only the idea that God exists, but that the nature of this God is in line with what the Bible reveals about Him.

4

NATURALISM VERSUS THE POSSIBILITY OF MIRACLES

Philosophical assumptions can dramatically impact a person's beliefs. If a person assumes that there is no supernatural, then probably no amount of evidence will convince him or her that God created the world, or that Jesus rose from the dead. The person's philosophical assumptions themselves prevent the possibility of accepting any related evidence. The relevance of this for atheism, agnosticism, and skepticism is obvious, because for most of these individuals, the philosophy of naturalism is the only game in town. We are told that all living creatures "are a direct product of the earth," and that "living things owe their origin entirely to certain physical and chemical properties of the ancient earth." We are assured that nothing supernatural—*no God*—was involved.[1]

Naturalism, as a philosophical system of thought, espouses the idea that all phenomena in the universe can be explained wholly in terms of natural causes and laws. Nature is the "whole show." There is no supernatural being that intervenes in the natural world. Miracles are rejected outright. Naturalists do not even ponder the possibility that anything (or anyone) outside the natural world (such as God) has influenced the natural world, for this natural world is all there is, and it is a closed system.

Naturalism has been called "the default position for all serious inquiry,"[2] and predominates in education, law, the arts, and, of course, science. Many of today's intellectual attacks against the Bible and Christianity are rooted in naturalism.

In this world where naturalism seems to reign, science is considered supreme. It is by scientific observation that we learn about the natural world. It is by scientific hypotheses that people speculate about causes and effects in the natural world. It is by scientific language that the natural world is described. Whatever conflicts with science today is viewed as unworthy of serious consideration.[3] Atheists, agnostics, and skeptics feel right at home in the atmosphere of naturalistic science.

In this chapter, we will explore some of the objections atheists, agnostics, and skeptics raise against the possibility of the supernatural and the miraculous.

Objection: Science proves that our universe is a closed system in which we witness purely material (natural) causes and effects. Dutch philosopher Benedict Spinoza (1632–77) argued that every event recorded in the pages of Scripture—

necessarily happened, like everything else, according to natural laws; and if anything is there set down which can be proved in set terms to contravene the order of nature, or not to be deducible therefrom, we must believe it to have been foisted into the sacred writings by irreligious hands; for whatsoever is contrary to nature is also contrary to reason, and whatsoever is contrary to reason is absurd, and, *ipso facto*, to be rejected.[4]

Spinoza's ideas have been repeated in virtually hundreds of articles and books written by atheists, agnostics, and skeptics.

Answering the Objection: Historically, in the early seventeenth century, Rene Descartes (1596–1650) propagated the idea that the universe was a purely mechanical system. Thus, it could be studied and measured. When Newtonian physics came on the scene some years later, naturalism swung into the mainstream. Scholar Del Ratzsch explains:

Many of Newton's followers interpreted both Newton and Newtonian physics as implying (1) that nothing was truly scientific except empirical observation and what could be logically supported by those observations, and (2) that (as Descartes had argued) nature was nothing but a vast, self-regulating physical machine. Although Newton himself held neither of those positions, they were nonetheless widely believed to have the authority of both Newton and his science behind them.[5]

Due to the influence of Descartes and Newtonian physics, the philosophy that came to predominate in intellectual circles was that the world of nature is a closed system where we witness purely material causes and effects. This natural world cannot be influenced by anything outside the natural world—such as God.

In responding to this line of argument, one cannot help but notice at the outset that dismissing the reality of God (and His influence on the universe) has the added benefit for naturalists that there is no moral accountability to a Supreme Being. Thomas Huxley—a champion of "aggressive secular materialism"[6]—was personally comforted by the philosophy of naturalism and the accompanying idea that there was no God he had to answer to at a future judgment. This is no doubt one of the appeals of naturalism: freedom from the weight of moral obligation.[7] (More on this later in the book.)

Aside from this, naturalism can be undermined by the very science it claims to hold in high regard. As Phillip E. Johnson puts it, the one thing that might suffice to bring naturalism to its knees is the fact that there is a widening gap between naturalism and the plain facts of scientific investigation. He suggests that the beginning of the end will come when naturalists are forced to face this one simple question: "What should we do if empirical evidence and materialist philosophy are going in different directions?"[8]

What would one do, for example, if hard scientific evidence were discovered that proved beyond any doubt that the universe is the result of intelligent design instead of just random mechanical processes? In fact, I believe we are witnessing this discovery in our own day. In a separate chapter in this book (chapter 6), I will provide extensive evidence regarding the intelligent design of the universe. In that chapter, I will demonstrate that the intelligent design theory punches a big hole in the wobbly boat of naturalism.

Without going into detail at this early juncture, intelligent design theory postulates that the same kinds of "signs of intelligence" discovered by crime scene investigators, archaeologists, cryptographers, and copyright offices are also clearly seen in the universe around us. There is clear *scientific* evidence—beginning at the molecular level and expanding into deep interstellar space—that an intelligent being intentionally brought our universe into existence, and that the universe was not the result of random chance or a cosmic accident.

Objection: Miracles are not possible. Claimed miracles are dismissed by naturalists in a number of ways. Some atheists say miracles are not possible because they violate the laws of nature. Others say the observers of alleged miracles are simply mistaken. Still others argue that just because we do not have a present explanation for some inexplicable event does not mean the supernatural was involved. As we grow in our understanding of the natural processes, we may come to a new natural understanding regarding what many previously thought were miraculous events.[9]

Sometimes we come across references to the "miracles of modern technology." It is argued that if our ancestors witnessed some of the advances we have today—airplanes, telephones, televisions, lasers, and the like—they would surely have considered such things as miraculous. Naturalists thus reason that the more scientific understanding we have, the less necessity there is to believe in the supernatural.

The possibility of miracles has long been denied by naturalist and humanistic thinkers. Benedict Spinoza, mentioned earlier, denied the possibility of miracles because they are irrational. Rudolph Bultmann said miracles were simply part of a mythological worldview that was part and parcel of biblical times. Immanuel Kant argued that miracles are not essential to religion.[10] Perhaps the most prolific denier of miracles, however, was David Hume.

Hume was a British empiricist (meaning he believed *all* knowledge comes from the five senses) and a skeptic of the Enlightenment period. In a chapter entitled "On Miracles" in *An Enquiry*

Concerning Human Understanding, he argued that, given the general experience of the uniformity of nature, miracles are highly improbable, and that the evidence in their favor is far from convincing.[11] He wrote, "A miracle is a violation of the laws of nature; and as a firm and unalterable experience has established these laws, the proof against a miracle, from the very nature of the fact, is as entire as any argument from experience can possibly be imagined."[12]

In Hume's thinking, since all of one's knowledge is derived from experience, and since this experience conveys the absolute regularity of nature, any report of a miracle is much more likely to be a false report than a true interruption in the uniform course of nature. Hence, a report of a resurrection from the dead (for example) is in all probability a deceptive report. Hume's arguments have been repackaged in the writings of innumerable atheists, agnostics, and skeptics.[13]

Answering the Objection: C.S. Lewis wrote, "If you begin by ruling out the supernatural, you will perceive no miracles."[14] Lewis was right. The philosophy of naturalism asserts that the universe operates according to uniform natural causes, and that it is impossible for any force outside the universe to intervene in the cosmos. This is an antisupernatural assumption that prohibits any possibility of miracles.

In answering the naturalist position, we begin with the fact that Christians *do* believe in the laws of nature. As theologian John Witmer said:

> The Christian position is not that the universe is capricious and erratic. Christians expect the sun to rise in the east tomorrow as it always has just as everyone else does. Christians recognize that this world is a cosmos, an orderly system, not a chaos. More

than that, Christians agree that the regularity of the universe is observable by men and expressible in principles or laws. As a result Christians do not deny the existence of what are called the laws of nature. Nor do they think that the occurrence of miracles destroys these laws or makes them inoperative.[15]

What Christians take exception to is the notion that the universe is a self-contained closed system with absolute laws that are inviolable. Christians believe that the reason there is regularity in the universe—the reason there are "laws" that are observable in the world of nature—is that God designed the universe that way. It is important to keep in mind, however, that the laws of nature are merely observations of uniformity or constancy in nature. They are not forces that *initiate* action. They simply describe the way nature behaves when its course is not affected by a superior power. God is not prohibited from taking action in the world, if He so desires.

Scripture tells us that God is the Sustainer and Governor of the universe (Acts 14:16-17; 17:24-28). Jesus is described in the Bible as "sustaining all things by his powerful word" (Hebrews 1:3) and the one in whom "all things hold together" (Colossians 1:17). That which from a human vantage point is called the "laws of nature" is in reality nothing more than God's normal cosmos-sustaining power at work! As Reformed scholar Louis Berkhof said, these laws of nature are "God's usual method of working in nature. It is His good pleasure to work in an orderly way and through secondary causes." However, Berkhof is careful to emphasize that this does not mean that God "cannot depart from the established order, and cannot produce an extraordinary effect, which does not result from natural causes, by a single volition, if He deems it desirable for the end in view. When God works miracles, He produces extraordinary effects in a supernatural way."[16]

When God miraculously intervenes in His creation, He is not "violating" the laws of nature. If one defines a miracle as a violation of the "absolute" laws of nature, as David Hume did, then the possibility of miracles occurring seems slim. However, as William Lane Craig notes, "Natural laws have implicit *ceteris paribus* conditions—that's Latin meaning, 'all other things being equal.' In other words, natural laws assume that no other natural or supernatural factors are interfering with the operation that the law describes."[17] In keeping with this, theologian Charles Ryrie explains that a miracle does not contradict nature because "nature is not a self-contained whole; it is only a partial system within a total reality, and a miracle is consistent within that greater system which includes the supernatural."[18]

When a miracle occurs, then, the laws of nature are not *violated*, but are rather *superseded* by a higher (supernatural) manifestation of the will of God. The forces of nature are not obliterated or suspended, but are only counteracted at a particular point by a force superior to the powers of nature.[19] As the famous physicist Sir George Stokes said, "It may be that the event which we call a miracle was brought on not by a suspension of the laws in ordinary operation, but by the super-addition of something not ordinarily in operation."[20] In other words, miracles do not go against the regular laws of cause and effect; they simply have a cause that *transcends* nature.[21]

Apologists Kenneth Boa and Larry Moody explain it this way:

> Since miracles, if they occur, are empowered by something higher than nature, they must supersede the ordinary processes or laws of nature. If you took a flying leap off the edge of a sheer cliff, the phenomenon that we call the law of gravity would surely bring you to an untimely end. But if you leaped off the same

cliff in a hang glider, the results would (hopefully!) be quite different. The principle of aerodynamics in this case overcomes the pull of gravity as long as the glider is in the air. In a similar way, the occurrence of a miracle means that a higher (supernatural) principle has overcome a lower (natural) principle for the duration of the miracle. To claim that miracles violate or contradict natural laws is just as improper as to say that the principle of aerodynamics violates the law of gravity.[22]

As for David Hume's point that given the general experience of the uniformity of nature miracles are highly improbable, one must note that Hume's experience was greatly limited. There is no way that all possible "experience" can confirm his naturalistic viewpoint unless he has access to all possible experiences in the universe, including those of the past and the future. Since (finite) Hume does not have access to this much broader (infinite) body of knowledge, his conclusion is baseless.[23]

Theologian Henry Clarence Thiessen makes this point with an illustration based on geology:

> The...proposition that miracles are incredible because they contradict human experience, wrongly assumes that one must base all his beliefs on *present* human experience. Geologists tell of great glacial activities in the past and of the formation of seas and bays by these activities; *we did not see this in our experience, but we do accept it*....Miracles do not contradict human experience unless they contradict *all* human experience, that in the past as well as that in the present. This fact leaves the door wide

open for well-supported evidence as to what did happen.[24]

Some scholars note that we could trust very little history if we were to believe only those things which we have personally observed and experienced. Unfortunately, however, this is the methodology modernistic critics still hold onto when it comes to the issue of the supernatural and miracles.

Norman Geisler and Ronald Brooks have noted that Hume essentially equates *probability* with *evidence*. Since people who die typically stay dead, a so-called miracle of resurrection is impossible. "That is like saying that you shouldn't believe it if you won the lottery because of all the thousands of people who lost. It equates evidence with probability and says that you should never believe that long shots win."[25] A miracle may be a "long shot," and it may not happen very often, but long shots make good sense when God is involved in the picture. What is impossible with man is possible with God (Matthew 19:26).

Objection: Miracles are rejected because they would disrupt any possibility of doing real science, since there would no longer be constancy in the world.[26]

Answering the Objection: There is constancy in the world precisely because God created the world that way. Miracles are unusual events that involve only a brief superseding of the natural laws. By definition, they are out of the norm. Unless there were a "norm" to begin with, miracles would not be possible. As apologists Peter Kreeft and Ronald Tacelli put it, "Unless there are regularities, there can be no exceptions to them."[27] Miracles are unusual, not commonplace events. A miracle is a unique event that stands out against the background of ordinary and regular occurrences. Hence, the possibility of miracles does not disrupt the possibility of doing real science because, again, God Himself has built constancy into the universe via the laws of nature.

Objection: The biblical miracles should be rejected because science disproves them.[28]

Answering the Objection: Science depends upon observation and replication. Biblical miracles, such as the incarnation and the resurrection, are by their very nature unprecedented events. No one can replicate these events in a laboratory. Hence, science simply cannot be the judge and jury as to whether or not these events occurred.

The scientific method is useful for studying nature but not *super*nature. Just as football stars are speaking outside their field of expertise when they appear on television to tell you what razor you should buy, so scientists are speaking outside their field when they address theological issues such as miracles or the resurrection.

Having said that, one must also note that there is a growing body of rather convincing scientific evidence that points to the truth of certain biblical claims. For example:

1. *The Second Law of Thermodynamics.* As noted in chapter 3, the second law of thermodynamics says that in an isolated system, the natural course of things is to degenerate. Our universe is headed toward an ultimate "heat death" in which there will be no more energy conversions.[29] The amount of usable energy will eventually deplete. Things are running down. Since this is the case, the universe must have had a beginning. As Lincoln Barnett said in his book *The Universe and Dr. Einstein,* "If the universe is running down and nature's processes are proceeding in just one direction [*entropy*], the inescapable inference is that everything had a beginning; somehow and sometime the cosmic processes were

started, the stellar fires ignited, and the whole vast pageant of the universe brought into being."[30] Here is a clear case of science supporting the miracle of God's creation of the universe.

2. *The Big Bang Theory.* The big bang theory holds that there was a massive cosmic explosion at a point in time, allegedly 13 to 15 billion years ago, that marked the beginning of the universe. Since whatever had a *beginning* must have had a *cause,* many reason that the big bang theory supports the idea of a Creator who caused the universe. If the big bang theory is correct, then it constitutes another example of science lending support to the miracle of God's creation of the universe.

3. *Intelligent Design Theory.* As I will demonstrate in chapter 6, intelligent design theory holds that an intelligent cause is empirically detectable in the universe by using a well-defined scientific method that focuses on *contingency, complexity,* and *specification.* In a capsule, if something were designed, we would expect to see evidence of *contingency*—meaning there is evidence that it did not result from an automatic, unintelligent process (such as natural selection). If something were designed, we would expect to see evidence that it is *complex* enough (with many interacting working parts) that random chance processes alone would not be able to cause its existence. We would also expect to see evidence of *specificity*—meaning that there was a detailed, precise pattern commonly associated with intelligent causes.[31] Here is yet another example of science supporting the miracle of God's creation of the universe.

4. *Archaeology.* As we will see in chapter 8, the Bible's accuracy and reliability have been proved and verified over and over again by archaeological finds produced by both Christian and non-Christian scholars and scientists. This includes verification for numerous customs, places, names, and events mentioned in the Bible. To date, over 25,000 sites in biblical lands have been discovered, dating back to Old Testament times, which have established the accuracy of innumerable details in the Bible. Hence, archaeology—classified as a science[32]—supports the accuracy of the Bible, which records the biblical miracles.

In view of these facts alone, atheists ought to be cautious about appealing to science against Christianity. They may find themselves being impaled by the very sword they have drawn against Christianity.

From a historical perspective, there is very good reason to believe in the miracles of Jesus. One highly pertinent factor is the brief amount of time that elapsed between Jesus' miraculous public ministry and the publication of the Gospels (see chapters 8 and 9 for information on the reliability of the biblical documents). This brief time was insufficient for the development of miracle legends. Many eyewitnesses to Jesus' miracles would have still been alive to refute any untrue miracle accounts (see 1 Corinthians 15:6).

One must also recognize the noble character of the men who witnessed these miracles (Peter, James, and John, for example). Such men—schooled from early childhood in the Ten Commandments, including the commandment against bearing false witness (Exodus 20:16)—were not prone to misrepresentation, and were willing to give up their lives rather than deny what they knew to be true about Jesus.

There were also hostile witnesses to the miracles of Christ. When Jesus raised Lazarus from the dead, for example, none of the chief priests or Pharisees disputed the miracle (John 11:45-48). (If they could have disputed it, they would have.) Rather, their goal was simply to stop Jesus (verses 47-48). Because there were so many hostile witnesses who observed and scrutinized Christ, successful fabrication of miracle stories in His ministry would have been impossible.

Regarding the issue of hostile witnesses, theologian James Oliver Buswell comments:

> In the biblical events strictly regarded as miracles, the adversaries of faith acknowledged the supernatural character of what took place. After the healing of the man "lame from his mother's womb," the rulers and elders and scribes, "beholding the man that was healed standing with them...could say nothing against it." But they said, "...that a notable miracle hath been done by them is manifest to all them that dwell in Jerusalem, and we cannot deny it" (Acts 3:1-4:22). In the case of the miracle at Lystra (Acts 14:8-23), the pagans said, "The gods are come down to us in the likeness of men." With reference to the resurrection of Christ, Paul could ask a Roman court of law to take cognizance of an indisputable, publicly attested fact, for, said he, "This thing was not done in a corner" (Acts 26:26).[33]

Further, in Acts 2:22, a bold Peter told a Jewish crowd, "Men of Israel, listen to this: Jesus of Nazareth was a man accredited by

God to you by miracles, wonders and signs, which God did among you through him, *as you yourselves know*" (emphasis added). If Peter were making all this up, the huge crowd surely would have shouted Peter down. They did not, however, for they knew that what he said was true.

On occasion, one might encounter an atheist or skeptic who responds by claiming that Peter and all the other New Testament personalities were just ignorant people who did not understand the laws of nature, and hence were easily fooled into believing in miracles. Such a claim, however, is preposterous. People in biblical times *did* know enough of the laws of nature to recognize bona fide miracles. As C.S. Lewis stated,

> When St. Joseph discovered that his bride was pregnant, he was "minded to put her away." He knew enough biology for that. Otherwise, of course, he would not have regarded pregnancy as a proof of infidelity. When he accepted the Christian explanation, he regarded it as a miracle precisely because he knew enough of the laws of nature to know that this was a suspension of them.[34]

Moreover, when the disciples beheld Christ walking on the water, they were frightened—something that would not have been the case unless they had been aware of the laws of nature and known that this was an exception. If one has no conception of a regular order in nature, then of course one cannot notice departures from that order.[35] Nothing can be viewed as "abnormal" until one has first grasped the "norm."[36]

In keeping with this, Josh McDowell and Don Stewart wrote:

> The people living at the time of Jesus certainly knew

that men born blind do not immediately receive their sight (John 9:32), that five loaves and a few fish would not feed 5,000 people (John 6:14), or that men do not walk on water (Matthew 14:2).

Doubting Thomas said, "Unless I see in his hands the print of the nails, and place my finger in the mark of the nails, and place my hand in his side, I will not believe" (John 20:25 RSV). He refused to accept the testimony of the unbelievable event of the resurrection, but changed his mind when confronted face-to-face with the resurrected Christ. Thus we are not expected to believe the ridiculous, and neither were the people of biblical times.[37]

Objection: The miracle claims of Christianity and the other world religions cancel each other out as evidence for truth. For example, there are accounts of Muhammad (the founder of Islam) doing miracles, just as there are accounts of Jesus (the founder of Christianity) doing miracles.

Answering the Objection: The Quran is often called "the miracle of Muhammad" because of the traditional belief that Muhammad was uneducated and was unable to write. (He was known as the "unlettered prophet.") The Hadith (Muslim tradition) records other alleged miracles of Muhammad, such as feeding a multitude of people with a handful of dates, healing blind eyes, healing sick people of their diseases, raising people from the dead, and causing barren fields to yield fruit.

Contrary to the claim of some Muslims, however, Muhammad was not a true miracle-worker. In fact, nowhere in the Quran do we find record of Muhammad performing *any* supernatural feats of nature. He explicitly disavowed such ability. When asked why he did not perform miracles like the other prophets did, he responded that the Quran was his miracle (Surah 29:48-50).

There is good reason for doubting the veracity of the miracle stories of Muhammad in Muslim tradition:

- Foundationally, the primary authoritative source for Muslims—the Quran—has no record of such miracles, but rather portrays Muhammad refusing to do miracles (Suras 3:181-84; 4:153; 6:8-9). Why should we consider the miracle legends contained in Muslim tradition authentic when the Quran—a higher authority—portrays Muhammad as refusing such miracles?

- Most of the individuals who collected the miracle stories of Muhammad lived between 100 to 200 years after Muhammad's time—meaning they were not eyewitnesses of Muhammad's deeds. This is plenty of time for miracle legends to develop.

- One must wonder whether some of these miracle stories were invented specifically to counter Christian apologists who spoke of Jesus' miracles.

- Many of these miracle stories seem quite similar to the legendary stories of Jesus contained in the New Testament Apocrypha, written long after the time of Jesus.[38] Such accounts are obviously inauthentic when compared to the historically verifiable documents of the New Testament. Because the Muslim traditions bear such strong similarity to the nature of the apocryphal books, they should be doubted every bit as much as the apocryphal books.

In contrast to the inauthentic miracle claims in Muslim tradition, there was an endless flow of eyewitnesses regarding the miracles performed by Jesus. John's Gospel tells us that Jesus' signs were done in the presence of His disciples to ensure that there was adequate witness to the events that transpired (John 20:30). "Witness" is a pivotal concept in this Gospel. The noun ("witness") is used 14 times and the verb ("testify") 33 times. The reason for this is clear: *The signs performed by Jesus are thoroughly attested.* There were many witnesses. Therefore, the signs cannot be simply dismissed or explained away. Even hostile witnesses admitted the veracity of the biblical miracles (Acts 4:16; 26:26).

We conclude, then, that there is no legitimate comparison between the historical miracles of Jesus and the legendary miracles of Muhammad (and leaders of other world religions).

THE REAL ISSUE

The real issue that is behind all this discussion of miracles is that of whether or not God exists. The bottom line, once you get rid of all the fancy philosophical arguments against miracles, comes down to this: If one admits the postulate of God, miracles are possible. Paul Little wrote, "Once we assume the existence of God, there is no problem with miracles, because God is by definition all-powerful."[39] Reformed scholar Charles Hodge, in his *Systematic Theology,* similarly wrote, "If theism [belief in a personal Creator-God] be once admitted, then it must be admitted that the whole universe, with all that it contains and all the laws by which it is controlled, must be subject to the will of God."[40] As Norman Geisler put it so well, "If there is a God who can *act,* then there can be *acts* of God. The only way to show that miracles are impossible is to disprove the existence of God."[41] That is something that naturalists and atheists cannot do.[42]

5

EVOLUTION:
A FLAWED THEORY

The theory of evolution caused Charles Darwin to lose his faith. Since his day, his experience has been repeated in the lives of countless other people. Philosopher Huston Smith suggested that evolutionary theory has caused more people to lose religious faith than any other factor.[1] Philosopher Daniel Dennett approvingly speaks of Darwinism as a "universal acid" that corrodes traditional spirituality.[2] "Like universal acid, the theory of evolution eats through just about every traditional religious idea."[3]

Atheist Richard Dawkins boasts that Darwinism enables a person to be an "intellectually fulfilled atheist."[4] Dawkins and other such atheists find no need for the supernatural. "We find insufficient evidence for belief in the existence of a supernatural; it is either meaningless or irrelevant to the question of the survival and fulfillment of the human race. As nontheists, we begin with humans not God, nature not deity."[5] These individuals promote a way of life that "systematically excludes God and all religion in the traditional sense. Man, for better or worse, is on his own in the universe. He marks the highest point to which nature has yet evolved, and he must rely entirely on his own resources."[6]

The idea that there is a Creator who brought the universe into being is scoffed at by evolutionists. Atheist Isaac Asimov, one of the most prolific authors and science writers of all time, tells us that the "universe can be explained by evidence obtained from the Universe alone...no supernatural agency need be called upon."[7] The explanation of humanity's origin is always the theory of evolution. We are told:

> Human beings are neither entirely unique from other forms of life nor are they the final product of some planned scheme of development....All life forms are constructed from the same basic elements, the same sorts of atoms, as are nonliving substances.... Humans are the current result of a long series of natural evolutionary changes, but not the only result or the final one. Continuous change can be expected to affect ourselves, other life forms, and the cosmos as a whole. There appears to be no ultimate beginning or end to this process.[8]

Atheists quite obviously derive substantial ammunition for their anti-god views from the theory of evolution.* In view of this, we will now examine key atheist objections to the Christian view of a Creator-God. Those who desire a far more comprehensive

---

* Note, however, that not all evolutionists are atheists. Some Christians subscribe to theistic evolution, a view that espouses the idea that God initially began creation, and then directed and controlled the processes of naturalistic evolution to produce the universe as we know it today.

treatment of creationism versus evolutionary theory are invited to consult my book *The 10 Things You Should Know About the Creation vs. Evolution Debate* (Harvest House Publishers).

Objection: Evolution must be true because it has been observed firsthand by scientists. Atheist and evolutionary theorist Stephen Jay Gould wrote an article entitled "Evolution as Fact and Theory" in *Discovery Magazine*, in which he stated that scientists now have "observational evidence of evolution in action."[9]

Answering the Objection: The examples Gould cites are actually examples of microevolution in action, not macroevolution. Microevolution refers to changes that occur within the same species, while macroevolution refers to the transition or evolution of one species into another. Macroevolution "consists of changes within a population leading to a completely new species with genetic information that did not exist in any of the parents."[10]

There is no question, even among creationists, that microevolution has taken place, for all the different races of human beings have descended from a single common human ancestor (Adam).[11] Likewise, all kinds of dogs have "microevolved" from the original dog species created by God.[12] In no case, however, has macroevolution ever been observed by scientists.[13] This is in keeping with the fact that the genetic pool of DNA in each species sets parameters beyond which the species simply cannot evolve (that is, dogs can take on new characteristics, but they cannot evolve into cats, for dog DNA always remains dog DNA, just as cat DNA always remains cat DNA).

Scripture indicates that God created the initial "kinds" of animals, and then reproduction took place, generation by generation, "according to its kind" (Genesis 1:21,24). This type of evolution is "micro" in the sense that *small changes* have taken place in the various species. So, for example, human DNA makes it possible for humans to have different eye colors, different hair colors, different heights, dark skin or light skin, a bulky frame or a scrawny frame, and so forth. The possibility for all kinds of variations such as these is encoded into the DNA of the human species.[14]

While microevolution is an observed fact, evolutionists have in the past tended to speak of evolution as a single unitary process (merging micro- and macroevolution into one basic category) such that proof for *microevolution* is viewed as proof for *macroevolution*. This conclusion is unwarranted.[15] This is an idea rejected even by many nontheistic biologists.[16]

Objection: Mutations, working in conjunction with natural selection, explain how evolution works. As one atheist put it, "Given enough time, and changing environmental conditions, mutation will add to mutation, and any species will gradually change into one or more new species."[17] A mutation involves a change of the DNA sequence such that a new character or trait emerges in the organism.[18] Such mutations are directly related to natural selection—a process involving survival of the fittest. Members of a species with superior traits survive, while members with inferior traits die out. By this ongoing process, inferior traits are eventually bred out of the species. The superior "winners" not only pass on their superior traits to offspring, but also allegedly develop ever-new characteristics that enhance the possibility of survival.[19] As this process repeats itself generation by generation, the organism grows increasingly complex and often evolves into an entirely different species with novel features.[20]

Answering the Objection: Natural selection *does* occur in the world, but it always involves limited changes *within* species—that is, there are microevolutionary mutations, but not macroevolutionary ones. John Morris explains: "Variation within a specific created type occurs all the time. Natural selection can select the variant best suited for an environment, but natural selection does not create anything new."[21] Genetic mutations can account for minor changes such as blue eyes rather than brown, or tall rather than short. But mutations can never account for the emergence of a characteristic *not already contained* in the gene pool of that species or "kind."[22] Yet what is contained in the gene pool of each "kind" (Genesis 1:24-25) is vast indeed:

> An essential feature of the creation model is the place-ment of considerable genetic variety in each created kind. Only thus can we explain the possible origin of horses, donkeys, and zebras from the same kind; of lions, tigers, and leopards from the same kind; of some 118 varieties of the domestic dog, as well as jackals, wolves, and foxes from the same kind. As each kind obeyed the Creator's command to be fruitful and multiply, the chance processes of recom-bination and the more purposeful process of natural selection caused each kind to subdivide into the vast array we now see.[23]

Even in terms of human beings alone, there is so much genetic variety built into human DNA that "the average human couple could have 10^{2017} children before they would have to have one child identical to another! That number, a one followed by 2017 zeroes, is greater than the number of sand grains by the sea, the number of stars in the sky."[24] The point is, then, that the gene pool of each species allows for plenty of variation within that species.

There are limits to such change, for the DNA in each member of the species will ensure that each member of the species *will remain* a member of that species, and not develop into a new spe-cies. There has not been, nor can there ever be, any crossing over of the "kinds" of Genesis 1. G.J. Mendel's experiments in plant genetics proved that the range of variation possible within a species was narrowly limited to the genetic parameters of that species, and offered no possibility of development into a different species.[25]

One must also note that the very process of natural selection, according to evolutionists, is blind and unguided. It has no ability to direct mutations. Therein lies the problem. Mutations only bring about one small change at a time, and the development of, for example, a complex organ like an eye would require thousands of positive mutations. How would natural selection, at each minimal step along the way over innumerable generations, know whether to keep each small mutational change, or breed that small muta-tional change out of the species? How would natural selection recognize the worth of a single mutation during a long process of multiple mutations, awaiting the eventual arrival of a complex organ like an eye? How would natural selection know that a small flap of skin on the side of the body would in many generations be a wing, and thus decide to keep that flap of skin?[26] Since at every step along the way the individual small mutational changes have no obvious immediate benefit, why wouldn't natural selection breed that change out of the species? I have not heard a good answer to this problem.

The problem becomes compounded when it is realized that the eye is only one among many complex organs in a human being. What about the ear? What about the brain? What about the heart? The liver? The kidney? The nervous system? The nose with its sense of smell? We are asked to believe that again and again, natural selection blindly and mindlessly brought about complex organs via a step-by-step, generation-by-generation process over an incal-culably long period of time. No wonder Darwin himself expressed doubt about how this could work.

To add to the woes of Darwin's "natural selection" theory, science proves that the great majority of mutations are, in fact, detrimental to the organism. Indeed, scientists have found that over 99 percent[27] are harmful, destructive, and disadvantageous to the organism.[28] One textbook notes:

> Experiments have conclusively shown that most mutations are harmful (about 99.9%), and some are even deadly. Mutations seem to result from "accidents" which occur in the genes, and the chance that such an accident could be helpful rather than harmful is very small indeed. Two-headed snakes and albino squirrels are considered to be genetic disasters instead of the beginnings of new and more advanced creatures.[29]

Most mutations cause deterioration and breakdown in the organism. Such changes tend to make the organism less well suited for its environment, thereby threatening its very survival. It does not take a genius to know that if most mutations are destructive to an organism, then any series of multiple mutations will, on average, have a much-increased chance of harming that organism. This fact greatly undermines evolutionary theory.

Still further, the impossibility of positive mutations bringing about new species is proven in the fact that this would require tremendous amounts of *new* information being added to the DNA (which carries genetic information). However, numerous studies and experiments have demonstrated that not only do mutations fail to produce *new* information, they actually *delete* information and thus bring harm to the organism.[30] Mutations generally involve some kind of copying error in the DNA, analogous to typing mistakes,[31] and hence are incapable of increasing information. It thus becomes absurd to think that, over a long period of time, enough information was added to cause a single-celled organism to eventually evolve into a complex human being with a brain, eyes, ears, a nose, a heart, kidneys, a liver, and all the other complex organs. Not only is it inconceivable how any of the above *individual* complex organs could develop through mutations, but the idea that these multiple complex organs evolved in a single species so as to *function synergistically with each other as an interrelated whole* through positive mutations is beyond all comprehension. How could these "parts" evolve in unison with the other parts?[32] Remember—natural selection, according to evolutionists, is mindless and blind.

Objection: The marked similarities between the anatomy of human beings and that of the higher vertebrata proves that human beings evolved from an animal ancestor. One atheist suggests that "most of the traditional evidences for the idea of common [evolutionary] descent came from comparative anatomy. It is still a powerful category of evidence with a wealth of examples that support the idea of evolution."[33]

Answering the Objection: In view of the fact that human beings and all the animals were created by the same Creator, it makes sense that there would be some similarities in their design. When we observe the paintings of da Vinci, we note certain similarities between them, even though they portray different subjects. When we observe the paintings of Picasso, we note certain similarities between them, even though they portray different subjects. Likewise, when we observe the creations of the Creator (a *divine* artist), we note certain similarities among species even though each species is different.[34]

Do not human engineers and designers do much the same in terms of incorporating similar design into various inventions?

Wheels work great on cars, buses, tractors, wagons, bicycles, and tricycles. Lightbulbs work great in houses, buildings, cars, outdoor stadiums, and street lamps. Air conditioners work fabulously in cars, houses, and buildings. Glass lenses work great for eyeglasses, telescopes, and microscopes. If human designers can incorporate similar items in the things they make, it is surely plausible that the divine Creator could do the same with the creatures He made.

A key factor that must be considered regarding similar design is the environment. It is reasonable to surmise that God, in His wisdom, knowing that various species would be living and moving about in a similar environment, would endow these various creatures with body parts suitable to survival in that environment. For example, God would give them lungs so they could all breathe the same air. God would give them stomachs and digestive tracts so they could eat the same kinds of food. He would give them eyes so they could see where they were going, and ears to hear sounds in their environment, and noses to detect aromas. In each case, God designed an organ or body part that effectively "worked," and put this effective working part in various creatures. A strong case can therefore be made that similar anatomy suggests a common Creator—an Intelligent Designer!

Objection: Since human bodies contain some organs for which there is no known use (vestigial organs), they must be "left over" organs from an earlier animal stage at which time they were useful. Atheists sometimes cite the appendix as an example: "The appendix is a vestigial organ....So, the question becomes, Why do humans have an appendix?...Evolution, the idea that we all have common ancestors, provides a meaningful answer."[35]

Answering the Objection: This view makes unwarranted assumptions. To begin, organs that are presently categorized as "vestigial" may serve a purpose that is yet unknown to science.[36] Scientists are not infallible, and are making new discoveries and revising older theories all the time. Significantly, scientists formerly categorized about 180 organs as "vestigial"—including the thyroid gland, the thymus, the pineal gland, the tonsils, the coccyx, the ear muscles, and the appendix.[37] Today, however, because scientists have discovered functional uses for many of these organs, the list has now dwindled to between zero and six, depending on who you talk to.[38]

Some atheistic evolutionists argue that vestigial organs can be removed from the human body without apparent loss. However, there may be losses that medical specialists are not yet aware of. It is hardly legitimate to argue that if the organ is removed and the person remains alive, then there is no need for the organ. The person may indeed remain alive, but he may not live as optimally as he would have if the organ had remained in his body. Further, medical specialists postulate that if an organ is removed from the body, it is always possible that another organ in the body will compensate for its loss. This compensation, however, should not be taken to mean that the removed organ served no useful purpose. Yet further, some organs—such as tonsils—may be more important in early childhood than in adulthood (for example, they may help young children ward off disease).[39]

Though I believe all these organs serve a purpose, even if I granted (for the sake of argument) that some organs are useless and "left over" from an earlier period of "human development," they should properly be understood as examples of *microevolution* (evolution within specific species), not *macroevolution* (evolution of one species into another). It could be postulated that as the species of man microevolved, some of these organs may have become less important. But this certainly offers no support for the naturalistic evolution of simple life forms into complex life forms.

There is one further point that bears mentioning. If evolution were true we would expect to see not just a loss of some organs ("devolution," involving the so-called vestigial organs) but also the development of some *new* organs. The persistent and longtime absence of any new organs would seem to argue against the evolutionary view.[40]

Objection: The fossil evidence does not support the book of Genesis. Atheists seem sure that the fossil record links modern humans to primitive primate relatives.[41]

Answering the Objection: Billions of fossils have been discovered virtually all over the world. There are dinosaur graveyards scattered all around, including such places as the Rockies, South Africa, Central Asia, and Belgium. Fossils of marine invertebrates are found almost everywhere. Fossils of ocean fish, mollusk shells, and even a whale have been discovered on various mountains.[42]

With this abundance of evidence, one would expect that if evolutionary theory were true, the fossil record would show a step-by-step progression from simple life forms to increasingly complex life forms. The record should show a step-by-step progression from common ancestors to the complex organisms of today. However, the fossil record actually shows that species throughout geologic history have remained remarkably stable (not changing) for exceedingly long periods of time, and that there was a sudden explosion of life forms during the Cambrian age (the first period of the Paleozoic Era).

So astonishing is the explosion of life forms during the Cambrian period that some refer to it as "biology's big bang." Stephen Jay Gould explains it this way: "In one of the most crucial and enigmatic episodes in the history of life—and a challenge to the old and congenial idea that life has progressed in a basically stately and linear manner through the ages—nearly all animal phyla make their first appearance in the fossil record at essentially the same time."[43] Many of the animal types that appear in the Cambrian era continue to the present day.[44]

An objective consideration of the Cambrian explosion reveals that there is no evolutionary descent of life forms, and no slow modifications taking place in life forms as a result of natural selection. Phillip E. Johnson is right in saying that "the prevailing characteristic of fossil species is *stasis*—the absence of change. There are numerous 'living fossils' which are much the same today as they were millions of years ago, at least as far as we can determine."[45]

Creationists therefore believe the fossil evidence is more in line with their view than with evolutionary theory.[46] There are certainly no intermediate fossils showing a transition of one species into another—such as a transition of a "primitive primate relative" into a human being—as one would expect if evolution were true.

Objection: The reason no fossil precursors exist prior to Cambrian times is that they were soft-bodied creatures, and hence would not have had any hard parts to be fossilized. Ernst Mayr, lifelong atheist and teacher of evolutionary theory, writes that "the absence of the ancestral types in Precambrian strata can be explained if one assumes that the earliest multicellular animals were microscopically small and soft-bodied."[47]

Answering the Objection: Single-celled organisms have been discovered in the Precambrian strata, and more than a hundred species of soft-bodied animals have been uncovered in the Cambrian (and later) strata. Bryn Nelson, for example, reports that "scientists have discovered some flattened soft-tissue fossils in late Precambrian and Cambrian phosphate-rich layers in Greenland and China."[48] In view of such evidence, it is unreasonable to argue that soft-bodied creatures could not have fossilized during pre-Cambrian times.[49]

Objection: Transitional fossils *have* been discovered, thereby proving the truth of evolution. An example is the Archaeopteryx. One atheist says the Archaeopteryx is "a marvelous connecting link between two-legged dinosaurs and modern birds. It had a long, lizard-like tail, teeth, clawed wing-digits still usable for climbing, and many other reptilian skeletal features too numerous to mention here. In fact, the only thing bird-like about it was its feathers."[50]

Answering the Objection: Atheistic evolutionists are making too much of the Archaeopteryx. One reason the Archaeopteryx is not a true transitional form is that all of its body parts are fully formed and fully functional. Its wings are fully formed (perfectly suited to flight), its tail is fully formed (it is not a mere stub), its claws are fully formed (no sharp stubs), and there is nothing on the creature indicating it is in the process of developing from one species into another. It is simply a unique creature, and it is perfectly compatible with a creationist scenario. In other words, the Archaeopteryx had all these unique features because God created it that way.

Further, there is evidence that birds have been around as long as or before the Archaeopteryx, and hence the Archaeopteryx could not have been the ancient ancestor of birds.[51] Indeed, researcher John Noble Wilford, based on a discovery in northeastern China, concluded that "by the time of Archaeopteryx, another bird lineage with perhaps much more ancient origins existed. That lineage seems to have led to modern birds." Wilford says this new evidence of a sparrow-size bird called the Liaoningornis—a virtual contemporary of the Archaeopteryx—"casts serious doubt on the widely held theory that birds are direct descendants of dinosaurs."[52]

It does not bode well for evolutionism that the Archaeopteryx is the best evolutionists can come up with in terms of a transitional fossil. If evolution were true, transitional fossils should be the *rule* and not the *exception*. In other words, one would expect to see a veritable *preponderance* of fossil records that show one life form transitioning into another. We should see fish transitioning into reptiles and some ancient ancestor life form transitioning into apes and humans. However, out of all the billions of fossils known and documented in the rocks of the earth's crust, there is no such evidence. In the British Museum of History alone, there are some 60 million fossil specimens, yet not one is a transitional form showing one species evolving into another.[53]

Rather, the evidence reveals a sudden appearance of life forms, and each of them exhibit all the features that distinguish that life form—fully formed and fully functional—with no "evolving" of body parts involved. We find no ancestors with stubs on their lower bodies that gave rise to species with legs. We find no ancestors with stubs on their sides that gave rise to species with wings. Such Darwinian "gradualism" is completely absent.

Stephen Jay Gould is an example of an evolutionist who has conceded that the lack of transitional evidence in the fossil record has been a problem for traditional evolutionism. He once commented that "all paleontologists know that the fossil record contains precious little in the way of intermediate forms; transitions between major groups are characteristically abrupt."[54] He said "the extreme rarity of transitional forms in the fossil record persists as the trade secret of paleontology."[55] He admitted that "the absence of fossil evidence for intermediary stages between major transitions in organic design, indeed our inability, even in our imagination, to construct functional intermediates in many cases, has been a persistent and nagging problem for gradualistic accounts of evolution."[56]

Objection: The theory of punctuated equilibrium is the correct

understanding of evolution. According to this theory, promoted by atheist Stephen Jay Gould, the development of new species occurred in spurts of major genetic alterations that punctuate long periods of little change. One atheist explains the theory this way:

> Most species are characterized by very long periods of relatively genetic inactivity—nothing much happens in their environment and so, lacking any particular evolutionary pressures, their genetic code doesn't really change much.
>
> However, these long times of relative equilibrium are "punctuated" every so often by dramatic changes in the environment which, in turn, exert strong evolutionary pressures on individuals. Essentially, those ill-equipped to deal with the new conditions are most likely to die, and what we have is basic natural selection put on fast-forward.[57]

Answering the Objection: An obvious problem for the theory of punctuated equilibrium is that it calls loud attention to the utter lack of transitional forms in the fossil record. It is like a giant neon sign pointing to the fact that *stasis* (no change) is what we witness in the fossil record. One cannot help but strongly suspect that because no true transitional forms have been found in the fossil record, this theory was formulated to explain away the lack of evidence. Certainly there is no overt empirical biological evidence for the theory. What the evidence does reveal is that there was a sudden explosion of animal phyla during the Cambrian era.

A second major problem with punctuated equilibrium is that it goes against all that is known regarding mutations. Studies in DNA and genetics indicate that there is sufficient genetic potential in a particular species to give rise to all kinds of variety *within* that species, but not to transform it into an *entirely new* species.[58] So, for example, there are variations that have occurred within the "dog kind," but we never witness the dog evolving into another species, even during times of severe environmental pressure. There are variations that have occurred within the "cat kind," but we never witness the cat evolving into another species, even during times of severe environmental pressure. In short, punctuated equilibrium is a theory that comes up short in terms of genuine scientific backing.

CONCLUSION

While atheists draw a great deal of ammunition for their anti-god view from the theory of evolution, more often than not they are "shooting blanks" at God. The evidence is on the side of creationism.

6

THE INTELLIGENT DESIGN OF THE UNIVERSE

Intelligent design theory involves the use of scientific methodology to uncover evidence that the universe was designed by an intelligent being. This evidence is massive, beginning at the molecular level and extending all the way to the deep recesses of interstellar space. Understandably, this theory has ignited a firestorm of response from the atheistic community. In what follows, I will briefly address some of the more notable objections atheists have voiced. Those interested in a more comprehensive treatment of the subject are invited to consult my book *The 10 Things You*

Should Know About the Creation-Evolution Debate (Harvest House Publishers).

Objection: Intelligent design theory is not reasonable. If it were reasonable, atheists say, "more scientists should be reaching the same kind of conclusion."[1]

Answering the Objection: Intelligent design theory *is* reasonable. In illustrating this, William Lane Craig paints an interesting word picture. Imagine you are trudging through the Sahara Desert and traversing miles upon miles of sand. *Sand is everywhere!* Suddenly, as you round a sand dune, you are confronted with a skyscraper the size of the Empire State Building. Would you conclude that it just randomly came together by chance? Or would you determine that somebody must have designed and built it? What is the more *reasonable* conclusion? The answer is obvious. There is too much order and there are too many signs of intelligent involvement for it to have been an accident.[2]

On a much grander scale, the incredible order and design of the universe provides clear signs of intelligence. Concisely put, the reasoning behind intelligent design theory involves two *premises* (1 and 2 below) and a *conclusion* (3):

1. All designs imply a designer.
2. There is great design in the universe.
3. Therefore, there must be a Great Designer of the universe.[3]

We might also put it this way:

1. Signs of intelligence always imply an intelligent being.
2. There are great signs of intelligence in the universe.

3. Therefore, there must be a Great Intelligence who created the universe.

In the modern world, there are various job professions and even whole industries that seek for clues of "intelligent design" and intentionality—that is, clues indicating that an intelligent being intentionally engaged in a particular action, as opposed to a chance occurrence.[4] A crime scene investigator (CSI), for example, examines all the evidence he or she can find at the scene of a death in order to answer the question, Was this person's demise *by design* or *by accident?* Life insurance companies also seek to ascertain whether a person's death was by design or by accident. Cryptographers seek to distinguish random signals from those that may carry encoded messages. Scientists who utilize radio telescopes at SETI (Search for ExtraTerrestrial Intelligence) seek to distinguish between random radio "noise" and signals from an intelligent source. Copyright offices seek to determine whether someone purposefully plagiarized a preexisting work. A teacher at an elementary school seeks to determine whether two nearly identical student tests were the result of someone cheating. The reality is that in many cases, we can detect signs of intelligence by the effects left behind.[5]

I remember the first time I traveled through South Dakota and saw the images of four U.S. presidents chiseled into a granite cliff on Mount Rushmore. The purposeful design in this giant rock is unmistakable. No one seeing this sight would conclude that wind or rain erosion caused it.[6] Such erosion might have caused the Grand Canyon, but not Mount Rushmore. Intelligent artistry is obvious in this case.

Likewise, if you look up at the sky during the day and see the words, "Free Concert in the Park Tonight," you can assume that these words were caused not by a random cloud formation but were spelled out by a skywriter. Clearly, such words indicate intelligent design at work.

The point I am driving at is that the same kinds of evidence that shows crime scene investigators, life insurance companies, cryptographers, SETI scientists, copyright offices, teachers, and people who see words in the sky that an intelligent being was involved are also clearly seen in the universe around us. Intelligent design researchers Phillip E. Johnson and Hugh Ross thus speak of a God who left His fingerprints all over the creation.[7] William Dembski speaks of a God who has left His footprints throughout the creation.[8] In our day, intelligent design theorists are finding increasing evidence for these fingerprints and footprints. It is therefore quite reasonable to believe in a divine Designer, and there are an increasing number of scientists who say so.[9]

Objection: Everything in the universe can be explained in terms of natural causes. There is no need to appeal to the existence of a divine designer, even in the case of complex body parts such as the human eye and a bird's wing. As one atheist put it:

> Neither wings nor eyes are miracles. Both organs betray the opportunistic nature of the evolutionary process. Just as there is more than one way to make a wing, so too there are many ways of making eyes. All this is intelligible if these structures are the result of natural selection acting upon randomly occurring mutations.[10]

Answering the Objection: The flaw in this line of thinking is that scientists in our day have discovered many structures that are *irreducibly complex,* and therefore could not have been caused by mere natural causes. According to Lehigh University biochemist Michael Behe, an irreducibly complex system is "a single system which is composed of several well-matched, interacting parts that contribute to the basic function, and where the removal of any one of the parts causes the system to effectively cease functioning."[11] In such a system, there are a number of components that interact with each other such that if any single component is missing from the system, it no longer operates correctly.[12]

Behe suggests that a good example of an irreducibly complex system is a common mechanical mousetrap.[13] Such a mousetrap has a number of components that are necessary to its functioning, such that if any component of the trap is missing, it no longer functions correctly.[14] In the case of a mousetrap, all its pieces have to be in place before you can actually catch a mouse.[15] If it is missing a spring, a hammer, or platform, for example, it will not work. It is hence irreducibly complex. Likewise, there are bodily organs and parts—such as the human eye and a bird's wing—that involve a variety of interacting components ordered in such a way that they accomplish a function beyond the individual components, and hence are irreducibly complex, thus giving evidence of being intelligently designed.[16] The atheistic claim that natural selection and random mutations can account for the eye and the wing is most unreasonable.

The Irreducibly Complex Eye. One of the best examples of a bodily organ that is irreducibly complex is the eye.[17] The more the eye is studied, the more impossible it seems that the eye could ever have come about as a result of Darwinian natural selection. A piece-by-piece development of this incredibly complex organ— resulting from infinitesimally small Darwinian improvements over an unimaginably long period of time, requiring untold thousands of random positive mutations—seems impossible to imagine. The sheer complexity of the eye indicates that an incredibly knowledgeable engineer planned it from beginning to end. Certainly the ability of the eye to focus on different objects at different distances alone is a complex procedure that requires fantastic engineering. As well, the ability of the eye to work in perfect and instant synergistic harmony with the brain so that sight is possible requires an engineering feat beyond anything human engineers could even begin to hope to accomplish.

Against evolutionary theory, Phillip E. Johnson observes that the initial steps toward a new bodily function such as seeing with an eye would provide virtually no advantage to an animal unless the various parts of the eye required for seeing *appeared at the same time*.[18] If the initial steps toward a new bodily function provided no advantage, one must assume that natural selection would weed such initial steps out of the body. Keep in mind that evolutionists themselves say that natural selection is purposeless and unguided, and cannot know the end result of these "initial steps." Put in the form of a question, How do the various parts of the eye know how to assemble themselves over a very long period in order to attain the function of seeing?

The Irreducibly Complex Wing. Evolutionists try to argue that the wing must have initially been a body appendage—a small flap or web—that served some useful purpose for the initial animal so that natural selection preserved it for future generations. Atheist Richard Dawkins speculates that perhaps the small flap helped the animal to jump farther than it could before, or perhaps catch some air to help it avoid breaking its neck in the event of a fall.[19] As long periods of time passed, the flap or web allegedly developed so that flight eventually became possible.

This seems to be wishful thinking. Even if a creature produced a small web or a flap, natural selection would likely weed it out as a useless body part long before the animal had the capability of flying. Mutations only bring about one tiny change at a time, and the development of a complex body part such as a wing would require untold thousands of random positive mutations. How would natural selection, at each minimal step along the way, know whether to keep each small mutational change, or breed that small mutational change out of the species? How would natural selection recognize the worth of a single mutation during a long process of multiple mutations, over innumerable generations, awaiting the eventual arrival of a complex body part such as a wing?[20]

Dawkins' explanation does not make sense when one considers that the initial small web would have likely been so small and insignificant that it would not have sufficient aerodynamic qualities to catch enough air to break a fall, or enable an animal to jump further. Moreover, growing a new appendage is not all that is required to fly. Both the bodily structure of the entire animal (such as developing new highly coordinated muscles on the side of the body) and the internal instincts of the (ground) animal must be altered in order to enable it to fly.[21] All things considered, natural selection simply cannot account for the origin of the wing. The wing gives every appearance of intelligent design.

Molecular Machines. We can make this same point with evidence at the molecular level. Historically, Darwinism emerged when there was little scientific knowledge about the inner workings of the cell. However, now that scientists have attained this knowledge, the fictional nature of Darwinism has become all too apparent.[22]

Nineteenth-century biologists believed the cell was composed of simple protoplasm.[23] Today, however, biologists have learned that the cell contains ultrasophisticated molecular machines.[24] In view of the complexity of molecular life, the key question has become this: Can Darwinism account for this complexity? Darwin once said that if a complex organ existed which could not have been formed by "numerous, successive, slight modifications,"[25] then his theory would break down. It is the contention of many today that the existence of complex, information-rich structures at the molecular level cannot be explained by Darwinism and calls for the existence of an intelligent designer.[26]

What kinds of complexity do we witness at the molecular level? William Dembski observes that we witness high-tech molecular systems that include such hallmarks as "information storage and transfer; functioning codes; sorting and delivery systems; self-regulation and feedback loops; signal transduction circuitry; and everywhere, complex arrangements of mutually-interdependent and well fitted parts that work in concert to perform a function."[27] This may sound complicated, but Dembski's point is that the complexity that we witness at the molecular level is every bit as "high-tech" as some of the high-tech electronic gadgets created by human beings. These ultrasophisticated molecular machines show just as much evidence of design as do modern computers.[28] Observations at the molecular level thus virtually beg for an explanation.[29]

Michael Behe likewise demonstrates complexity at the molecular level with his discussion of the ion-powered rotary engines that turn the whiplike flagella of certain bacteria. He notes that this complex machinery includes such components as a rotor, a stator, O-rings, bushings, and a drive shaft.[30] He argues that since multiple independent protein parts are necessary in order for this molecular mechanism to function—and since the absence of any single component of this mechanism would cause it not to function—there is no way that gradualistic natural selection, through multiple intermediate stages over a long period of time, can explain the emergence of such mechanisms. With a cell, it is "all or nothing."[31] The only explanation that makes sense is that an intelligent designer is behind such irreducibly complex mechanisms. Such molecular mechanisms must have been created fully formed, with all parts in place, or else they would not function.

Objection: DNA emerged strictly via natural causes. Atheist Keith Parson asks:

> What grounds could there possibly be for holding that DNA cannot have originated in a purely naturalistic fashion?...Proponents of the view that life arose naturalistically do not hold that the first DNA molecule arose...in a single step through a random shuffling of its constituent parts. Rather, they hold that the first DNA molecule developed from a slightly simpler molecule, which in turn developed from a slightly simpler molecule, and so on. Life developed through a process of cumulative evolution, not in one big leap.[32]

Answering the Objection: DNA is a nucleic acid that carries genetic information in the cell and is capable of self-replication. The volume of information contained in DNA staggers the mind. There is enough information capacity in a single DNA cell to store all 30 volumes of the *Encyclopædia Britannica,* three or four times over.[33] Put another way, "The amount of information that could be stored in a pinhead's volume of DNA is equivalent to a pile of paperback books 500 times as tall as the distance from Earth to the Moon, each with a different, yet specific content."[34] We must therefore ask: *Where* did this staggering amount of information—much like computer software code inside a computer[35]—come from? The evidence points to the existence of a divine programmer.[36]

To expand on the software analogy, Microsoft founder Bill Gates says that "DNA is like a computer program, but far, far more advanced than any software we've ever created."[37] Computer programs do not write themselves. A programmer is always involved. Even if plenty of time is provided, a computer program still cannot write itself. A software program cannot write a simple version of itself (beta 1), and from there improve on itself until a slightly better version is completed (beta 2), and so on until the final software program, with all its millions of lines of computer code, is completed. The same is true regarding the information in DNA. Somebody *had* to program that information into the DNA.

Objection: There is no scientific basis for intelligent design theory. Atheists claim there is no way to measure, count, repeat, and/or test results in intelligent design theory, and therefore it cannot be true science.[38] Design arguments "don't lead to anything that's empirically investigable."[39] "The scientific method of testing hypotheses requires observation," and intelligent design cannot be "demonstrated clearly through a laboratory test."[40] Hence, atheists are sure that intelligent design "has nothing to offer us scientifically."[41]

Answering the Objection: There are a number of areas of scientific study in which repetition is impossible. Many scientists presently believe in the big bang theory, but this event happened (allegedly) only once some 13 to 15 billion years ago. No one was around to observe it firsthand, no one was available to take measurements, and there is certainly no way of repeating the event in a laboratory so that it can be tested over and over again. Yet no one balks at including the big bang theory within the realm of science.

Likewise, simply because we cannot repeat in a laboratory the fossilization process of ancient life forms does not exclude paleontology from the realm of science. Simply because we cannot repeat the inscription on the Rosetta Stone does not exclude archaeology from the realm of science.[42] Simply because no one was on hand to observe a so-called extinct common ancestor does not exclude evolution from science. Likewise, simply because we cannot repeat the work of the original Intelligent Designer in a laboratory does not exclude intelligent design from science. The reality is that *science is far more than repetition.*

Intelligent design theory holds that an intelligent cause of the universe is empirically detectable by using a well-defined scientific method that focuses on *contingency, complexity,* and *specification.* Simply put, if something were designed, we would expect to see evidence of *contingency,* meaning there is evidence that it did not result from an automatic, unintelligent process (such as natural selection). If something were designed, we would expect to see evidence that it was *complex* enough (with many interacting working parts) that random-chance processes alone would not be able to cause its existence. If something were designed, we would also expect to see evidence of *specificity*—meaning that it possesses a detailed, precise pattern commonly associated with intelligent causes.[43]

We might illustrate "specified complexity" this way:

- The letter "C" is *specified* without being *complex.*
- The random sequence of letters "WQNRAZ" is *complex* without being *specified.*
- The phrase "Houston, we have a problem" is both *complex* and *specified.* We can easily discern that an intelligent mind is behind this sequence of letters.
- What all this is leading up to is that *specified complexity is our means of empirically detecting design in the universe.*[44]

Many scholars from the fields of science and philosophy believe there are evidences for specified complexity in the number of perfect "circumstances" there are in this universe for life to emerge.

Jimmy Davis and Harry Poe suggest that specified complexity is evident in "the universe's coincidences of having the right atoms, the right molecules, enough time, and enough space for life to occur." Specified complexity is also seen "in the earth's coincidences of the right galaxy type, the location in the galaxy, the type of star, the earth's distance from the sun, the location of Jupiter, the size of the moon, and the composition of the earth."[45]

Our universe is literally fine-tuned for the possibility of human life.[46] This is called the "anthropic principle" (from the Greek word *anthropos,* meaning "man"). There are numerous highly improbable factors that have to be *precisely in place* in a *balanced fashion* for the survival of life on earth. Eliminate any one of these factors, and life would not be possible. As one scholar put it, "almost everything about the basic structure of the universe...is balanced on a razor's edge for life to occur."[47] Another scholar notes, "The astonishing intricacy, harmony, and organization of the cosmos in allowing for human life is evidenced from the fine-tuning of the fundamental constants of physics, to the 'just-so' nature of the galaxy and solar system, to the information-laden building blocks known as the DNA code, to perhaps the crowning teleological (relating to design) achievement: the incredible and delicate complexity of the human brain-mind relationship."[48] Yet another comments, "One could think of the initial conditions of the universe and the fundamental parameters of physics as a dartboard that fills the whole galaxy, and the conditions necessary for life to exist as a small one-foot wide target: unless the dart hits the target, life would be impossible."[49] Well, life has emerged on earth because the dart in fact "hit the target."

For example, our universe is expanding at the precise rate necessary to enable the formation of galaxies. (If it were to expand too slowly, it would collapse into one big lump. If it were to expand too rapidly, the matter would quickly disperse so efficiently that no galaxies could form.[50]) Further, if our moon were significantly larger, its gravitational pull would be greater, and this would cause flooding from tidal waves as well as severe climatic instabilities.[51] Likewise, if earth had more than one moon, there would be great tidal instability. If earth were significantly closer to the sun, temperatures would increase to the point that life could not survive on earth. There is just enough oxygen on earth—comprising 21 percent of the atmosphere—for creatures to be able to breathe. Norman Geisler and Frank Turek explain: "That precise figure is an anthropic constant that makes life on earth possible. If oxygen were 25 percent, fires would erupt spontaneously; if it were 15 percent, human beings would suffocate."[52]

It has also been pointed out that the sheer size of the planet Jupiter causes such a gravitational pull that it attracts asteroids and comets that otherwise might strike Earth. If there were more water vapor in the atmosphere than there is now, it would cause a runaway greenhouse effect and become too hot on earth to allow for human life. If there were less water vapor in the atmosphere, it would become too cold because there would be an insufficient greenhouse effect.[53]

In short, everything about our earth and the universe seems tailor-made for the existence of human life (and other life forms). As William Lane Craig put it, "The existence of intelligent life depends on a conspiracy of initial conditions that must be fine-tuned to a degree that is literally incomprehensible and incalculable."[54] There is no plausible explanation for all this other than the existence of a cosmic Designer.

Objection: Those who hold to intelligent design theory have a creationist bias in their examination of the evidence.[55]

Answering the Objection: *All* people have some biases,

including secular scientists. Astronomer Robert Jastrow made a highly revealing comment in this regard:

> Theologians generally are delighted with the proof that the Universe had a beginning, but astronomers are curiously upset. Their reactions provide an interesting demonstration of the response of the scientific mind—supposedly a very objective mind—when evidence uncovered by science itself leads to a conflict with the articles of faith in our profession. It turns out that the scientist behaves the way the rest of us do when our beliefs are in conflict with the evidence. We become irritated, we pretend the conflict does not exist, or we paper it over with meaningless phrases.[56]

The fact is, scientists have biases like everybody else does. Physicist Fritjof Capra, author of *The Turning Point* and *The Tao of Physics,* once admitted, "My presentation of modern physics has been influenced by my personal beliefs and allegiances."[57]

Let us be honest in admitting that the accusation of bias is a sword that can cut both ways. The key question that should concern all of us is this: What does the evidence truly reveal?

Objection: The fact that the universe is not perfectly designed proves there was no divine Designer. Because the design of certain aspects of the universe could be improved upon (that is, they are imperfect), they could not have been created by a *perfect* Designer. Because our universe has "design flaws," it could not have come from the hands of a flawless, divine Creator.

Answering the Objection: This line of argumentation is faulty. I might look at a particular model of a car and think of various ways the car could have a better design, but that does not mean the car itself did not come from the hands of a designer. I might look at the floor plan of a house and decide the plan could be better in some ways, but that does not mean the floor plan did not come from the hands of an intelligent designer. So it is with the universe. Just because someone might imagine how a structure in the universe might have had a better design does not mean the structure did not come from an intelligent source.

One should consider that even in regard to humanly designed structures, we might think we have a better design in mind for a particular item, but upon talking to the designer, we might discover some important variables we had not previously considered that casts the design in a different (more favorable) light. For example, I might think that a computer casing would have a better design if it were much smaller. But then, upon talking to the design engineer, he informs me that the larger size better accommodates the internal cooling system for the components that generate heat. This new information adjusts my thinking so that I now know my idea is not necessarily a better design.

In the same way, we may think we can come up with better designs for structures in the universe, but there are likely variables involved that we know nothing about, and that the Intelligent Designer is fully aware of. Maybe we do not know as much as we think we do. And besides, how do we know whether our suggested change would actually make a structure better? Introducing a new element might result in a malfunction we had not anticipated.

CONCLUSION

Because all designs imply a designer, and because there is great design in the universe, our inescapable conclusion is that there is a Great Designer behind the universe. Belief in God is therefore reasonable.

7

MORALITY AND THE ABSOLUTELY MORAL LAWGIVER

Can humankind's sense of morality be accounted for by strictly social factors? Or is such morality impossible without the existence of a Moral Lawgiver? The debate between atheists and Christians on this issue is a heated one. In this chapter, we will briefly address some of the more common objections atheists voice about the Christian viewpoint on morality.

Objection: Christians are in no position to criticize the morality of atheists since there are so many moral atrocities recorded in the Bible. Atheists say the Bible accepts and even regulates the institution of slavery, oppresses gays and lesbians, and is sexist in its oppression of women.[1]

Answering the Objection: The atheistic objection misrepresents the facts. On the issue of slavery, God from the very beginning declared that *all* humans are created in the image of God (Genesis 1:27 NKJV). The apostle Paul also declared that "we are the off-spring of God" (Acts 17:29 NKJV), and God "has made from one blood every nation of men to dwell on all the face of the earth" (verse 26 NKJV). Moreover, despite the fact that slavery was coun-tenanced in the Semitic cultures of the day, the law in the Bible demanded that slaves eventually be set free (Exodus 21:2; Leviticus 25:40). Likewise, servants had to be treated with respect (Exodus 21:20,26). Israel, itself in slavery in Egypt for a prolonged time, was constantly reminded by God of this (Deuteronomy 5:15), and their emancipation became the model for the liberation of all slaves (see Leviticus 25:40).

In the New Testament, Paul declared that in Christianity "there is neither Jew nor Greek, there is neither slave nor free, there is nei-ther male nor female; for you are all one in Christ Jesus" (Galatians 3:28 NKJV). All social classes are broken down in Christ; we are all equal before God. Though the apostle Paul urges, "Bondservants, be obedient to those who are your masters" (Ephesians 6:5 NKJV), he is not thereby approving of the institution of slavery, but simply alluding to the *de facto* situation in his day. He is instructing ser-vants to be good workers, just as believers should be today, but he was not thereby commending slavery. Paul also instructed all believers to be obedient to the government (even if unjust) for the Lord's sake (Romans 13:1; see also Titus 3:1; 1 Peter 2:13). But this in no way condones oppression and tyranny, which the Bible repeatedly condemns (Exodus 2:23-25; Isaiah 10:1).

Atheists also misrepresent Christianity's view toward women. Women were certainly mistreated during ancient Jewish times. The woman is "in all things inferior to the man," said first-century

Jewish historian Flavius Josephus.[2] Rabbi Judah, a contemporary of Josephus, said "a man must pronounce three blessings each day: 'Blessed be the Lord who did not make me a heathen; blessed be he who did not make me a woman; blessed be he who did not make me an uneducated person.'"[3]

Jewish rabbis in the first century were encouraged not to teach or even to speak with women. Jewish wisdom literature tells us that "he that talks much with womankind brings evil upon himself and neglects the study of the Law and at the last will inherit Gehenna [hell]."[4] One reason for the avoidance of women was the belief that they could lead men astray: "From garments cometh a moth and from a woman the iniquities of a man" (Ecclesiasticus 42:13). Indeed, men were often viewed as intrinsically better than women, for "better is the iniquity of a man than a woman doing a good turn" (Ecclesiasticus 42:14).[5]

In view of this low status of women, it is not surprising that they enjoyed few legal rights in Jewish society. Women were not even allowed to give evidence in a court of law, except in extraordinary circumstances. Moreover, according to the rabbinic school that followed Rabbi Hillel, a man could legally divorce his wife merely for burning his dinner.

It was in this oppressive context that Christianity was born. Many people—both men and women—have hailed Jesus as a feminist because of His elevation of women in a male-chauvinist society. In a Jewish culture where women were discouraged from studying the law, Jesus taught women right alongside men as equals (Matthew 14:21; 15:38). And when He taught, He often used women's activities to illustrate the character of the kingdom of God, such as baking bread (Luke 13:20-21), grinding corn (Luke 17:35), and sweeping the house to find a lost coin (Luke 15:8-10). Some Jewish rabbis taught that a man should not speak to a woman in a public place, yet Jesus not only spoke to a woman (who, incidentally, was a Samaritan), but also drank from her cup in a public place (John 4:1-30). The first person He appeared to after His resurrection from the dead was Mary and not the male disciples (Matthew 28:9-10). Clearly, Jesus had a very high view of women.

Likewise, Galatians 3:28 tells us that there is neither male nor female in Jesus Christ. First Peter 3:7 says men and women are fellow heirs of grace. Ephesians 5:21 speaks of mutual submission between man and wife. According to John 7:53–8:11, Jesus would not permit the double standard of the woman being taken in adultery and letting the man go free. In Luke 10:38, we read that Jesus let a woman sit at His feet, which was a place typically reserved for the male disciples. Verses such as these show that in God's eyes, men and women are spiritually equal. Hence, the Bible can hardly be charged with condoning the oppression of women.

As for homosexuality, this is unquestionably a moral issue that God addresses quite sternly in Scripture. The Bible states that "neither fornicators...nor homosexuals...will inherit the kingdom of God" (1 Corinthians 6:9-10 NKJV). The Scriptures repeatedly and consistently condemn homosexual practices (see Leviticus 18:22 and Romans 1:26). God loves all persons, including homosexuals, but He hates homosexuality. The Bible condemns *all* types of fornication—which would therefore include homosexuality (Matthew 15:19; Mark 7:21; John 8:41; Acts 15:20,29; Galatians 5:19-21; 1 Thessalonians 4:3; Hebrews 13:4).

It is noteworthy that sex is defined *biologically* in Scripture from the very beginning. In Genesis 1 we read that God created "male and female" and then told them to "be fruitful and multiply" (Genesis 1:27-28). This reproduction was possible only if He was referring to a biological male and female. Second, sexual orientation is understood biologically when God said, "For this reason a man will leave his father and mother and be united to his wife, and they will become one flesh" (Genesis 2:24). Only a biological father and mother can produce children, and the reference to "one flesh" speaks of a physical marriage. From the very beginning, then, heterosexuality is God's standard for the human race. Homosexuality, by contrast, is viewed as sin and is forbidden by God. Yet again, God loves *all* people, and He does not condone the oppression of anyone, including homosexuals.

Objection: Christians aren't so moral. The hypocrisy of Christians constitutes a powerful argument against Christianity.[6] Indeed, "the number one cause of atheism is Christians. Those who proclaim God with their mouths and deny Him with their lifestyles are what an unbelieving world find simply unbelievable."[7] As Friedrich Nietzsche put it, "I will believe in the Redeemer when the Christian looks a little more redeemed."[8]

Answering the Objection: It is regrettably true that some Christians are hypocritical. However, a Christian's success or failure in living up to the ethical principles set forth by Christ should not be *the* decisive factor in evaluating whether or not Christianity is true. The more important issue is whether the historical, factual, and theological claims of Christianity are true. Important questions include: Is there historical evidence to suggest that the Bible is, in fact, the Word of God and can be trusted? Is there evidence to suggest that Jesus was a historical person? Is there evidence to suggest that Jesus was God in human flesh? Is there evidence to suggest that Jesus was crucified and rose from the dead? It is the answers to these kinds of questions that ought to guide one in evaluating Christianity. Christian apologist Kenneth Samples writes:

Logically, a Christian's ethical inconsistency (while

never to be condoned and understandably discon-
certing) has little or no bearing on the objective
truth-claims of Christianity. To put it more directly—
the negative, sinful, or evil actions of individual
Christians (real or so-called) do not falsify the historic
claims about Christ—his perfect life, sacrificial death,
and bodily resurrection. Because some Christians act
in a hypocritical manner, it does not follow that Jesus
ceases to be the Son of God and the Savior of the
world.[9]

Actually, the fact that some Christians are hypocritical is a
reflection of one of the primary doctrinal planks of Christianity:
All human beings are fallen in sin (Romans 3:23). When a person
becomes a Christian, his sin nature does not vanish. He becomes
redeemed but he is still a sinner. Thankfully, there are many
Christians in the world who are not hypocritical, and are a strong
witness for the truth of Christianity. Again, however, the more
important point is whether the historical, factual, and theological
claims of Christianity are true. I believe the evidence presented in
this book establishes that Christianity is indeed true.

Objection: Atheists are not less moral than Christians are. One
atheist wrote, "There is no evidence that atheists are any less moral
than believers. Many systems of morality have been developed
that do not presuppose the existence of a supernatural being."[10]

Answering the Objection: Christians grant that all people—
themselves included—have been tainted by sin. Therefore, all
people—Christians included—do some immoral things. There is
no argument here. Yet it is also true that where there is no moral
constraint (for example, when people jettison the absolute moral
commands of Scripture), sinful behavior more easily flourishes.

I find it highly relevant that a number of atheists themselves have admitted that their worldview of atheism makes it more comfortable for them to live the kinds of lives they like—that is, without moral accountability. They essentially suppress evidence for God in order to protect their comfortable lifestyle. They realize that becoming a Christian would require a change in thinking, friends, priorities, lifestyle, and morals, and they are not willing to make that change.[11]

Former atheist Lee Strobel reveals that this was a motivating factor when he chose to believe in atheistic Darwinism: "I was more than happy to latch onto Darwinism as an excuse to jettison the idea of God so I could unabashedly pursue my own agenda in life without moral constraints."[12] He reflects:

> I had a lot of motivation to find faults with Christianity when I was an atheist. I knew that my hard-drinking, immoral, and self-obsessed lifestyle would have to change if I ever became a follower of Jesus, and I wasn't sure I wanted to let go of that. After all, it was all I knew. Consequently, instead of trying to find the truth, I found myself attempting to fend off the truth with fabricated doubts and contrived objections.[13]

Some atheists would rather seek liberated, unfettered living than embrace the meaning in life that Christianity can bring. Atheist Aldous Huxley admitted,

> I had motives for not wanting the world to have a meaning; consequently assumed that it had none, and was able without any difficulty to find satisfying reasons for this assumption. The philosopher who finds no meaning in the world is not concerned exclusively

with a problem in pure metaphysics, he is also concerned to prove that there is no valid reason why
he personally should not do as he wants to do....
For myself, the philosophy of meaninglessness was
essentially an instrument of liberation, sexual and
political.[14]

No wonder Christian scholar J. Budziszewski concluded that
"not many people disbelieve in God and then begin to sin; most
atheists adopt some favorite sin and then find reasons to disbelieve in God."[15] This brings to mind Psalm 14:1: "The fool says in
his heart, 'There is no God.'" Notice this verse is not saying that
a person is a fool for denying the existence of God. Rather, he is
called a fool for *saying in his heart* that there is no God. The implication is that he knows better. He *says* there is no God, despite
the fact that he knows there likely is one. Such is an act of great
folly. Verse 3 then tells us that such people have become corrupt.
Scripture draws a very close connection between a corrupt lifestyle
and a denial of God's existence (see, for example, Romans 1:20-
25).

**Objection: Admitting to the existence of God is not necessary in
order for a person to have morality or to make sense of one's life.**
As atheist Kai Nielsen put it, "You can make perfectly good sense
of your lives and of your moral beliefs without belief in God."[16]

Answering the Objection: I concede that atheists can hold
to certain moral principles. I do not believe, however, that they
can ultimately *justify* these principles. One can outwardly claim
that hate, racism, and genocide are wrong, but if there is no ultimate standard of morality (God), how can these things *actually* be
wrong? As Samples put it, "Atheism has no foundation upon which
to ground man's conscious awareness of moral obligation. Without

God, objective moral values have no metaphysical anchor and thus cannot be accounted for."[17] Put another way, how can there be a moral prescription without a Moral Prescriber.[18] How can there be moral law without a Moral Lawgiver? Moral law extends from the cosmic Moral Lawgiver. The God revealed in Scripture is the morally perfect Person who stands behind the objective moral order discovered in the universe.

Objection: Contrary to the claims of Christians, atheists do believe there are some things that are objectively wrong. Atheist Walter Sinnott-Armstrong argues that behaviors such as rape and discrimination against gays and lesbians are morally wrong, even if there are some people who do not consider them wrong. These behaviors are *objectively* wrong. Such an admission, however, implies nothing about God.[19]

Answering the Objection: Christians do not argue that one must believe in God in order to live a moral life. Nor do Christians argue that it is impossible to recognize moral values without believing in God. Nor do Christians argue that it is impossible to construct a system of ethics without God. What Christians *do* challenge, as noted earlier, is the claim that atheists can hold to objective rights and wrongs *without having a basis or foundation for such a belief or worldview*. Ultimately, for the atheist, all morals are based on social conventions. It could just have easily been decided that cars should go on a red light and stop on a green light.[20] The "right choice" is subjectively determined by society. There is no *ultimate* ground or basis for either green or red meaning "go." And so it is with *all* ethics in the atheist worldview.

For Walter Sinnott-Armstrong to say it is "objectively wrong" to discriminate against gays and lesbians is to express nothing but his own subjective, ungrounded opinion. There are feasibly others who would say it is objectively wrong to give gays and lesbians the same considerations in society as heterosexuals. Sinnott-Armstrong says that even if some disagree with the idea that it is objectively wrong to discriminate against gays and lesbians, it is nevertheless objectively wrong. But who says this must be the case? Sinnott-Armstrong could say that legitimately only if there were some ultimate standard of right and wrong. But since he denies such an ultimate standard of right and wrong (that is, God), he has no ultimate basis for saying it is objectively wrong to discriminate against gays and lesbians. William Lane Craig is thus right when he says:

> If God does not exist, then objective moral values do not exist. When I speak of objective moral values, I mean moral values that are valid and binding whether anybody believes in them or not. Thus, to say, for example, that the Holocaust was objectively wrong is to say that it was wrong even though the Nazis who carried it out thought that it was right and that it would still have been wrong even if the Nazis had won World War II and succeeded in exterminating or brainwashing everyone who disagreed with them. Now if God does not exist, then moral values are not objective in this way.[21]

In this same line of thought, C.S. Lewis commented:

> If no set of moral ideas were truer or better than any other, there would be no sense in preferring civilized morality to savage morality, or Christian morality to Nazi morality. In fact, of course, we all do believe that some moralities are better than others....The moment you say that one set of moral ideas can be better than

another, you are, in fact, measuring them both by
a standard...comparing them both with some Real
Morality, admitting that there is such a thing as a real
Right, independent of what people think, and that
some people's ideas get nearer to that real Right than
others.[22]

**Objection: Morality is something that evolves and is based on social
instinct.** Some atheists take a Darwinian approach to morality,
arguing that our sense of morality evolves much in the same way
that our physical beings have evolved—by natural selection.[22] It is
also suggested by some that the development of ethics is a result
of a social instinct that is within each of us. As we work through
common struggles with other people, moral principles emerge
from within our social instincts and become socially acceptable on
a broad level.[24]

Answering the Objection: Objective rights and wrongs do not
evolve. It is highly revealing that people seem to have a universal
and inherent sense of right and wrong. Various cultures around
the world recognize honesty, wisdom, courage, and justice as vir-
tues. As C.S. Lewis said, "Human beings, all over the earth, have
this curious idea that they ought to behave in a certain way, and
cannot really get rid of it."[25]

Scripture reveals that God's moral law is written on every
human heart (Romans 2:12-16). Every person has an inherent sense
of right and wrong—*an inner sense of moral oughtness*—in their
heart. Everyone knows intuitively, for example, that love is right
and hate is wrong, that saving lives is good and taking lives is evil,
that telling the truth is good and lying is evil, that wisdom is good
and foolishness is evil. The changeless character of God is the only
true source of such universal and objective moral principles. Mere

social instinct cannot account for these universal, objective moral principles.

Christian apologist Dan Story helps us understand the necessity of God's absolute moral standard:

> We could not know what evil is, in any universal sense, unless a moral standard exists outside of us. Without a moral absolute—namely—independent of human consciousness, there would be no criteria to determine what is right or wrong, whether what is wrong today will be wrong tomorrow, whether what is wrong for me is also wrong for you, and whether what is wrong in my culture is also wrong in yours. In short, I could not justify telling you what you ought to do unless there was an absolute standard of moral behavior independent of individual persons and cultures. But such a standard does exist.[26]

That standard is God Himself!

Objection: Either morality is beyond God or it is arbitrary. Atheist Bertrand Russell once inquired where God got the moral law. He believed there were only two options. The first option is that moral law is beyond God, and hence He Himself must be subject to it. In this case, God could not be considered the "ultimate good" of which Christians speak. The second option is that moral law involves an arbitrary selection of codes that simply originated in God's will or choice—that is, something is "wrong" simply because God decided it was wrong. We must conclude, Russell says, that either morality is beyond God or it is arbitrary.[27]

Answering the Objection: The either/or nature of this objection does not exhaust the possibilities for a proper solution. Christians believe that moral law is rooted in the *intrinsic* morality of God

Himself. Goodness is ultimately rooted in the *intrinsic* goodness of God Himself. Love is ultimately rooted in the *intrinsic* love of God Himself. Hence, morality, goodness, and love are not beyond God, nor are they arbitrary choices on His part, but these are a *part of His very nature,* and hence what He commands must be in keeping with that nature. It is impossible for God to "will" something that is not in accordance with His nature. Because of God's intrinsic love, goodness, and morality, He simply cannot "will" anything arbitrarily.[28]

WHAT CAN WE CONCLUDE?

It is reasonable for us to conclude that the existence of an objective moral law points to the existence of a Moral Lawgiver. This argument can be summarized in two premises (1 and 2 below) and a conclusion (3):

1. If God does not exist, objective moral values do not exist.

2. Objective moral values *do* exist.

3. Therefore, God exists.[29]

8

THE RELIABILITY OF
THE BIBLE—PART 1

The Bible is not a single volume, but is rather an entire library of books, including letters, histories, poems, prayers, and other kinds of writing. These writings were penned by numerous different authors, living in different lands, in a variety of different circumstances. Yet from Genesis to Revelation, the Bible tells one primary story of redemption. This story is a thread that runs through the entire Bible. Though God deals with different people in each of the biblical books, in each case we read of God's interaction among them for the purpose of bringing redemption to them.

Not unexpectedly, atheists, agnostics, and skeptics expend a great deal of effort in seeking to undermine the reliability of the Bible and its message. In what follows, I will address some of their more common objections.

Objection: The oral tradition from which the New Testament was written was unreliable. Michael Shermer, editor of *The Skeptic Magazine,* made a case for this on Lee Strobel's *Faith Under Fire* television show.[1]

Answering the Objection: Among the ancient Jews, much attention was paid to accuracy and reliability in carrying on the oral tradition because it was by this means that customs, practices, and teachings were handed down generation to generation. Even from an early age, Jewish children were taught to remember oral material accurately.

One might concede that the memory of a single individual in the community could become faulty. One must not forget, however, that oral tradition was handed down collectively to the entire community of believers. The fact that many people received the same oral tradition served as a safeguard against the faulty transmission of the tradition. It is unlikely that the memories of *all* those in the community would become faulty, especially since the goal of each person was to be dead accurate.

Even while oral tradition was being handed down, one must recognize that it was always God's will for His revelations to be written down and preserved for coming generations. "Moses wrote all the words of the LORD" (Exodus 24:4 NKJV). Joshua, too, "wrote these words in the Book of the Law of God" (Joshua 24:26). Samuel "told the people the ordinances of the kingdom, and wrote them in the book and placed it before the LORD" (1 Samuel 10:25 NASB). The Lord instructed Isaiah, "Take for yourself a large tablet and write on it in ordinary letters…" (Isaiah 8:1 NASB). What the apostle Paul wrote was at "the Lord's command" (1 Corinthians 14:37). The apostle John was commanded by the Lord to "write, therefore, what you have seen…" (Revelation 1:19). What all this means is that the prophets and apostles who initially communicated to people via oral tradition went on to quickly record their revelations from God by writing them down.

It is also critical to grasp that when the human penmen wrote down the words of Scripture, they did not do so merely by human memory, but their writings were inspired by God. I realize atheists, agnostics, and skeptics reject miracles, including the miracle of the inspiration of Scripture by the Holy Spirit. The reader is urged to review the case for miracles found in chapter 4 of this book.

Biblical inspiration may be defined as God's superintending of the human authors so that, using their own individual personalities—and even their writing styles—they composed and recorded without error His revelation to humankind in the words of the original autographs. In other words, the original documents of the Bible were written by men, who, though permitted to exercise their own personalities and literary talents, wrote under the control and guidance of the Holy Spirit, the result being a perfect and errorless recording of the exact message God desired to give to humankind.

Hence, the writers of Scripture were not mere writing machines. God did not use them like keys on a typewriter to mechanically reproduce His message. Nor did He dictate the words, page by page. The biblical evidence makes it clear that each writer had a style of his own. (Isaiah had a powerful literary style; Jeremiah had a mournful tone; Luke's style had medical overtones; and John was very simple in his approach.) The Holy Spirit infallibly worked through each of these writers and their individual styles to inerrantly communicate His message to humankind.

To what extent were the biblical writers controlled by the Holy Spirit as they wrote? Second Peter 1:21 provides a key insight regarding the human-divine interchange in the process of inspiration. This verse informs us that "prophecy [or Scripture] never had its origin in the will of man, but men spoke from God as they were carried along by the Holy Spirit." The phrase "carried along" in this verse literally means "forcefully borne along."

Even though human beings were used in the process of writing down God's Word, they were all literally "carried along" by the Holy Spirit. The human wills of the authors were not the originators of God's message. God did not permit the will of sinful human beings to misdirect or erroneously record His revelation. Rather, "God *moved* and the prophet *mouthed* these truths; God *revealed* and man *recorded* His word."[2]

Interestingly, the Greek word for "carried along" in 2 Peter 1:21 is the same as that found in Acts 27:15-17. In this passage, we read of experienced sailors who could not navigate their ship because the wind was so strong. The ship was being driven, directed, and carried along by the wind. This is similar to the Spirit's driving, directing, and carrying the human authors of the Bible as He wished. The word is a strong one, indicating the Spirit's complete superintendence of the human authors. Yet just as the sailors were active on the ship (though the wind, not the sailors, ultimately controlled the ship's movement), so the human authors were active in writing as the Spirit directed.

The evidence indicates that the New Testament writers were aware that their writings were inspired by God. In 1 Corinthians 2:13 the apostle Paul said he spoke "not in words taught us by human wisdom but in words taught by the Spirit, expressing spiritual truths in spiritual words." In this passage Paul (who wrote over half the New Testament) affirmed that his words were authoritative because they were rooted not in fallible men but infallible God (the Holy Spirit). The Holy Spirit is the Spirit of truth who was promised to the apostles to teach and guide them into all the truth (see John 16:13).

Later, in 1 Corinthians 14:37, Paul said, "If anybody thinks he is a prophet or spiritually gifted, let him acknowledge that what I am writing to you is the Lord's command." In 1 Thessalonians 2:13 Paul likewise said, "We also thank God continually because, when you received the word of God, which you heard from us, you accepted it not as the word of men, but as it actually is, the word of God, which is at work in you who believe." Again, the reason Paul's words were authoritative is that they were rooted in God, not in man. God used Paul as His instrument to communicate His word to man.

Because the Scriptures were inspired by the Holy Spirit, the various books of the Bible possess an amazing unity. One must consider the fact that the Bible's authors were from all walks of life—including kings, peasants, philosophers, fishermen, physicians, statesmen, scholars, poets, and farmers. These individuals lived in different cultures, had vastly different experiences, and often were quite different in character. Yet, as noted earlier, the Bible has a continuity that can be observed from Genesis to Revelation. How could this be? How did God accomplish this? It is all related to the fact that God the Holy Spirit inspired Scripture.

Objection: The gospel writers were biased with theological motives in what they wrote, and hence the New Testament is unreliable. This point was argued by skeptic Michael Shermer on *Faith Under Fire,* and is a favorite argument on many atheist Web sites.

Answering the Objection: The fallacy here is to imagine that to give an account of something one believes in passionately necessarily forces one to distort history. This is simply not true. In modern times, some of the most reliable reports of the Nazi Holocaust were written by Jews who were passionately committed to seeing such genocide never repeated.[3]

The reality is that everyone has a point of view. Just because a person holds to a particular point of view does not mean that his or her analysis of some event he or she witnessed is untrustworthy.

The New Testament is not made up of fairy tales, but is rather based on eyewitness testimonies. In 2 Peter 1:16 we read, "We did not follow cleverly invented stories when we told you about the power and coming of our Lord Jesus Christ, but we were eyewitnesses of his majesty." First John 1:1 affirms, "That which was from the beginning, which we have heard, which we have seen with our eyes, which we have looked at and our hands have touched—this we proclaim concerning the Word of life."

Further, it is highly relevant that many of the New Testament writers gave up their lives in defense of the truth they witnessed. "Theological biases" hardly explain why these people were *so* committed to their beliefs that they made the ultimate sacrifice in defending them.

A powerful evidence against the idea that the biblical writers were biased and influenced by "theological motives" is that they included embarrassing details about themselves in the Bible. For example, those who wrote the Old Testament included reports of the Jewish people's total unfaithfulness during the wilderness sojourn as well as their participation in idolatry. The New Testament writers included reports of Peter denying Christ three times, Peter being addressed as "Satan" by Jesus, the disciples scattering like a bunch of faithless cowards when Christ was arrested, and Thomas' doubt about the resurrection of Jesus. Surely if the biblical documents were influenced by biases, these biases would have caused the biblical writers to remove such unflattering elements from the Old and New Testaments.

Contrary to atheist claims, archaeological evidence supports the historical accuracy of the four Gospels. Let us consider the book of Luke as an example. Modern archaeologists who have studied the

Gospel of Luke have concluded that Luke, a doctor, was extremely accurate in his writings, and wrote in an erudite and eloquent way, approaching classical Greek. At the very outset of his Gospel, Luke is careful to emphasize that his account was based upon reliable, firsthand sources (Luke 1:1-4). He wanted to make sure that the truth about Jesus was communicated in an ordered and accurate way. It is noteworthy that in the past, there were a number of instances in which archaeologists thought Luke might have been wrong about a particular issue, but eventually, newly unearthed archaeological evidence vindicated Luke.[4]

Many scholars have pointed to the relevance of a doctor writing this Gospel. As a doctor, Luke would be interested in both scientific *and* historical accuracy. As a doctor, he was certainly fully aware that a woman does not get pregnant without having physical relations with a man. It is therefore highly significant that he expresses unflinching belief in his Gospel that Jesus was virgin-born, and that Mary became pregnant as a result of the Holy Spirit overshadowing her (Luke 1:35). It is also significant that Luke as a doctor expressed steadfast belief in the many miracles of Jesus (see 4:38-40; 5:15-25; 6:17-19; 7:11-15).

Top-rate scholars have studied the Gospel of Luke and have concluded that Luke was an amazingly accurate historian. Sir William Ramsay, originally a liberal and a skeptic, did 30 years of study on Luke and concluded that "Luke is a historian of the first rank; not merely are his statements of fact trustworthy...this author should be placed along with the very greatest of historians."[5] Ramsey noted that the critics of Luke are "pre-archaeological." One should note that Luke also wrote the book of Acts, which, taken with the Gospel of Luke, constitutes about one-fourth of the New Testament being written by this amazingly accurate historian.

In support of the accuracy of Luke as a historian, classical scholar and historian Cohn Hemer painstakingly identified 84 facts in the final 16 chapters of Luke's book of Acts that have been archaeologically verified.[6] Since Luke has a proven track record on these 84 points, he should be given the benefit of the doubt on other issues he speaks of that have not yet been archaeologically verified.[7] Luke's critics certainly have an uphill battle.

Objection: Archaeological evidence is lacking regarding key events found in the Bible. One atheist asks: "Has archaeology proven the historical accuracy of the Bible? If you listened only to biblical inerrantists, you would certainly think so. Amateur apologists have spread this claim all over the internet."[8] The article concedes that a small portion of the Bible has been confirmed by archaeology, but this is far from confirming the Bible as a whole. The clear implication is that there is a plethora of inaccuracies in the Bible.

Answering the Objection: The word *archaeology* literally means "study of ancient things." Biblical archaeology, then, involves a study of ancient things related to biblical people, places, and events.

Contrary to the low view expressed by atheists, the Bible's accuracy and reliability have been proved and verified over and over again by archaeological finds produced by both Christian and non-Christian scholars and scientists. This includes the verification of numerous customs, places, names, and events mentioned in the Bible. To date, over 25,000 sites in biblical lands have been discovered, dating back to Old Testament times, which have established the accuracy of innumerable details in the Bible. Notable examples include:

The Hittites. For many years the existence of the Hittites, a powerful people who lived during the time of Abraham (Genesis 23:10-20), was questioned because no archaeological digs had uncovered anything about them. Critics claimed the Hittites were pure myth. Today the critics are silent. Abundant archaeological evidence for the existence of the Hittites during the time of Abraham has been uncovered. One can even obtain a doctorate in Hittite Studies from the University of Chicago.

Handwriting During the Time of Moses. It was once claimed that Moses could not have written the first five books of the Bible (Genesis, Exodus, Leviticus, Numbers, and Deuteronomy) because handwriting had not been invented yet. However, archaeological discoveries of ancient inscriptions now conclusively prove that there indeed was handwriting during the time of Moses.

Sodom and Gomorrah. Critics used to say that Genesis 10, 13, 14, 18, and 19 are mythological because of a lack of evidence that Sodom and Gomorrah ever existed. These critics have now been silenced in view of the abundant archaeological evidence for the former existence of these cities.

Floors of Ancient Homes. It has now been discovered that many ancient floors in homes were cobbled. On such a floor, it would be quite easy for someone to lose a small object, such as a coin, between the stones on the floor. This archaeological discovery helps us to better understand Jesus' parable of the lost coin in Luke 15:8-10.

There are many other such archaeological evidences that confirm the accuracy and reliability of the Bible. Fossil graveyards around the world attest to the reality of the universal flood during Noah's day. The grave of Abraham's wife, Sarah, has been discovered in southern Israel. Illustrations have been discovered of Hebrew slaves making bricks for the cities of Pithom and Rameses in Egypt. Overwhelming evidence has been discovered regarding David and Solomon and their respective empires. Many believe the house of Joseph (Jesus' father) has been discovered in Nazareth. The grave box of the high priest Caiaphas has been discovered. The synagogue in Capernaum where Jesus often taught has been discovered. A stone discovered at a Roman theater in Caesarea bears the name of Pontius Pilate. Many believe the tomb of Lazarus, whom Jesus raised from the dead, has been discovered. The Pool of Siloam (John 9:7) and Jacob's Well (John 4:12) have been unearthed.

In view of these and multiple other discoveries, we can conclude that archaeology is a true friend of the Bible, but is not so friendly to atheists, agnostics, and skeptics. Nelson Glueck, a specialist in archaeology, did an exhaustive study and concluded, "It can be stated categorically that no archaeological discovery has ever controverted a biblical reference."[9] Well-known scholar William F. Albright, following a comprehensive study, wrote, "Discovery after discovery has established the accuracy of innumerable details, and has brought increased recognition of the value of the Bible as a source of history."[10] Since the Bible as a whole has a proven track record in terms of archaeological discoveries, it should be given the benefit of the doubt on people, places, and events that have not yet been archaeologically confirmed.

Objection: The Bible is lacking in legitimate extrabiblical support.
Atheists and skeptics are unimpressed with the few references to *Christos* (Christ) in early literature, and suggest these references may not even relate to the Christ of the Bible.[11]

Answering the Objection: The truth is that there are both Christian and secular extrabiblical references that date very close to the time of Christ and lend support to the accuracy of the Bible. Christian sources include the following:

1. *Clement* was a leading elder in the church at Rome. In his epistle to the Corinthians (c. A.D. 95), he cites portions of Matthew, Mark, and Luke, and introduces them as *the actual words of Jesus.*[12]

2. *Papias,* the bishop of Hierapolis in Phrygia and author of *Exposition of Oracles of the Lord* (c. A.D. 130), cites the Gospels of Matthew, Mark, Luke, and John, presumably as canonical. He specifically refers to John's Gospel as containing the words of Jesus.[13]

3. *Justin Martyr,* foremost apologist of the second century (c. A.D. 140), considered all four Gospels to be Scripture.

4. *The Didache,* an ancient manual of Christianity that dates between the end of the first century and the beginning of the second, cites portions of the three synoptic Gospels and refers to them as the words of Jesus. This manual quotes extensively from Matthew's Gospel.

5. *Polycarp,* a disciple of the apostle John, quotes portions of Matthew, Mark, and Luke, and refers to them as the words of Jesus (c. A.D. 150).

6. *Irenaeus,* a disciple of Polycarp (c. A.D. 170), quotes from 23 of the 27 New Testament books, omitting only Philemon, James, 2 Peter, and 3 John.[14]

Clearly, there are many early Christian sources dating between A.D. 95 and 150 that refer to Matthew, Mark, Luke, and John as containing the actual words of Christ. History is therefore on the side of the New Testament Gospels and argues against the skeptical claim that these Gospels are unreliable.

There are also secular extrabiblical sources that mention various aspects of Jesus' life, thus lending support to the Bible. These include ancient historians such as Tacitus, Jewish sources such as Josephus and the Talmud, and government officials such as Pliny the Younger. Let us consider a few details:

Josephus, a Jewish historian born in A.D. 37, wrote his literary works—including *The Antiquities,* a history of the Jews up until his time—toward the end of the first century. In *The Antiquities* (Book 20, Chapter 9, Paragraph 1), we read that the high priest "convened the judges of the Sanhedrin, and brought before them the brother of Jesus, the one called Christ, whose name was James, and certain others, and accusing them of having transgressed the law delivered them up to be stoned."[15] Notice that this reference to Christ is definitely the Christ of the New Testament Gospels, contrary to the claim of some atheists and skeptics. Note also that James was not originally a believer in Jesus (John 7:5), but became one after Jesus' resurrection (see 1 Corinthians 15:7).

Earlier in *The Antiquities* (Book 18, Chapter 3), we read:

> Now there was about this time Jesus, a wise man, if it be lawful to call him a man; for he was a doer of wonderful works, a teacher of such men as receive the truth with pleasure. He drew over to him both many of the Jews and many of the Gentiles. He was [the] Christ. And when Pilate, at the suggestion of the principal men amongst us, had condemned him to the cross, those that loved him at the first did not forsake him; for he appeared to them alive again the third day; as the divine prophets had foretold these and ten thousand other wonderful things concerning him. And the tribe of Christians, so named from him, are not extinct at this day.

Most scholars believe this passage to be mostly authentic—that is, most of it came from the pen of Josephus, although there are likely a few interpolations (inserted words) made by some early Christian copyists, probably around the third century A.D. Possible interpolations include the following:

- "if it be lawful to call him a man"—This may be an interpolation because it is unlikely that Josephus, a Jew, believed Jesus to be God in human flesh.

- "He was [the] Christ"—In the previously mentioned citation from Josephus (*The Antiquities,* Book 20, Chapter 9, Paragraph 1), Josephus concedes that Jesus is "the one called Christ." It is therefore unlikely that he himself would actually refer to Jesus as "the Christ." This is likely a Christian interpolation.

- "he appeared to them alive again the third day"—This may be an interpolation by early Christian copyists, since it is unlikely that Josephus believed in the resurrection.[16]

Aside from these three interpolations, scholars believe that Josephus' words about Jesus are thoroughly authentic. The information that is left corroborates that Jesus was the leader of Christians, that He did wonderful works, and that He was a martyr (by crucifixion) for the Christian cause. Hence, Josephus' words constitute extrabiblical corroboration for New Testament teachings about Jesus.

The Talmud. There are some references to Jesus in the Talmud, a collection of ancient rabbinic writings on Jewish law and tradition that constitute the basis of religious authority in Orthodox Judaism. As a backdrop, one must keep in mind that since Jewish leaders were against Jesus, what found its way into the Talmud was understandably unflattering, to say the very least. Still, the fact that certain information found its way into the Talmud does offer us extrabiblical corroboration of Jesus.

Keeping Jewish hostility in mind, the Talmud claims that "on the eve of the Passover Yeshu was hanged. For forty days before the execution took place, a herald...cried, 'He is going forth to be

stoned because he has practiced sorcery and enticed Israel to apos-
tasy.'"[17] Elsewhere, Mary is called an adulteress.[18]

The reference to Yeshu (Jesus) being "hanged" is simply a
synonym for crucifixion (see Galatians 3:13). The Talmudic text
indicates that Jesus was crucified "on the eve of the Passover." The
reference to sorcery is an understandable accusation from hostile Jews seeking to explain away Jesus' miracles. The reference to
Mary being called an adulteress is no doubt meant to explain away
the virgin birth. The reference to stoning apparently reflects Jewish
intentions, though these intentions obviously did not come to pass.

Pliny the Younger (A.D. 62–113) was a Roman governor who,
in some of his personal correspondence to his friend Trajan, made
reference to Christians he arrested. He asked Trajan for advice
about how Christians should be treated in legal proceedings. Here
is what Pliny had learned about these Christians:

> They were in the habit of meeting on a certain fixed
> day before it was light, when they sang in alternate
> verses a hymn to Christ, as to a god, and bound them-
> selves by a solemn oath, not to any wicked deeds, but
> never to commit any fraud, theft or adultery, never to
> falsify their word, nor deny a trust when they should
> be called upon to deliver it up; after which it was their
> custom to separate, and then reassemble to partake of
> food—but food of an ordinary and innocent kind.[19]

This paragraph constitutes extrabiblical corroboration that
Christians...

- met for worship on a "certain fixed day" (which would be
  Sunday),
- worshipped Jesus as "a god,"

- changed their behavior as a result of their commitment to Christ, and

- celebrated the Lord's Supper with "food of an ordinary and innocent kind."

Tacitus, a Roman historian, wrote the following words regarding the Emperor Nero's blame of the Christians for the fire that destroyed Rome in A.D. 64:

> Nero fastened the guilt...on a class hated for their abominations, called Christians by the populace. Christus, from whom the name had its origin, suffered the extreme penalty during the reign of Tiberius at the hands of...Pontius Pilatus, and a most mischievous superstition, thus checked for the moment, again broke out not only in Judaea, the first source of the evil, but even in Rome.[20]

This constitutes extrabiblical evidence that Christians derived their name from a historical person named Jesus Christ ("Christus"). He "suffered the extreme penalty"—a reference to Roman crucifixion. It occurred "during the reign of Tiberius" at the hands of "Pontius Pilatus." All of this is in keeping with the New Testament documents. Some believe the reference to "a most mischievous superstition" to be the early church's belief that the crucified Jesus had risen from the dead.[21]

One final extrabiblical reference worthy of mention involves the ancient historian Thallus. In about A.D. 52, he made reference to the darkness that engulfed the land at the time of Christ's resurrection. While we do not possess actual copies of Thallus' work, some of his writings have been preserved in the writings of others. In A.D. 221 Julius Africanus quoted Thallus: "On the whole world there pressed a most fearful darkness, and the rocks were rent by an earth-quake, and many places in Judea and other districts were thrown down. This darkness Thallus, in the third book of his *History*, calls, as appears to me without reason, an eclipse of the sun."[22]

We can conclude that the extrabiblical evidence provides rather significant information that corroborates the New Testament record. Norman Geisler and Frank Turek have noted that we can derive at least 12 basic facts from the extrabiblical literature:

1. Jesus lived during the time of Tiberius Caesar.
2. He lived a virtuous life.
3. He was a wonder-worker.
4. He had a brother named James.
5. He was acclaimed to be the Messiah.
6. He was crucified under Pontius Pilate.
7. He was crucified on the eve of the Jewish Passover.
8. Darkness and an earthquake occurred when He died.
9. His disciples believed He rose from the dead.
10. His disciples were willing to die for their belief.
11. Christianity spread rapidly as far as Rome.
12. His disciples denied the Roman gods and worshiped Jesus as God.[23]

Objection: There is no good reason to believe that the Bible has been accurately transmitted down through the centuries. Some atheists question whether *any* biblical manuscripts can be trusted.[24]

Answering the Objection: There is overwhelming manu-script evidence that points to the reliability of the Bible. There are 5,686 known partial and complete manuscript copies of the New

Testament. These manuscript copies are very ancient and they are available for inspection now. Following are some highlights:

- The Chester Beatty papyrus (P45) dates to the third century A.D., and contains the four Gospels and the book of Acts (chapters 4–17). (P = papyrus.)

- The Chester Beatty papyrus (P46) dates to about A.D. 200, and contains ten Pauline epistles (all but the pastoral epistles) and the book of Hebrews.

- The Chester Beatty papyrus (P47) dates to the third century A.D., and contains Revelation 9:10–17:2.

- The Bodmer Papyrus (P66) dates to about A.D. 200, and contains the Gospel of John.

- The Bodmer Papyrus (P75) dates to the early third century, and contains Luke and John.

- The Sinaiticus uncial manuscript dates to the fourth century, and contains the entire New Testament.

- The Vaticanus uncial manuscript dates to the fourth century, and contains most of the New Testament except Hebrews 9:14ff., the pastoral epistles, Philemon, and Revelation.

- The Washingtonianus uncial manuscript dates to the early fifth century, and contains the Gospels.

- The Alexandrinus uncial manuscript dates to the fifth century, and contains most of the New Testament.

- The Ephraemi Rescriptus uncial manuscript dates to the fifth century, and contains portions of every book except 2 Thessalonians and 2 John.

- The Bezae/Cantabrigiensis uncial manuscript dates to the fifth century, and contains the Gospels and Acts.

- The Claromontanus uncial manuscript dates to the sixth century and contains the Pauline epistles and Hebrews.

If one adds into the mix over 10,000 Latin Vulgate manuscripts and at least 9,300 other early versions (including Ethiopic, Slavic, Armenian, and other versions), the total approximates 25,000 manuscripts that cite portions of the New Testament. This far exceeds the number of manuscripts of other ancient documents, which, in most cases, numbers less than ten.[25]

There are also some 86,000 quotations from the New Testament found in the writings of the early church fathers, and there are several thousand lectionaries (church-service books containing Scripture quotations used in the early centuries of Christianity). In fact, there are enough quotations from the early church fathers that even if we did not have a single manuscript copy of the Bible, scholars could still reconstruct all but eleven verses of the entire New Testament from material written within 150 to 200 years from the time of Christ.

Early Patristic Quotations of the New Testament

Writer	Gospels	Acts	Pauline Epistles	General Epistles	Revelation	Totals
Justin Martyr	268	10	43	6	3	330
Irenaeus	1,038	194	499	23	65	1,819
Clement of Alexandria	1,017	44	1,127	207	11	2,406
Origen	9,231	349	7,778	399	165	17,922
Tertullian	3,822	502	2,609	120	205	7,258

Hippolytus	734	42	387	27	188	1,378
Eusebius	3,258	211	1,592	88	27	5,176
Grand Totals	19,368	1,352	14,035	870	664	36,289

As this chart indicates, we have over 36,000 quotations from a mere seven church fathers alone. Can any other ancient document boast of such widespread and reliable support? Such overwhelming support for the New Testament deals a deathblow to the claim that we have insufficient evidence in support of the reliability of the Bible.

The Dead Sea Scrolls provide even further evidence. In these scrolls discovered at Qumran in 1947, we have Old Testament manuscripts that date about 1,000 years earlier (150 B.C.) than the other Old Testament manuscripts previously in our possession (which dated to A.D. 980). What is significant is that when one compares the two sets of manuscripts, it is clear that they are essentially the same, with very few changes. The fact that manuscripts separated by 1,000 years are essentially the same indicates the incredible accuracy of the Old Testament's manuscript transmission.

The copy of the book of Isaiah discovered at Qumran illustrates this accuracy. Dr. Gleason Archer, who personally examined both the A.D. 980 and 150 B.C. copies of Isaiah, comments:

> Even though the two copies of Isaiah discovered in Qumran Cave 1 near the Dead Sea in 1947 were a thousand years earlier than the oldest dated manuscript previously known (A.D. 980), they proved to be *word for word identical* with our standard Hebrew Bible in more than 95 percent of the text. The 5

percent of variation consisted chiefly of obvious slips of the pen and variations in spelling.[26]

Similarly, Christian apologist Paul Little comments:

> In comparing the Qumran manuscript of Isaiah 38–66 with the one we had, scholars found that the text is extremely close to our Massoretic text. A comparison of Isaiah 53 shows that only 17 letters differ from the Massoretic text. Ten of these are mere differences in spelling, like our "honor" or "honour," and produce no change in the meaning at all. Four more are very minor differences, such as the presence of the conjunction, which is often a matter of style. The other three letters are the Hebrew word for 'light' which is added after "they shall see" in verse 11. Out of 166 words in this chapter, only this one word is really in question, and it does not at all change the sense of the passage. This is typical of the whole manuscript.[27]

The Dead Sea Scrolls prove that the copyists of biblical manuscripts took great care in going about their work. These copyists knew they were duplicating God's Word. Hence, they went to incredible lengths to insure that no error crept into their work. In the course of creating copies, the scribes carefully counted every line, word, syllable, and letter to ensure accuracy.[28]

Objection: There are many variants in the biblical manuscripts, and hence the Bible is unreliable. How can one possibly trust the Bible, atheists ask, when there are some 200,000 variants in the various biblical manuscripts?[29]

Answering the Objection: In the many thousands of manuscript copies we possess of the New Testament, it is true that scholars have discovered that there are some 200,000 variants. This may seem like a staggering figure to the uninformed mind. To those who study the issue, however, the numbers are not so damning as they may initially appear. Indeed, a look at the hard evidence shows that the New Testament manuscripts are amazingly accurate and trustworthy.

To begin, one must recognize that because of the way variants are counted, the 200,000 figure may be misleading. The reality is that if a single word is misspelled in 2,000 manuscripts, that counts as 2,000 variants.[30] This fact alone *substantially* reduces the severity of the variant problem.

Further, one must emphasize that out of these 200,000 variants, 99 percent hold virtually no significance whatsoever. Many of these variants simply involve a missing letter in a word; some involve spelling a word differently (such as "honour" instead of "honor"); some involve reversing the order of two words (such as "Christ Jesus" instead of "Jesus Christ"); some may involve the absence of one or more insignificant words. When all the facts are put on the table, only about 40 of the variants have any real significance—and even then, no doctrine of the Christian faith or any moral commandment is affected by them. For more than 99 percent of the cases, the original text can be reconstructed to a practical certainty.

We must also emphasize that the sheer volume of manuscripts we possess greatly narrows the margin of doubt regarding what the original biblical document said. As New Testament scholar F.F. Bruce stated, "If the number of [manuscripts] increases the number of scribal errors, it increases proportionately the means of correcting such errors, so that the margin of doubt left in the process of recovering the exact original wording is not so large as might be feared; it is in truth remarkably small."[31]

By practicing the science of textual criticism—comparing all the available manuscripts with each other—we can come to an assurance regarding what the original document must have said. Perhaps an illustration might be helpful.

Let us suppose we have five manuscript copies of an original document that no longer exists. Each of the manuscript copies is different. Our goal is to compare these five copies and ascertain what the original must have said. Here are the words we find in the five copies:

MANUSCRIPT #1: Jesus Christ is the Savior of the whole world.

MANUSCRIPT #2: Christ Jesus is the Savior of the whole world.

MANUSCRIPT #3: Jesus Christ s the Savior of the whole world.

MANUSCRIPT #4: Jesus Christ is th Savior of the whle world.

MANUSCRIPT #5: Jesus Christ is the Savor of the whole world.

Could you, by comparing the manuscript copies, ascertain what the original document said with a high degree of certainty that you are correct? Of course you could.

This illustration is admittedly extremely simplistic, but a great majority of the 200,000 variants are solved by methodology similar to that used in the illustration. By comparing the various manuscripts, all of which contain minor differences, it becomes fairly clear what the original must have said.

With regard to the variants that exist among the New Testament manuscripts, Metzger says that many relate to word order, often due to a scribe inadvertently putting the right words in the wrong place in the sentence, or perhaps due to a lapse in memory in the scribe. Such variants, Metzger says, are rather inconsequential in terms of the original Greek text:

> It makes a whale of a difference in English if you say, "Dog bites man" or "Man bites dog"—sequence matters in English. But in Greek it doesn't. One word functions as the subject of the sentence regardless of where it stands in the sequence; consequently, the meaning of the sentence isn't distorted if the words are out of what we consider to be the right order. So yes, some variations among manuscripts exist, but generally they're inconsequential variations like that. Differences in spelling would be another example.[32]

Objection: The New Testament gospels and manuscripts are dated late and are therefore unreliable. Atheistic Harvard professor Michael Martin makes this point in his book *The Case Against Christianity.*[33]

Answering the Objection: There are two issues we need to address here: the dating of the manuscript copies of the original autographs, and the dating of the original autographs themselves. Let us first consider the dating of the manuscript copies.

As a backdrop, most ancient classical literary works have a gap of 700 years or more between the writing of the original document and the earliest extant manuscript copy. Some works written by such well-known thinkers as Plato and Aristotle have a span of over twice that between the original writing and the earliest extant manuscript copy.

By comparison, the Chester Beatty papyrus (Papyrus 45)— containing the four Gospels and much of the book of Acts—

dates to the third century A.D., within 150 years of the original New Testament documents.[34] The Chester Beatty papyrus (Papyrus 46), which contains ten Pauline epistles (all but the pastoral epistles) and the book of Hebrews, dates to about A.D. 200, which is also quite close in time to the original writing of the New Testament documents. Clearly, no other piece of ancient literature can stand up to the Bible. Manuscript support for the Bible is unparalleled!

Norman Geisler tells us that "there are more [New Testament] manuscripts copied with greater accuracy and earlier dating than for any secular classic from antiquity."[35] French theologian René Pache adds, "The historical books of antiquity have a documentation infinitely less solid."[36] Benjamin Warfield concludes, "If we compare the present state of the text of the New Testament with that of no matter what other ancient work, we must...declare it marvelously exact."[37] Consider the data in the following chart:

Comparison of Ancient Texts[38]

Ancient Author	Date Written	Earliest Copy	Number of Copies	Accuracy of Copies
Caesar	1st cent. B.C.	A.D. 900	10	——
Livy	1st cent. B.C.	——	20	——
Tacitus	c. A.D. 100	A.D. 1100	20	——
Thucydides	5th cent. B.C.	A.D. 900	8	——
Herodotus	5th cent. B.C.	A.D. 900	8	——
Demosthenes	4th cent. B.C.	A.D. 1100	200	——

Mahabharata	—	—	—	90%
Homer	9th cent. B.C.	—	643	95%
New Testament	1st cent. A.D.	2nd cent. A.D.	5,000	99+%

From this documentary evidence, it is clear that the New Testament manuscript copies are superior to comparable ancient writings. The records for the New Testament are vastly more numerous, dated much earlier, and are considerably more accurate in their text. No wonder the late Sir Frederic Kenyon, world-renowned scholar who specialized in ancient manuscripts, concluded that the interval "between the dates of original composition and the earliest extant evidence becomes so small as to be in fact negligible, and the last foundation for any doubt that the Scriptures have come down to us substantially as they were written has now been removed. Both the authenticity and the general integrity of the books of the New Testament may be regarded as finally established."[39]

There is also substantial evidence that the original autographs of the New Testament Gospels were written very close in time to the events on which they report. One evidence for this is that the apostle Paul died during the Neronian persecution, which took place in A.D. 64. Paul was certainly still alive as of the end of the book of Acts. This means Acts was written *prior* to A.D. 64. We further know that Luke wrote his Gospel before he wrote the book of Acts, which means his Gospel was written around A.D. 60. This places Luke's Gospel within 30 years of the life of Christ.

Scholars have also pointed out that all four canonical Gospels must date prior to A.D. 70 for one simple reason: All four fail to mention anything at all about the destruction of Jerusalem and its temple in A.D. 70 at the hands of Titus and his Roman warriors. The destruction of Jerusalem and the temple would be on a par with the Holocaust in modern times. For this horrific event not to be mentioned can mean only one thing: the four canonical Gospels must have been written *prior* to this time. J.P. Moreland comments:

> In recent years there has been a growing number of New Testament scholars who date the Gospels from A.D. 40 to A.D. 70, including the late W.F. Albright at Johns Hopkins, the dean of American archaeology. The bulk of the letters of the New Testament date from A.D. 48 to 64. This means that we have clear widespread testimony to a miracle-working, supernatural, resurrected Jesus no later than fifteen to twenty years after the events of His life.[40]

Such evidence renders false the claim by atheists that the New Testament Gospels are of late origin.

Objection: No one knows for sure which books belong in the biblical canon. One atheist, seeking to undermine belief in the Bible, asks, "How can one know which books are 'inspired' and should be part of the Scriptural canon?" He noted that certain books—including Hebrews, Jude, James, 2 Peter, and 3 John—were doubted for a time.[41]

Answering the Objection: There were five primary canonical tests that were applied in the course of determining which books belonged in the New Testament: Here they are, listed in question format:

1. *Was the book written or backed by a prophet or apostle of God?* This is the single most important test. The reasoning here is that the Word of God, which is inspired by the Spirit of God for the people of God, must be com-

municated through a man of God. Deuteronomy 18:18 informs us that God appoints prophets to speak His word. Second Peter 1:20-21 assures us that Scripture is written only by men of God. In Galatians 1:1-24, the apostle Paul argued support for the book of Galatians by appealing to the fact that he was an authorized messenger of God, an apostle.

2. *Is the book authoritative?* In other words, can it be said of this book as it was said of Jesus, "The people were amazed at his teaching, because he taught them as one who had authority, not as the teachers of the law" (Mark 1:22)? Put another way, does this book ring with a sense of, "Thus saith the Lord"?

3. *Does the book tell the truth about God and doctrine as it is already known by previous revelation?* The Bereans searched the Old Testament Scriptures to see whether Paul's teaching was true (Acts 17:11). They knew that if Paul's teaching did not accord with the Old Testament canon, it could not be of God. Agreement with all earlier revelation is essential (Galatians 1:8).

4. *Does the book give evidence of having the power of God?* The reasoning here is that any writing that does not exhibit the transforming power of God in the lives of its readers could not have come from God. Scripture says that the Word of God is "living and active" (Hebrews 4:12). Second Timothy 3:16-17 indicates that God's Word has a transforming effect. If the book in question did not have the power to change a life, then, it was reasoned, the book could not have come from God.

5. *Was the book accepted by the people of God?* In Old

Testament times, Moses' scrolls were placed immediately into the Ark of the Covenant (Deuteronomy 31:24-26). Joshua's writings were added in the same fashion (Joshua 24:26). In the New Testament, Paul thanked the Thessalonians for receiving the apostle's message as the Word of God (1 Thessalonians 2:13). Paul's letters were circulated among the churches (Colossians 4:16; 1 Thessalonians 5:27). It is the norm that God's people—that is, the majority of them and not simply a faction—will initially receive God's Word as such.

Many of the New Testament books were recognized as Scripture right during the general time they were written. In 1 Timothy 5:18, for example, the apostle Paul joined an Old Testament reference and a New Testament reference and called them both (collectively) "Scripture" (Deuteronomy 25:4 and Luke 10:7). It would not have been unusual in the context of first-century Judaism for an Old Testament passage to be called "Scripture." But for a passage from a New Testament book to be called "Scripture" so soon after it was written says volumes about Paul's view of the authority of contemporary New Testament books.

More specifically, only three years had elapsed between the writing of Luke's Gospel and the writing of 1 Timothy (Luke was written around A.D. 60; 1 Timothy was written around A.D. 63). Yet despite this, Paul (himself a Jew—a "Hebrew of Hebrews") did not hesitate to place Luke on the same level of authority as the Old Testament book of Deuteronomy.

Further, the writings of the apostle Paul were recognized as Scripture by the apostle Peter (2 Peter 3:16). Paul, too, understood that his own writings were inspired by God and therefore authoritative (1 Corinthians 14:37; 1 Thessalonians 2:13). Paul, of course, wrote over half the New Testament.

The reality is that God determined the canon, and that many living in biblical times recognized that the individual books written by the prophets and apostles were indeed Scripture. While God *determines* the canon, human beings *discover* the canon. While God *regulates* the canon, human beings *recognize* the canon.

What about the atheist claim that certain books were doubted as being canonical for a time? While this claim is true, an examination of the facts greatly deflates the force of this objection:

- Hebrews was doubted because the author of the book was unknown. However, the book eventually came to be viewed as having apostolic authority, if not apostolic authorship.

- James was doubted because of its seeming conflict with Paul's teaching about salvation by faith alone. The conflict is resolved when we understand the works James speaks of as an outgrowth of real faith.

- Second Peter was doubted because the style of the book differs from that of 1 Peter. It seems clear, however, that Peter used a scribe to write 1 Peter (see 1 Peter 5:12). A style conflict is therefore not a problem.

- Second and 3 John were doubted because the author of these books is called "elder," not "apostle." However, Peter (an apostle) is also called "elder" in 1 Peter 5:1. It is therefore clear that the same person can be both an elder and an apostle.

- Jude was doubted because it refers to two noncanonical books—the Book of Enoch and the Assumption of Moses. This objection was eventually overcome because even Paul quoted from pagan poets (see Acts 17:28 and Titus 1:12). Moreover, Jude enjoyed early acceptance by most of the early believers.

- The book of Revelation was doubted because it teaches a 1,000-year reign of Christ. Since there was a local contemporary cult that taught the same, it was reasoned that Revelation must not be true Scripture. However, because many of the earliest church fathers believed in a 1,000-year reign of Christ too, this objection was eventually seen as being without merit.

Christians believe that the same God who supernaturally inspired the Scriptures in the first place also providentially guided human beings in the selection of the correct books for admission into the Scriptural canon.

WHAT CAN WE CONCLUDE?

In this chapter, we have established the following facts:

- Oral tradition was reliable.
- It was always God's will for His revelations to be written down, and this took place under the inspiration of the Holy Spirit.
- The New Testament Gospels cannot be discredited by accusations of bias on the part of the writers.
- Archaeology provides powerful support for the reliability of the Bible.
- There is both Christian and secular extrabiblical support for the Bible.
- The Bible has been accurately transmitted via manuscript copies through the centuries.
- The variants in the biblical manuscripts do not pose a serious problem, and do not affect a single tenet of the Christian faith.

• The New Testament Gospels are all dated prior to A.D. 70, very close to the timing of the events on which they report.

• The biblical books that comprise the Old and New Testaments are canonical.

9

THE RELIABILITY OF
THE BIBLE—PART 2

In the previous chapter, I answered atheistic objections against the Bible—including ones dealing with oral tradition, alleged biases on the part of the New Testament authors, archaeology, historical references in extrabiblical literature, manuscript transmission, the dating of the Gospels, and the issue of canonicity. In each case, I demonstrated the weakness of the atheistic position against the Bible.

There are two further arguments in the atheist arsenal of objections against the Bible: Bible prophecy is unreliable, and there are many contradictions in the Bible. It is to these issues that I now turn my attention.

Objection: Prophecy does not prove a supernatural influence on the Bible, for many prophecies were manufactured after the fact. Atheist George Smith wrote: "The Bible as we have it today is the result of much editing and interpolation....There is considerable reason to suppose that many alleged prophecies...were manufactured after the fact in question."[1]

Answering the Objection: Scholars are practically unanimous that the prophetic books of the Old Testament were completed at least 400 years before Christ was even born, with many of the books dating as far back as the eighth and ninth centuries B.C. The exception to this is the book of Daniel, which some scholars date at 167 B.C. However, no matter whether a prophetic book dates 167 years before Christ's birth or 800 years, either way, it is equally hard to predict a future event. For a prophecy to be fulfilled perfectly requires that it come from God alone, who knows the end from the beginning.[2]

Let us consider the book of Isaiah as an example. In days past, the earliest available manuscript copy of Isaiah was dated at A.D. 980. Following the discovery of the Dead Sea Scrolls in 1947, however, scholars could examine a manuscript copy of Isaiah dated at 150 B.C. This manuscript is but a *copy* of an original document that dates back to the seventh century B.C. Hence, any specific prophecies of the coming divine Messiah that are recorded in Isaiah—including the facts that Jesus would be born of a virgin (7:14), that He would be called Immanuel (7:14), that He would be anointed by the Holy Spirit (11:2), that He would have a ministry in Galilee (9:1-2), that He would have a ministry of miracles (35:5-6), that He would be silent before His accusers (53:7), that He would be crucified with thieves (53:12) and accomplish a sacrificial atonement for humankind (53:5), and then be buried in a rich man's tomb (53:9)—cannot possibly have been recorded

it does not mean He will come from Sodom, or Tyre, or some other city. It means Bethlehem. No ambiguity here. When Isaiah 7:14 says the Messiah will be born of a virgin and will be called "Immanuel," no one can accuse this prophecy of being so obscure that any number of events could be the fulfillment of it. Atheists are grasping at straws when they argue about the obscurity of biblical prophecies. I find it most impressive that virtually hundreds of very specific prophecies were fulfilled in the one person of Jesus Christ.

Keep in mind that the odds of one person fulfilling *just eight* of the hundreds of Old Testament messianic prophecies is astronomical—a 1 in 10^{17} chance. Peter Stoner, author of *Science Speaks,* provides an illustration to help us understand the magnitude of such odds:

> Suppose that we take 10^{17} silver dollars and lay them on the face of Texas. They will cover all of the state two feet deep. Now mark one of these silver dollars and stir the whole mass thoroughly, all over the state. Blindfold a man and tell him that he can travel as far as he wishes, but he must pick up one silver dollar and say that this is the right one. What chance would he have of getting the right one? Just the same chance that the prophets would have had of writing these eight prophecies and having them all come true in any one man, from their day to the present time, providing they wrote using their own wisdom.[5]

This is a key point. The fact that *virtually hundreds* of very precise messianic prophecies (and not just eight) were fulfilled in an exact way in the person of Jesus Christ leads to two well-grounded conclusions: 1) Jesus is the promised Messiah, and

2) the prophecies must have had a divine origin. Therefore, *God exists!*

Objection: There are many mistaken and unfulfilled prophecies found in the Bible. In support of this claim, one atheist cites Jesus' "failed" prophecy in Matthew 24:34 that "the end" would come in his lifetime.[6]

Answering the Objection: In Matthew 24:34, Jesus states: "I tell you the truth, this generation will certainly not pass away until all these things have happened." Evangelical Christians have generally held to one of two interpretations of this verse. One is that Christ is simply saying that those people who witness the signs stated earlier in Matthew 24 (all of which deal with the future Tribulation period) will see the coming of Jesus Christ within *that very generation.* In other words, the generation that's alive at the time of the abomination of desolation (verse 15), the Great Tribulation (verse 21), and the sign of the Son of Man in heaven (verse 30) will still be alive when these prophetic judgments are completed. Since the Tribulation is a period of seven years (Daniel 9:27; Revelation 11:2), then Jesus would be saying that the generation alive at the beginning of the Tribulation will be the same generation that sees the end of the Tribulation, at which time the second coming of Christ occurs.

Other evangelicals say the word "generation" in this verse is to be taken in its secondary meaning of "race," "kindred," "family," "stock," or "breed." Jesus' statement could mean that the Jewish race would not pass away until all things are fulfilled. Since many divine promises were made to Israel, including the eternal inheritance of the land of Palestine (Genesis 12; 14–15; 17) and the Davidic kingdom (2 Samuel 7), then Jesus could be referring to God's preservation of the nation of Israel in order to fulfill His promises to the nation. This would go along with the apostle Paul's words about a future of the nation of Israel when the Jews will be reinstated in God's covenantal promises (Romans 11:11-26). Either way, this verse certainly does not represent a mistaken prophecy, as atheists try to argue.

Objection: The biblical writers conspired to make it appear that Jesus was a fulfillment of Bible prophecy. One atheist wrote, "The biblical authors went to great lengths to pound Jesus into the mold of Jewish messianic expectation. In their enthusiasm, however, they resorted to blatant distortions."[7]

Answering the Objection: This allegation does not fit the biblical facts. First, note that the writers of Scripture were God-fearing Jews who gave every evidence of possessing the highest moral character, each having been raised since early childhood to obey the Ten Commandments (including the commandment against bearing false witness—Exodus 20:16). It breaches all credulity to say that these men were deceitful and sought to fool people into believing Jesus was the Messiah when He really was not. It also breaches credulity to argue that these men chose to suffer and give up their lives in defense of what they knew to be untrue.

Further, there are many prophecies fulfilled in the person of Jesus that the biblical writers could not have manipulated, such as His birthplace in Bethlehem (Micah 5:2), His direct descent from David (2 Samuel 7:12-16) and from Abraham (Genesis 12:2), being born of a virgin (Isaiah 7:14), the identity of His forerunner, John the Baptist (Malachi 3:1), the Sanhedrin's gift of 30 pieces of silver to Judas, the betrayer (Zechariah 11:12), the soldiers gambling for His clothing (Psalm 22:18), and His legs remaining unbroken (Psalm 22:17).

Still further, concerning prophecies related to Jesus' resurrection from the dead (Psalm 16:10; 22:22), it is unlikely that the writers of Scripture could have stolen the body in order to give the appearance of a resurrection. After all, the tomb had a huge stone weighing several tons blocking it; it bore the seal of the Roman government (with an automatic penalty of death for anyone who broke it); and it was guarded by brawny Roman guards trained in the art of defense and killing. To say Jesus' Jewish followers overcame these guards, moved the stone, and stole the body does not seem like a credible scenario.

Objection: One can only believe what can be seen, and therefore much of what is recorded in the Bible cannot be believed. (This objection sometimes surfaces on atheist and skeptic Web sites.)

Answering the Objection: This objection has been more than adequately answered by Kenneth Samples, who is correct in observing that "I only believe in what I see" is a self-contradictory statement. In other words, the statement "I only believe in what I see" *cannot be seen,* and therefore it cannot be believed. The statement thus reduces to absurdity.[8]

There is another problem with this objection:

> A number of science-related entities cannot be seen but, nevertheless, are still considered a necessary part of reality. Magnetism, gravity, electricity, electrons, and neutrinos, to name just a few. Moral values such as justice and goodness exist, but they cannot be seen. People judge human actions to be evil or good, without actually seeing these values. The concept of truth is an undeniable invisible reality.[9]

Objection: The New Testament abounds in contradictions and therefore cannot be trusted.[10]

Answering the Objection: While the Gospels may have some *apparent* contradictions, they do not have *genuine* contradictions.

There are differences in the accounts, yes, but actual contradictions, no.

Foundationally, one must keep in mind that inspiration (the fact that Scripture is "God-breathed"—2 Timothy 3:16) and inerrancy are, strictly speaking, ascribed *only* to the original autographs of Scripture. Certainly I believe the copies we have of the original autographs are extremely accurate (see chapter 8). But theologians have been careful to say that the Scriptures, in their original autographs and properly interpreted, will be shown to be wholly true in everything they teach.

Having provided this qualification, I want to emphasize that if all four Gospels were the same, with no differences, atheist and skeptic critics would be screaming "collusion" all over the place. The fact that the Gospels have differences shows there was no collusion but rather represent four different (but inspired) accounts of the same events.

One should not assume that a *partial* account in a book of the Bible is a *faulty* account. One book might provide some details on an event, and another biblical book might provide other, different details regarding the event. Just because they provide different details does not mean one or another of the accounts is faulty. Augustine wisely said, "If we are perplexed by any apparent contradiction in Scripture, it is not allowable to say, the author of this book is mistaken; but either the manuscript is faulty, or the translation is wrong, or you have not understood."[11]

Back in the early 1980s, I had the privilege of taking a Bibliology course under Dr. Norman Geisler, widely recognized as a top authority in the field. In that class, Professor Geisler provided us a list of seventeen mistakes people often make that lead to so-called "contradictions." This list later made its way into printed form.[12] Following is a brief summary of it:

- *Mistake 1: Assuming that the Unexplained Is Not Explainable.* In many cases, archaeology, linguistics, and historical studies have cleared up what was formerly unexplainable. It is likely that this will continue with future studies.

- *Mistake 2: Presuming the Bible Guilty Until Proven Innocent.* The Bible should be presumed innocent until it is proven guilty.

- *Mistake 3: Confusing Our Fallible Interpretations with God's Infallible Revelation.* Humans are finite; God is infinite. Humans make mistakes (we have erasers on pencils and delete keys on computers); God does not make mistakes. We should not confuse our finite misinterpretations with God's perfect revelation.

- *Mistake 4: Failing to Understand the Context of the Passage.* Divorced from its context, any verse can be twisted to say something that it does not really intend to say. Failure to consult the context accounts for many so-called contradictions.

- *Mistake 5: Neglecting to Interpret Difficult Passages in the Light of Clear Ones.* The clearer we are on the clear passages, the easier it is to make sense of the difficult passages.

- *Mistake 6: Basing a Teaching on an Obscure Passage.* In Scripture, the main things are the plain things, and the plain things are the main things. We should base our beliefs on the plain things rather than on obscure passages.

- *Mistake 7: Forgetting that the Bible Is a Human Book with Human Characteristics.* Though all of Scripture is inspired by the Holy Spirit, each biblical writer retained his own writing style when recording God's revelation. Isaiah had a powerful literary style; Jeremiah had a mournful tone; Luke's style had medical overtones; Paul had a pastoral tone when he wrote to Timothy, and John was very simple in his approach. The Holy Spirit infallibly worked through each of these writers, through their individual styles, to inerrantly communicate His message to humankind. In interpreting Scripture, however, we must be mindful of the different writing styles so we will understand the authors' words as they were intended to be understood.

- *Mistake 8: Assuming that a Partial Report Is a False Report.* Different writers of the Bible spoke of the same events from different perspectives. Sometimes writers may provide only a partial account. When accounts are taken together, we can construct a composite, comprehensive account.

- *Mistake 9: Demanding that New Testament Citations of the Old Testament Always Be Exact Quotations.* Citations need not be exact quotations. Sometimes a later writer would provide the essence of an earlier biblical statement without intending to provide a quote. This is perfectly acceptable in modern literature, and it is perfectly acceptable in biblical literature.

- *Mistake 10: Assuming that Divergent Accounts Are False Ones.* Accounts can differ without being wrong, and differing accounts are not necessarily mutually exclusive. Taking different accounts together, we can construct a composite, comprehensive account of an event.

- *Mistake 11: Presuming that the Bible Approves of All It Records.* For example, the Bible accurately records some of the lies of Satan (Genesis 3:4; John 8:44), but that does not mean the Bible condones or approves of those statements.

- *Mistake 12: Forgetting that the Bible Uses Nontechnical, Everyday Language.* The Bible does not attempt to use scientific language, but rather communicates in common, everyday language. "The use of observational, nonscientific language is not unscientific, it is merely *prescientific.*"[13]

- *Mistake 13: Assuming that Round Numbers Are False.* The use of round numbers has always been acceptable in everyday, common speech. It is also acceptable in the biblical accounts.

- *Mistake 14: Neglecting to Note that the Bible Uses Different Literary Devices.* There are a variety of literary genres in the Bible, each of which has peculiar characteristics that must be recognized in order to interpret the text properly. Bible genres include the historical (Acts), the dramatic epic (Job), poetry (Psalms), wise sayings (Proverbs), and apocalyptic writings (Revelation). An incorrect genre judgment will lead one far astray when interpreting the Scriptures.

- *Mistake 15: Forgetting that Only the Original Text, Not Every Copy of Scripture, Is Without Error.* Manuscript copies may have some minor errors, but this does not mean the original documents had errors.

- *Mistake 16: Confusing General Statements with Universal Ones.* General statements were never intended to be applicable in all situations, but rather are held to be generally true. For example, the book of Proverbs contains many general maxims of wisdom, but there are certainly exceptions to some of the maxims.

- *Mistake 17: Forgetting that Later Revelation Supersedes Previous Revelation.* The Old Testament, for example, emphasizes the oneness of God, but in the unfolding of progressive revelation, God went on to reveal that within the unity of the Godhead are three co-eternal and co-equal persons: the Father, the Son, and the Holy Spirit.

A Sampling of So-Called Contradictions. Following is a brief sampling of some alleged "contradictions" that might surface during dialogue with atheists, agnostics, and skeptics. In each case, I follow with a biblical resolution:

Genesis 2:17—Did Adam Die the Same Day? Some point out that Genesis 2:17 says Adam would die the same day he ate of the forbidden fruit, but Genesis 5:5 says Adam lived to the age of 930 years. There is no real contradiction here, for Adam and Eve *did* die the day they ate the fruit. They did not die *physically,* but they died *spiritually.*

The word "death" carries the idea of *separation.* Physical death involves the separation of the soul or spirit from the body. Spiritual death involves the separation of a person from God. When Adam and Eve partook of the forbidden fruit, they were immediately separated from God in a spiritual sense. (Their consequent action of trying to hide from God in the Garden of Eden indicates their awareness of this spiritual separation.) The moment of their sin, they became "dead in...transgressions and sins" (Ephesians 2:1). Their spiritual separation from God eventually led to their physical deaths.

Exodus 33:11—Can We See God? Exodus 33:11 says Moses saw God "face to face," while other verses say no one has ever seen God (for example, John 1:18).

The apostle Paul said that God the Father is invisible (Colossians 1:15; 1 Timothy 1:17) and "lives in unapproachable light, whom no one has seen or can see" (1 Timothy 6:16). John's Gospel likewise tells us that "no one has ever seen God [the Father], but God the One and Only [Jesus Christ], who is at the Father's side, has made him known" (John 1:18, inserts added). John 5:37 similarly tells us that no one has ever seen the Father's form.

Does the fact that Moses spoke to God "face to face" mean that God has a physical body that Moses beheld (Exodus 33:11)? No. The phrase "face to face" is simply a figurative way of indicating Moses spoke to God "personally," "directly," or "intimately." Moses was in the direct presence of God and interacted with Him on a personal and intimate basis. The word *face,* when used of God, is an anthropomorphism—that is, it is a word used to figuratively describe God in humanlike terms. Seen in this light, there is no contradiction in the Bible in this regard.

Second Samuel 24:1—Did God or the Devil Incite David? Second Samuel 24:1 says the Lord incited David to number Israel, while 1 Chronicles 21:1 says Satan incited David to do so. These accounts are not contradictory, but rather, complementary. Both are true, but both reflect different aspects of a larger truth.

Satan was the actual instrument used to incite David to number Israel (1 Chronicles 21:1), but God permitted Satan to do this. In the Hebrew mind-set, whatever God *permits,* God *commits.* By allowing this census, God is viewed as having brought about the act Himself (2 Samuel 24:1). (Keep in mind that the Hebrews were not too concerned about distinguishing between "first causes" and "secondary causes.") Satan did what he did because he wanted to destroy David and the people of God. God's purpose, however, was simply to humble David and teach him and his people a valuable spiritual lesson.

The same is true of Job's sufferings. It was Satan who directly caused the suffering of Job. As the text of Scripture clearly indicates, however, God permitted Satan to do this.

Matthew 1:1-17—A Contradictory Genealogy? Some atheists point out that the genealogy contained in Matthew's Gospel (1:1-17) contradicts that found in Luke's Gospel (3:23-38). Christians respond that the genealogies are *different,* but not *contradictory.* Up to David, the two genealogies are very similar—they are practically the same. In fact, they share some 18 or 19 common names, depending on whether *Matthan* and *Matthat* are the same person. From David on, they are very different. Almost none of the names from David to Joseph coincide. (In fact, only two of the names—Shealtiel and Zerubbabel—coincide.) Why are they different?

Matthew's genealogy traces Joseph's line of descendants, and deals with the passing of the legal title to the throne of David (David → Solomon → Jehoikim → Coniah → Joseph → Jesus). As Joseph's adopted Son, Jesus became his legal heir so far as his inheritance was concerned. The "of whom was born Jesus" (Matthew 1:16) is a feminine relative pronoun, clearly indicating that Jesus was the physical child of Mary and that Joseph was not His physical father.

Matthew traced the line from Abraham and David in 41 links to Joseph. Matthew obviously did not list every individual in the genealogy. Jewish reckoning did not require every name be included in order to satisfy a genealogy.

Abraham and David were the central figures of the two unconditional covenants pertaining to the Messiah. Matthew's Gospel was written to Jews, and Matthew wanted to prove to Jews that Jesus was the promised Messiah. This would demand a fulfillment of the Abrahamic Covenant (Genesis 12) and the Davidic Covenant (2 Samuel 7). Matthew was calling attention to the fact that Jesus came to fulfill the covenants made with Israel's forefathers.

Luke's genealogy traces Mary's lineage, and carries all the way back beyond the time of Abraham to Adam and the commencement of the human race. Whereas Matthew's genealogy pointed to

Jesus as the Jewish Messiah, Luke's genealogy points to Jesus as the Son of Man, a name often used of Jesus in Luke's Gospel. Whereas Matthew's genealogy was concerned with the Messiah as related to the Jews, Luke's genealogy was concerned with the Messiah as related to the entire human race.

Matthew 12:40—In the Tomb Three Days and Three Nights? Some atheists argue that Matthew 12:40 is in error in saying Jesus was in the tomb for three days and three nights. The Gospel accounts are clear that Jesus was crucified and buried on Friday sometime before sundown. This means Jesus was in the grave for part of Friday, the entire Sabbath (Saturday), and part of Sunday. In other words, He was in the tomb for two full nights, one full day, and part of two days. How do we reconcile this with Jesus' words in Matthew 12:40: "For as Jonah was three days and three nights in the belly of a huge fish, so the Son of Man will be three days and three nights in the heart of the earth"?

In the Jewish mind-set, any part of a day was reckoned as a complete day. The Babylonian Talmud (a set of Jewish commentaries) tells us that "the portion of a day is as the whole of it." Hence, though Jesus was really in the tomb for part of Friday, all of Saturday, and part of Sunday, according to Jewish reckoning He was in the tomb for "three days and three nights." Seen in this light, this verse poses no problem for the veracity of the Bible.

In Matthew 16:28 Jesus said: "I tell you the truth, some who are standing here will not taste death before they see the Son of Man coming in his kingdom." Some atheists point out that Jesus has not come in His kingdom, and hence the people standing with Jesus all died before seeing Christ come.

Christians respond that there was a sense in which Christ's contemporaries saw "the Son of Man coming in his kingdom" (Matthew 16:28). It is likely that when Jesus said this He had in mind the transfiguration, which happened precisely one week later. In fact, in Matthew's account the transfiguration (Matthew 17:1-13) immediately follows the prediction itself (16:28). If this interpretation is correct, as the context seems to indicate, the transfiguration served as a preview or foretaste of the kingdom in which the divine Messiah would appear in a state of glory. More specifically, in the transfiguration, the power and the glory within Jesus broke through the veil of His flesh and shone out, until His very clothing kindled to the dazzling brightness of the light. This very same glory will be revealed to the world when Christ comes to this earth again to set up His kingdom (see Matthew 24:30; 25:31).

Some atheists note that Matthew 20:29-34 says Jesus healed two blind men as He left Jericho, while Mark 10:46-52 and Luke 18:35-43 say Jesus healed one man as He entered Jericho. Properly interpreted, this is not a contradiction. There are several possible explanations. One is that the healing took place as Jesus was leaving old Jericho and was nearing new Jericho (there were two Jerichos in those days). If Jesus were at a place between the two Jerichos, then, depending on one's perspective, He could be viewed as "leaving" one Jericho or "entering" the other Jericho. Now, there were apparently two blind men in need of healing, but Bartimaeus was the more aggressive of the two, and hence two of the gospel accounts (Mark and Luke) mention only him. If the blind men were healed between the two Jerichos, this would clear up the apparent contradiction between the Gospel accounts.

Another possible explanation is that the blind men pled with Jesus as He entered (either the old or new) Jericho, but they did not receive their actual healings until Jesus was leaving Jericho. It is also possible that Jesus healed one blind man as He was entering Jericho, and healed two other blind men as He was leaving Jericho. Clearly, there are a number of ways of reconciling the Gospel accounts.

Matthew 27:5—How Did Judas Die? Atheists point out that Matthew 27:5 says Judas died by hanging himself, while Acts 1:18 says Judas died by falling headlong in a field and bursting open. Properly interpreted, there is no real contradiction. Apparently Judas first hanged himself. Then, at some point, the rope either broke or loosened so that his body slipped from it and fell to the rocks below and burst open. Neither account is complete. Taken together, we have a full picture of what happened to Judas.

Some atheists argue that some verses in the Bible say faith in Christ alone brings salvation (Romans 3:20; Galatians 2:16), whereas other verses, such as James 2:14-26, say people are justified by works.

Properly interpreted, there is no contradiction. The passage in James merely says faith without works is dead. Martin Luther explained that James 2 is not teaching that a person is saved by works. Rather a person is "justified" (declared righteous before God) by faith alone, but not by a faith that is alone. In other words, genuine faith will always result in good works in the saved person's life.

James is writing to Jewish Christians ("to the twelve tribes"— James 1:1) who were in danger of giving nothing but lip service to Jesus. His intent, therefore, is to distinguish true faith from false faith. He shows that true faith results in works, which serve as visible evidences of faith's invisible presence. In other words, good works are the "vital signs" indicating that faith is alive. Apparently some of these Jewish Christians had made a false claim of faith. It is the counterfeit boast of faith that James condemned. Merely claiming to have faith is not enough; genuine faith is evidenced by works.

Other "Contradictions." In the preceding pages, I have touched on a few of the more notable "contradictions" found in the Bible.

There are others that could come up in your discussions with atheists. For this reason, I urge you to consider obtaining some or all of the following books, which you many find helpful as you defend the faith:

- Ron Rhodes, *The Complete Book of Bible Answers* (Harvest House Publishers).

- Norman Geisler and Thomas Howe, *When Critics Ask: A Popular Handbook on Bible Difficulties* (Baker Book House).

- Gleason Archer, *An Encyclopedia of Bible Difficulties* (Zondervan).

- Walter C. Kaiser, *Hard Sayings of the Old Testament* (InterVarsity Press).

- Walter C. Kaiser, *More Hard Sayings of the Old Testament* (InterVarsity Press).

- Robert H. Stein, *Difficult Passages in the New Testament* (Baker Book House).

- William Arndt, *Bible Difficulties and Seeming Contradictions* (Concordia).

- Manfred T. Brauch, *Hard Sayings of Paul* (InterVarsity Press).

- F.F. Bruce, *The Hard Sayings of Jesus* (InterVarsity Press).

- John W. Haley, *Alleged Discrepancies of the Bible* (Baker Book House).

These books will help you answer the great majority of alleged Bible contradictions brought up by atheists, agnostics, and skeptics.

10

THE EVIDENCE
FOR JESUS

On five different occasions, Jesus claimed to be the theme of
the entire Old Testament (Matthew 5:17; Luke 24:27; Luke 24:44;
John 5:39; Hebrews 10:7). Because Christ is the theme of the Old
Testament, the relationship between the Old and New Testaments
is inseparably connected in the person of Jesus Christ. The Bible is
a "Jesus book."

> The Bible, opening with the words, "In the begin-
> ning God" (Gen. 1:1), and closing with reference to
> "the Lord Jesus" (Rev. 22:20-21), is preeminently
> a revelation of Jesus Christ. Though the Bible obvi-
> ously treats many subjects—including the history of

man, the existence of angels, the revelation of God's purposes for the nations, Israel, and the church, and includes in its revelation facts from eternity past to eternity future—Jesus Christ is revealed as the Center. He is presented as the Creator, the Messiah of Israel, the Savior of the saints, the Head of the church, and King of kings over all creation. As the theme of divine revelation, the person and work of Jesus Christ threads its way from the first to the last book of the Bible.[1]

In view of the preeminence of Jesus in the Bible, it is understandable that atheists, agnostics, and skeptics would target many of their objections toward Him. In what follows, I will address some of the more common objections.

Objection: Many claims about Jesus in the New Testament documents are simple legends. According to one atheist, "the Gospels themselves contain some clues which suggest that the stories of Jesus as a miracle worker evolved after His death."[2]

Answering the Objection: Only a very brief time elapsed between Jesus' miraculous public ministry and the publication of the Gospels. This time was insufficient for the development of miracle legends. Many eyewitnesses to Jesus' miracles would have still been alive to refute any untrue miracle accounts (see 1 Corinthians 15:6).

One must also recognize the noble character of the men who witnessed these miracles—Peter, James, and John, for example. Such men were not prone to misrepresentation, having been schooled from early childhood in the Ten Commandments (including God's commandment against bearing false witness—Exodus 20:16), and were willing to give up their lives rather than deny what they knew to be true about Jesus.

There were also hostile witnesses to the miracles of Christ. When Jesus raised Lazarus from the dead, for example, none of the chief priests or Pharisees disputed the miracle (John 11:45-48). (If they could have disputed it, they would have.) Rather, their goal was simply to stop Jesus (verses 47-48). Because there were so many hostile witnesses who observed and scrutinized Christ, successful fabrication of miracle stories in His ministry would have been impossible.

C.S. Lewis suggests that the one who claims there are legends in the New Testament documents is simply unfamiliar with the nature of legends:

> If he [the biblical critic] tells me that something in a Gospel is legend or romance, I want to know how many legends and romances he has read, how well his palate is trained in detecting them by the flavor; not how many years he has spent on that Gospel.... Read the dialogues [in John]: that with the Samaritan woman at the well, or that which follows the healing of the man born blind. Look at its pictures: Jesus... doodling with his finger in the dust....I have been reading poems, romances, vision-literature, legends, and myths all my life. I know what they are like. I know that not one of them is like this.[3]

Objection: Many New Testament claims about Jesus were derived from pagan myths. Atheist and skeptic critics say that the virgin birth, Jesus' turning water into wine, Jesus' walking on water, and even the resurrection were all derived from Greek mythology and paganism.[4]

Answering the Objection: Such critics are distorting the facts. In terms of the virgin birth, Greek mythology and paganism hold that the male Greek gods would come to earth and have sex with human women, who in turn would give birth to hybrid beings. This bears no resemblance to the virgin birth of Jesus Christ. Jesus is *eternal deity.* When the Holy Spirit overshadowed Mary (Luke 1:35), it was specifically to produce a human nature within her womb for the eternal Son of God to step into, after which He was born as the God-Man (100 percent God and 100 percent man) nine months later. This is entirely different from Greek paganism.

Many alleged similarities between Christianity and the Greek pagan religions are either greatly exaggerated or fabricated. For example, some critics often describe pagan rituals in language they borrowed from Christianity, thereby making them falsely *appear* to be "parallel."

Furthermore, the chronology for such claims is all wrong. Scholar Ronald Nash, widely considered an expert on ancient mythology and paganism, wrote, "Almost all of our sources of information about the pagan religions alleged to have influenced early Christianity are dated very late. We frequently find writers quoting from documents written 300 years [later]." Nash said "we must reject the assumption that just because a cult had a certain belief or practice in the third or fourth century after Christ, it therefore had the same belief or practice in the first century."[5] Moreover, as New Testament scholar Bruce Metzger notes, "It must not be uncritically assumed that the Mysteries always influenced Christianity, for it is not only possible but probable that in certain cases, the influence moved in the opposite direction."[6] It should not be surprising that leaders of cults that were being successfully challenged by Christianity should do something to counter the challenge. What better way to do this than by offering a pagan substitute? Pagan attempts to counter the growing influence of Christianity by imitating it are clearly apparent in measures instituted by Julian the Apostate.[7]

Regarding claims of resurrection among pagan gods, Nash comments, "Which mystery gods actually experienced a resurrection from the dead? Certainly no early texts refer to any resurrection of Attis. Nor is the case for a resurrection of Osiris any stronger."[8] William Lane Craig agrees: "Orientalists have questioned whether it is proper to speak of 'resurrection' at all with regard to these deities," noting that "the idea of resurrection is late and tenuous in the case of Adonis, practically non-existent in the case of Attis, and inapplicable in the case of Osiris."[9] One can speak of a so-called "resurrection" in the stories of Osiris, Attis, and Adonis only in the *loosest* of senses: "For example, after Isis gathered together the pieces of Osiris's dismembered body, Osiris became 'Lord of the Underworld.' This is a poor substitute for a resurrection like that of Jesus Christ. And, no claim can be made that Mithras was a dying and rising god."[10]

In view of the evidence, the tide of scholarly opinion has turned dramatically against attempts to make the Christian doctrine of resurrection dependent on the so-called dying and rising gods of Hellenistic paganism. Such mythological resurrections always involved nonhistorical, fictional, mythological characters that came to life "once upon a time," which is in dire contrast to the flesh-and-blood historical Jesus who died and was physically resurrected from the dead.

Unlike mythical accounts, the New Testament accounts are based on eyewitness testimony. In 2 Peter 1:16 we read, "We did not follow cleverly invented stories when we told you about the power and coming of our Lord Jesus Christ, but we were eyewitnesses of his majesty." First John 1:1 affirms, "That which was from the beginning, which we have heard, which we have seen with our eyes, which we have looked at and our hands have touched—this we proclaim concerning the Word of life." These eyewitnesses gave up their lives defending what they knew to be the truth about Jesus Christ. No one would make the ultimate sacrifice for what they knew to be a pagan myth.

Objection: Jesus was primarily a good moral teacher.[11]

Answering the Objection: As Christian apologists have long pointed out, no mere "example" or "moral teacher" would ever claim that the destiny of the world lay in His hands, or that people would spend eternity in heaven or hell depending on whether they believed in Him (John 6:26-40). The only "example" this would provide would be one of lunacy. And for Jesus to convince people that He was God (John 8:58) and the Savior of the world (Luke 19:10) when He really was not would be the ultimate *im*morality. Hence, to say that Jesus was primarily a good moral teacher makes no sense.

The primary reason Jesus came into the world was not to be some kind of moral influence, but rather to die for the sins of humankind. Jesus affirmed that it was for the very purpose of dying that He came into the world (John 12:27). Moreover, He perceived His death as being a sacrificial offering for the sins of humanity (He said His blood "is poured out for many for the forgiveness of sins," Matthew 26:26-28). He took His sacrificial mission with utmost seriousness, for He knew that if He did not die on the cross, humanity would certainly perish (Matthew 16:25; John 3:16) and spend eternity apart from God in a place of great suffering (Matthew 10:28; 11:23; 23:33; 25:41; Luke 16:22-28).

Jesus therefore described His mission this way: "The Son of

Man did not come to be served, but to serve, and to give his life a ransom for many" (Matthew 20:28). "The Son of Man came to seek and to save what was lost" (Luke 19:10). "God did not send his Son into the world to condemn the world, but to save the world through him" (John 3:17).

In John 10, Jesus compared Himself to a good shepherd who not only gives His life to save the sheep (John 10:11) but lays His life down of His own accord (John 10:18). This is precisely what Jesus did at the cross: He laid His life down to atone for the sins of humanity.

Certainly this is how others perceived His mission. When Jesus began His three-year ministry and was walking toward John the Baptist at the Jordan River, John said, "Look, the Lamb of God, who takes away the sin of the world!" (John 1:29). John's portrayal of Christ as the Lamb of God is a graphic affirmation that Jesus Himself would be the sacrifice that would atone for the sins of the lost (see Isaiah 53:7).

Objection: If Jesus was the divine Messiah, why didn't He make claims that are more overt in this regard?[12]

Answering the Objection: Many have wondered why Jesus did not perpetually and forthrightly claim to be the divine Messiah promised in the Old Testament Scriptures. One very important consideration that helps us understand Jesus' *modus operandi* is that in the first century, many popular misunderstandings were circulating about the Messiah. There was a high expectation among the Jews to the effect that when the Messiah came, He would deliver them from Roman domination (see John 6:15). The people were expecting a political Messiah/deliverer. For news that Jesus was the Messiah to circulate at an early juncture in His ministry would immediately excite people's preconceived imaginations about what this Messiah-figure was supposed to do. This could have caused the Roman governing authorities to mark Him as a rebel leader.

Seeking to avoid an erroneous popular response to His words and deeds, Jesus—especially early in His ministry—was cautious about how much He revealed about Himself. He did not want anyone prematurely speaking of His identity until He had had sufficient opportunity to make the character of His mission clear to the masses. As time passed on, Christ's identity became increasingly clear to those who encountered Him.

There is another reason Jesus was cautious about revealing His identity too quickly. By the time Jesus came on the scene, there had been only glimpses of the doctrine of the Trinity in Old Testament times (for example, Isaiah 48:16). Revelation in the Bible is *progressive* in nature, and the primary emphasis about the doctrine of God in Old Testament times was God's oneness. For Jesus to come right out and say, "I am the divine Messiah" or "I am God" would have caused incredible confusion. People would not have understood His claim in the context of Him being the second person of the Trinity. Hence, Jesus went slowly in terms of revealing all that needed to be revealed about Himself and His relationship with the Father and the Holy Spirit. To do otherwise would have caused a huge distraction for people and thus would have been counterproductive to His overall ministry.[13]

An examination of the New Testament evidence reveals that Jesus did, in fact, go on to clearly reveal His divine nature to people. For example, Jesus implicitly ascribed the divine name, Yahweh, to Himself during a confrontation He had with a group of hostile Jews. Someone in the group said to Him, "Abraham died and so did the prophets, yet you say that if anyone keeps your word, he will never taste death. Are you greater than our father Abraham?" (John 8:52-53). Jesus responded, "Your father Abraham rejoiced at the thought of seeing my day; he saw it and was glad" (verse 56). The Jews mockingly replied, "You are not yet fifty years old and you have seen Abraham!" (verse 57). To which Jesus replied, "I tell you the truth, before Abraham was born, I am" (verse 58).

The Jews immediately picked up stones with the intention of killing Jesus, for they recognized He was identifying Himself as Yahweh.[14] The Jews were acting on the prescribed penalty for blasphemy in Old Testament law: death by stoning (Leviticus 24:16).

The name *Yahweh,* which occurs over 5,300 times in the Old Testament, is connected with the Hebrew verb "to be." We first learn of this name in Exodus 3, where Moses asked God by what name He should be called. God replied to him, "I AM WHO I AM.... Thus you shall say to the sons of Israel, 'I AM has sent me to you'" (verse 14 NKJV).

I AM may seem like an odd name to the modern ear. But Moses understood in some measure what God was saying to him. The name clearly conveys the idea of eternal self-existence.[15] Yahweh never came into being at a point in time, for He has always existed. He was never born; He will never die. He does not grow older, for He is beyond the realm of time. To know Yahweh is to know the Eternal One.

All of this adds significance to Jesus' encounter with the Jews. Knowing how much they venerated Abraham, Jesus in John 8:58 deliberately contrasted the created origin of Abraham with His own eternal, uncreated nature. "It was not simply that he was older than Abraham, although his statement says that much too, but that his existence is of a different kind than Abraham's—that Abraham's existence was created and finite, beginning at a point in time, while Christ's existence never began, is uncreated and infinite, and therefore eternal."[16] In Jesus, therefore, "we see the timeless

God, who was the God of Abraham and of Isaac and of Jacob, who was before time and who will be after time, who always is."[17]

It is noteworthy that Jesus began His assertion of deity with the words, "*I tell you the truth*...before Abraham was born, I am" (emphasis added). In the King James Version, the phrase "I tell you the truth" is rendered "verily, verily." Jesus used such language only when He was making an important and emphatic statement. These words tell us He was stating the strongest possible oath and claim.[18] We might paraphrase it, "I assure you, most solemnly I tell you." Jesus did not want there to be any confusion over the fact that He claimed to be eternal God. He claimed in the strongest possible terms that He had independent continuous existence from before time.

Notice also that when the Jews picked up stones to attempt to kill Jesus for what they perceived to be blasphemy, Jesus did not say, "Oh, no, you've got it all wrong. I was not claiming to be deity." Rather, Jesus let His meaning stand because He indeed *was* claiming to be God.

The Septuagint provides us with additional insights on Christ's identity as Yahweh. The Septuagint is a Greek translation of the Hebrew Old Testament that dates prior to the birth of Christ. It renders the Hebrew phrase for "I AM" in Exodus 3:14 as *ego eimi*.[19] On a number of occasions in the Greek New Testament, Jesus used this same term as a way of identifying Himself as God.[20] For example, in John 8:24 (NASB) Jesus declared, "Unless you believe that I am [*ego eimi*] He, you shall die in your sins." The original Greek text for this verse does not have the word *he*. The verse is literally, "If you do not believe that I am, you shall die in your sins."

Then, according to verse 28 (NASB), Jesus told the Jews, "When you lift up the Son of Man, then you will know that I am [*ego eimi*] He." Again, the original Greek text reads, "When you lift up the

Son of Man, then you will know that I am" (there is no *he*). Jesus purposefully used the phrase as a means of identifying Himself as Yahweh.[21]

A more subtle—but nevertheless powerful—claim to deity is found in the fact that Jesus forgave sins, a prerogative that belongs *only* to God. An example is Mark 2:1-12, where we find Jesus forgiving the sins of a paralytic. In this passage, we read that a paralytic was lowered through a roof by his friends in order to get close to Jesus in hopes of a healing. Jesus' first words to the paralytic were, "Son, your sins are forgiven" (Mark 2:5). Upon first reading, such words may seem out of place because the paralytic was seeking healing. Further investigation indicates that Jesus was making an important statement. He knew that all those present were aware that only God could pronounce someone's sins as being forgiven. (In Isaiah 43:25, for example, God said, "I, even I, am he who blots out your transgressions, for my own sake, and remembers your sins no more.") Hence, when Jesus said, "Your sins are forgiven," He was clearly placing Himself in the position of God. The scribes who were present understood Jesus' words this way, for they reasoned, "Why does this man speak that way? He is blaspheming; who can forgive sins but God alone?" (Mark 2:7 NASB). Of course, Jesus' subsequent healing of the paralytic served to substantiate His claim to be God (verse 10).

The rest of the New Testament provides powerful witness to Jesus' identity as God. For example:

1. Many Scripture verses point to Jesus' identity as Yahweh:

- In Revelation 1:7 Jesus is seen to be the "pierced" Yahweh who is described in Zechariah 12:10.

- The prophetic reference to "Lord" ("Yahweh") and "God"

("Elohim") in Isaiah 40:3 is fulfilled in the person of Jesus (Mark 1:2-4).

- "Calling upon Yahweh" (Joel 2:32) is identical and parallel to "calling upon Jesus" (Romans 10:13).

- The glory of Yahweh in Isaiah 6:1-5 is recognized as the glory of Jesus in John 12:41.

- Yahweh's voice "like the roar of rushing waters" (Ezekiel 43:2) is identical to Jesus' voice "like the sound of rushing waters" (Revelation 1:15).

- While Yahweh in the Old Testament is portrayed as the *only* Creator (Isaiah 44:24), Jesus in the New Testament is portrayed as the agent of creation (John 1:3; Colossians 1:16).

- While Yahweh in the Old Testament is portrayed as the *only* Savior (Isaiah 43:11), Jesus is portrayed as our great God and Savior in Titus 2:13-14.

- David F. Wells, in his book *The Person of Christ,* points us to even further parallels between Christ and Yahweh:

> If Yahweh is our sanctifier (Exodus 31:13), is omni-present (Psalms 139:7-10), is our peace (Judges 6:24), is our righteousness (Jeremiah 23:6), is our victory (Exodus 17:8-16), and is our healer (Exodus 15:26), then so is Christ all of these things (1 Corinthians 1:30; Colossians 1:27; Ephesians 2:14). If the gospel is God's (1 Thessalonians 2:2, 6-9; Galatians 3:8), then that same gospel is also Christ's (1 Thessalonians 3:2; Galatians 1:7). If the church is God's (Galatians 1:13; 1 Corinthians 15:9),

then that same church is also Christ's (Romans 16:16). God's Kingdom (1 Thessalonians 2:12) is Christ's (Ephesians 5:5); God's love (Ephesians 1:3-5) is Christ's (Romans 8:35); God's Word (Colossians 1:25; 1 Thessalonians 2:13) is Christ's (1 Thessalonians 1:8; 4:15); God's Spirit (1 Thessalonians 4:8) is Christ's (Philippians 1:19); God's peace (Galatians 5:22; Philippians 4:9) is Christ's (Colossians 3:15; cf. Colossians 1:2; Philippians 1:2; 4:7); God's "Day" of judgment (Isaiah 13:6) is Christ's "Day" of judgment (Philippians 1:6,10; 2:16; 1 Corinthians 1:8); God's grace (Ephesians 2:8,9; Colossians 1:6; Galatians 1:15) is Christ's grace (1 Thessalonians 5:28; Galatians 1:6; 6:18); God's salvation (Colossians 1:13) is Christ's salvation (1 Thessalonians 1:10); and God's will (Ephesians 1:11; 1 Thessalonians 4:3; Galatians 1:4) is Christ's will (Ephesians 5:17; cf. 1 Thessalonians 5:18). So it is no surprise to hear Paul say that he is both God's slave (Romans 1:9) and Christ's (Romans 1:1; Galatians 1:10), that he lives for that glory which is both God's (Romans 5:2; Galatians 1:24) and Christ's (2 Corinthians 8:19, 23; cf. 2 Corinthians 4:6), that his faith is in God (1 Thessalonians 1:8,9; Romans 4:1-5) and in Christ Jesus (Galatians 3:22), and that to know God, which is salvation (Galatians 4:8; 1 Thessalonians 4:5), is to know Christ (2 Corinthians 4:6).[22]

2. Many Scripture verses point to Jesus as having all the attributes of deity, including:

- *Self-existence.* As the Creator of all things (John 1:3), Christ Himself must be *un*created. Because He is "before all things" (Colossians 1:17), He does not depend on anyone or anything outside Himself for His existence.

- *Immutability.* Christ, as God, is unchanging in His divine nature (Hebrews 1:10-12; 13:8).

- *Omnipresence.* Christ promised His disciples that "where two or three come together in my name, there am I with them" (Matthew 18:20). The only way He could be simultaneously present with believers worldwide is if He is omnipresent.

- *Omniscience.* Jesus' disciples acknowledged, "Now we can see that you know all things" (John 16:30). Jesus knew exactly where the fish were in the water (Luke 5:4,6) and exactly which fish contained the coin (Matthew 17:27). He knows the Father as the Father knows Him (John 7:29; 8:55; 10:15; 17:25).

- *Omnipotence.* Christ created the entire universe (Colossians 1:16) and sustains it by His power (Colossians 1:17). During His earthly ministry, Christ exercised power over nature (Luke 8:25), physical diseases (Mark 1:29-31), demonic spirits (Mark 1:32-34), and death (John 11:1-44).

3. Many Scripture verses portray Jesus as having the names of deity:

- *Elohim* (Old Testament Hebrew term for "God"). *Elohim*

literally means "strong one," and its plural ending (*im* in Hebrew) indicates fullness of power. Jesus is clearly identified as Elohim in Isaiah 9:6 and 40:3.

- *Yahweh* (Old Testament Hebrew term for "Lord"). Jesus told some Jews, "I tell you the truth, before Abraham was born, I am" (John 8:58). The Jews immediately picked up stones with the intention of killing Jesus, for they understood He was identifying Himself as Yahweh—the "I am" of Exodus 3:14. Isaiah 40:3 presents another clear allusion to Jesus being Yahweh: "In the desert prepare the way for the Lord [*Yahweh*]; make straight in the wilderness a highway for our God [*Elohim*]." Mark's Gospel tells us that Isaiah's words were fulfilled in the ministry of John the Baptist preparing the way for Jesus (Mark 1:2-4).

- *Theos* (New Testament Greek term for "God"). The New Testament Greek word for God, *Theos,* is the corresponding parallel to the Old Testament *Elohim.* Jesus is recognized as *Theos* by doubting Thomas (John 20:28), a jailer (Acts 16:31-34), the apostle Paul (Titus 2:13), Peter (1 Peter 1:1), and others.

- *Kurios* (New Testament Greek term for "Lord"). The New Testament equivalent of *Yahweh* is *Kurios.* The apostle Paul points us to the close relationship between *Yahweh* and *Kurios* in Philippians 2, where he tells us that Christ was given a name above every name, "that at the name of Jesus every knee should bow, in heaven and on earth and under the earth, and every tongue confess that Jesus Christ is Lord [*Kurios*]" (verses 9-11). Paul, an Old Testament scholar par excellence, is alluding to Isaiah 45:22-24: "I am God, and there is no other....Before me every knee will bow; by me every tongue will swear." Drawing on his vast knowledge of the Old Testament, Paul made the point that Jesus is Yahweh, the Lord of all humankind.

4. Many Scripture verses portray Jesus doing only what God can do. Jesus' miracles provide further evidence of His divine identity. His miracles are often called "signs" in the New Testament, for signs always *signify* something—in this case, that Jesus is the divine Messiah. Some of Jesus' more notable miracles include turning water into wine (John 2:7-8); walking on water (Matthew 14:25); calming a stormy sea (Mark 4:39); feeding 5,000 men and their families (Luke 9:16); raising Lazarus from the dead (John 11:43-44); and causing the disciples to catch a great number of fish (Luke 5:5-6).

5. Many Scripture verses portray Jesus as receiving the worship that belongs only to God. Jesus Christ was worshiped (Greek: *proskuneo*) as God many times according to the Gospel accounts, and He always accepted such worship as perfectly appropriate. Jesus accepted worship from Thomas (John 20:28), the angels (Hebrews 1:6), some wise men (Matthew 2:11), a leper (Matthew 8:2), a ruler (Matthew 9:18), a blind man (John 9:38), an anonymous woman (Matthew 15:25), Mary Magdalene (Matthew 28:9), and the disciples (Matthew 28:17). All these verses contain the word *proskuneo*, the same word used of worshiping the Father in the New Testament.

The fact that Jesus willingly received (and condoned) worship on various occasions says a lot about His true identity, for it is the consistent testimony of Scripture that only God can be worshiped. Exodus 34:14 tells us, "Do not worship any other god, for the LORD, whose name is Jealous, is a jealous God" (see also Deuteronomy 6:13; Matthew 4:10). In view of this, the fact that

Jesus accepted worship on numerous occasions testifies to His identity as God.

Objection: Jesus could not have been omniscient because He admitted He did not know the day or hour of His return.[23]

Answering the Objection: The fact that Jesus said no one knows the day or hour of His return except the Father (Mark 13:32) does not disprove His deity. We gain a proper perspective on this issue by understanding the nature of the incarnation.

The eternal Son of God was, prior to the incarnation, one in person and nature (wholly divine). In the incarnation (when He was born of Mary), He became two in nature (divine and human) while remaining one person. In the incarnation, the person of Christ is the partaker of the attributes of both natures, so that whatever may be affirmed of either nature—human or divine—may be affirmed of the one person of Jesus Christ.

Though Christ sometimes operated in the sphere of His humanity and at other times in the sphere of His deity, in all cases what He did and what He was could be attributed to His one person. Thus, though Christ in His human nature knew hunger (Luke 4:2), weariness (John 4:6), and the need for sleep (Luke 8:23), and though in His divine nature He was omniscient (all-knowing) (John 2:24), omnipresent (everywhere-present) (John 1:48), and omnipotent (all-powerful) (John 11)—all this was experienced *by the one person* of Jesus Christ.

The Gospel accounts are clear that Christ operated at different times under the major influence of one or the other of His two natures. Indeed, Christ operated in the human sphere to the extent that it was necessary for Him to accomplish His earthly purpose as determined in the eternal plan of salvation. At the same time, He operated in the divine sphere on numerous occasions to openly demonstrate that He was (is) the divine Messiah (see Philippians 2:6-9).

It is interesting to observe that both of Christ's natures come into play in many events recorded in the Gospels. For example, Christ's initial approach to the fig tree to pick and eat a fig to relieve His hunger reflected the natural limits of the human mind (Matthew 21:19a). (That is, in His humanity He did not know from a distance that there was no fruit on that particular tree.) But when He saw the tree had no fruit, He immediately exercised His divine omnipotence by causing the tree to wither (verse 19b).

On another occasion, Jesus in His divine omniscience (all-knowingness) knew that His friend Lazarus had died, and He set off for the town of Bethany (John 11:11). When Jesus arrived in Bethany, He asked (in his humanness, without exercising omniscience) where Lazarus had been laid (verse 34).

All this serves as a backdrop to a proper understanding of Jesus' comment in Mark 13:32 (NASB): "Of that day or hour no one knows, not even the angels in heaven, nor the Son, but the Father alone." Jesus was here speaking from the vantage point of His humanity. In His humanity, Jesus was not omniscient but was limited in understanding just as all human beings are. If Jesus had been speaking from the perspective of His divinity, He would not have stated those words.

Scripture is abundantly clear that in His divine nature, Jesus *is* omniscient—just as omniscient as the Father is. The apostle John said that Jesus "did not need man's testimony about man, for he knew what was in a man" (John 2:25). Jesus' disciples said, "Now we can see that you know all things..." (16:30). After the Resurrection, when Jesus asked Peter for the third time if Peter loved Him, Peter responded, "Lord, you know all things; you know that I love you" (21:17). Jesus also knew the Father as the

Father knew Him (Matthew 11:27; John 7:29; 8:55; 10:15; 17:25), which quite clearly requires the attribute of omniscience.

One might wonder why Jesus chose on some occasions not to use His divine attributes. The scriptural testimony is that Jesus submitted to a *voluntary* nonuse of some of His divine attributes on some occasions in keeping with His purpose of living among human beings and their limitations, and in keeping with His role as the Mediator between God (the Father) and human beings (see Philippians 2:5-11; 1 Timothy 2:5). Mark 13:32 mentions one example of Jesus' voluntary nonuse of the divine attribute of omniscience. On other occasions, however, Jesus did exercise His omniscience (for example, Matthew 17:27).

Objection: Jesus was not omnipotent because He was unable to do miracles in His own hometown.[24]

Answering the Objection: In Mark 6:4-5, Jesus affirmed that a prophet is without honor in his hometown, and in view of that reality, He Himself could not perform any miracles in Nazareth except for healing a few sick people. Apparently the people of Nazareth were plagued by unbelief and paid little attention to His claims. At first glance, one might get the impression that Jesus' miraculous power was utterly dependent upon peoples' faith in order for it to work. That is not the meaning of this passage, however. It is not that Jesus was unable to perform miracles in Nazareth. Rather, Jesus "could not" do miracles there in the sense that He *would not* do so in view of the pervasive unbelief in that city.

Miracles serve a far greater purpose, from the divine perspective, than merely providing a raw display of power. Indeed, Jesus' miraculous deeds are often called "signs" in the New Testament because they served to signify His identity as the Messiah. But because the people of Nazareth had already made up their minds against Jesus, and had provided more than ample evidence of their lack of faith in Him, Jesus chose not to engage in miraculous acts there except for healing a few sick people. He refused to bestow miraculous deeds on a city that had rejected the miraculous Messiah. Unbelief excluded the residents of Nazareth from the dynamic disclosure of God's grace that residents of other cities had experienced.

Because of Nazareth's rejection of the person and message of Jesus Christ, He went on to other cities that did respond to and receive Him. There is no evidence that Jesus ever again returned to Nazareth.

Objection: Jesus may have claimed to be God, but He was deluded. As one atheist put it, Jesus was a "deluded visionary and fanatic, even stooping to fraud."[25]

Answering the Objection: Jesus was not deluded. Almost without exception, people who study the life of Jesus recognize His great wisdom. This is acknowledged even by those who reject His deity. Further, Jesus has consistently been recognized as a good man. His goodness is evident in the words He spoke and in His actions toward others. Such characteristics as wisdom and goodness do not fit the profile of a deluded person.

In their *Handbook of Christian Apologetics,* Peter Kreeft and Ronald Tacelli wrote, "The 'divinity complex' is a recognized form of psycho-pathology. Its character traits are well known: egotism, narcissism, inflexibility, dullness, predictability, inability to understand and love others as they really are and creatively relate to others. In other words, this is the polar opposite of the personality of Jesus!"[26] Clearly, Jesus does not fit the profile of a deluded person.

In keeping with this, there are innumerable people who encountered Jesus and chose not only to follow Him, but to even suffer and die rather than retract their allegiance to Him (including highly educated people such as Saul of Tarsus). People do not respond in this way to deluded men. The only way we can explain their actions is by recognizing that Jesus truly is who He claimed to be—the divine Messiah.

Objection: The claim that Jesus is "the only way" is arrogant and narrow-minded. Former atheist Lee Strobel said, "When I was an atheist, I bristled at assertions by Christians that they held a monopoly on the only correct approach to religion. 'Who do they think they are?' I'd grouse. 'Who are they to judge everyone else? Where's the love of Jesus in that?'"[27] Aren't all religions essentially the same?

Answering the Objection: It is true that in John 14:6 Jesus said, "I am the way and the truth and the life. No one comes to the Father except through me." Jesus *did* claim to be the only way of salvation. This claim was confirmed by those who followed Him. A bold Peter said in Acts 4:12, "Salvation is found in no one else, for there is no other name under heaven given to men by which we must be saved." The apostle Paul said, "There is one God and one mediator between God and men, the man Christ Jesus" (1 Timothy 2:5). Moreover, Jesus sternly warned His followers about those who would try to set forth a different "Christ" (Matthew 24:4-5). Jesus then proved the veracity of all He said by rising from the dead (Acts 17:31). None of the leaders of the other world religions have ever done this. Jesus' resurrection proved that He was who He claimed to be—the divine Messiah (Romans 1:4).

In the interest of fairness, it is important to recognize that Christianity is not the only religion that claims exclusivity. Muslims claim Allah is the only true God, that Muhammad is His ultimate prophet, and that the Koran is God's ultimate revelation to humankind. Hinduism is unbending in its commitment to the Vedas as scriptures, and reincarnation and the law of karma as the means of salvation. Atheism, for that matter, is exclusivist in its view that all religions that believe in God are wrong, and that atheism alone is the correct view. To chastise Christianity as being the only exclusivistic group is therefore unfair.

The very act of criticizing Christianity for its belief in the exclusive nature of truth itself constitutes a truth claim. As Ravi Zacharias said, "To deny the exclusive nature of truth is to make a truth claim, and is that person then not arrogant too? That's the boomerang effect that the condemner often doesn't pause to consider."[28]

Christians do not believe that sharing Jesus as the one way of salvation makes them "arrogant." Christians are much like postal carriers. They only deliver the mail. They did not write the letter. Jesus wrote the letter, and there is no arrogance involved in simply passing it on to others.

While saying Jesus is the "only way" may seem narrow-minded, there are many "narrow options" in life that are not necessarily bad. For example, sometimes there is only one operation that can save your life. Sometimes there is only one road out of a forest. There is only one correct formula for Pepsi. When I take a flight to the Dallas-Fort Worth airport, I desire the pilot to land only at that airport. I want my wife Kerri to remain faithful to me (her "one and only") for the rest of her life. All these things are narrow, but that doesn't make them bad. So it is with the wonderful gift of salvation in Jesus Christ. The same gift is offered to all people, but people must choose to accept or reject this one gift. The act of sharing about this gift with other people does not make one a narrow-minded, arrogant person, but rather a *caring* person.

Though it is not politically correct to say so, it is simply not true that all religions are essentially the same. They may possess certain ethical similarities (due to God Himself planting His moral law in the hearts of all human beings), but on a doctrinal level, the various world religions are quite different. For example, the leaders of the different world religions taught different (and contradictory) ideas about God: Jesus taught that there is only one God and that He is triune in nature (Matthew 28:19). Muhammad taught that there is only one God, but that God is *not* a Trinity and cannot have a son. Krishna in the Bhagavad Gita (a Hindu scripture) indicated he believed in a combination of polytheism (there are many gods) and pantheism (all is God). Confucius believed in many gods. Zoroaster taught that there is both a good god and a bad god. Buddha taught that the concept of God was essentially irrelevant. Clearly, then, all religions are *not* essentially the same.

Further, Christianity teaches that Jesus is the Son of God and is absolute deity. Islam teaches that Jesus was not the Son of God, and was only a prophet to Israel. Hinduism teaches that Jesus was an enlightened man. The Baha'i Faith teaches that Jesus is one of many manifestations of God throughout human history.

Still further, Christianity teaches that one is saved by faith in Christ alone. Islam teaches that one becomes saved through submission to Allah. Hindus teach that salvation is rooted in reincarnation and karma. I could provide numerous other examples. The point I am trying to make is that these religious leaders cannot be said to be teaching the same basic truth. If one is right, all the others are wrong. If Jesus was right (as I believe He is), then all the others are wrong.

This brings me to echo a point made by Ravi Zacharias some years ago: All the world's other religions seek to take bad men and make them better by ethics. Christianity, by contrast, seeks to take dead men and make them alive. More specifically, Christianity seeks to take people who are spiritually dead (separated from God because of sin), and make them spiritually alive so they can enjoy a personal relationship with the God who created them.[29] *This* is what makes Christianity unique.

On a number of atheist and skeptic Web sites, one objection often raised against Jesus being the only way of salvation is this: How can infants and young children who die, retarded people, and those who have never heard the gospel be saved? To be frank, Christians, too, have expressed concern over these categories of people. How can these individuals be saved if they don't know or understand Jesus' "only way" statements?

This is a critically important issue and calls for an extended answer. I will first deal with those who lack the capacity to exercise cognitive faith in Christ—such as an infant or a young child (the same arguments would hold true for a retarded person). I believe the Scriptures teach that every young child who dies is immediately ushered into God's glorious presence in heaven. I believe that at the moment of death, Jesus applies the benefits of His sacrificial death to that child, thereby saving him or her.

At the outset, though, we must recognize that the whole of Scripture points to the universal need of salvation—even among little children. All of us—including infants who cannot believe— are lost (Luke 19:10), perishing (John 3:16), condemned (John 3:18), and are under God's wrath (John 3:36). This is rooted in the fact that *all* human beings are born into the world with a sin nature (Psalm 51:5; Ephesians 2:3). In view of this, we cannot say that little children are in a sinless state. That is why it is necessary for Christ to apply the benefits of His sacrificial death to each child that dies.

In attaining a balanced perspective on this issue, one must keep in mind that God's primary purpose in saving human beings is to display His wondrous grace. One must ask, Would the "riches of God's grace" be displayed in "wisdom and understanding" (Ephesians 1:7-8) in sending little children to hell? I think not. It would be a cruel mockery for God to call upon little children to do—and to hold them responsible for doing—what they *could not* do. Very young children simply do not have the capacity to exercise saving faith in Christ. I believe it is the uniform testimony of Scripture that those who are not capable of making a decision to receive Jesus Christ, and who have died, are now with Christ in heaven, resting in His tender arms, enjoying the sweetness of His love.

Several factors support this viewpoint. First, in all the descriptions of hell in the Bible, we never read of infants or little children there. Only people capable of making decisions are seen there. Nor do we read of infants and little children standing before the Great White Throne judgment, which is the judgment of the wicked dead and the precursor to the Lake of Fire (Revelation 20:11-15). The complete silence of Scripture regarding the presence of infants in eternal torment militates against their being there.

Moreover, as we examine instances in which Christ encountered children during His earthly ministry, it appears that children have a special place in His kingdom. Jesus even said, "Unless you change and become like little children, you will never enter the kingdom of heaven" (Matthew 18:3). He also said, "Whoever welcomes a little child like this in my name welcomes me" (verse 5). I do not believe there is any way someone could read Matthew 18 and conclude that it is within the realm of possibility that Jesus could damn such little ones to hell!

Certainly King David in the Old Testament believed he would one day be reunited with a son who died very young (2 Samuel 12:22-23). David firmly believed in life after death, and he had no doubt that he would spend eternity with his beloved little one.

Another consideration that points to the assurance of infant salvation relates to the *basis* of the judgment of the lost. We read in Revelation 20:11-13 that the lost are judged "according to what they had done." The basis of the judgment of the wicked involves deeds done while on earth. Hence, infants and young children cannot possibly be the objects of this judgment because they are not responsible for their deeds. Such a judgment against infants would be a travesty. We conclude, then, that babies and young children go straight to heaven at the moment of death.

What about those—"the heathen"—who have never heard the gospel? Since Jesus is "the only way" (John 14:6), are they saved or lost? In answering this question, we must begin with the recognition that if the heathen are not really lost, then many of Christ's teachings become absurd. For example, John 3:16—"For God so loved the world that he gave his one and only Son, that whoever believes in him shall not perish but have eternal life"—becomes meaningless. If the heathen are not lost, Christ's postresurrection and pre-ascension commands to His disciples are a mockery. In Luke 24:47 Christ commanded "that repentance and forgiveness of sins should be preached in his name among all nations." Similarly, in Matthew 28:19 He said, "Therefore go and make disciples of all nations, baptizing them in the name of the Father and of the Son and of the Holy Spirit." These verses might well be stricken from the Scriptures if human beings without Christ are not lost. If the heathen are not really lost, then the Lord's words were meaningless when He said to His disciples, "As the Father has sent me, I am sending you" (John 20:21). Why did the Father send Him? Jesus Himself explained that "the Son of Man came to seek and to save what was lost" (Luke 19:10). If the heathen do not need Christ and His salvation, then neither do we. Conversely, if we need Him, so do they. The Scriptures become a bundle of contradictions, the Savior becomes a false teacher, and the Christian message becomes "much ado about nothing" if the heathen are not lost. As noted above, Scripture makes it very plain that "salvation is found in no one else, for there is no other name under heaven given to men by which we must be saved" (Acts 4:12). The Bible says, "There is one God and one mediator between God and men, the man Christ Jesus" (1 Timothy 2:5).

Other religions do not lead to God. The one sin for which God judged the people of Israel more severely than any other was that of participating in heathen religions. The Bible repeatedly states that God hates, despises, and utterly rejects anything associated with heathen religions and practices. Those who follow such idolatry are not regarded as groping their way to God but rather as having turned their backs on Him, following the ways of darkness.

Because God loves and cares for all the people in the world, He has given a certain amount of revelational "light" to *every single person.* Everyone has some sense of God's law in his or her heart. As John Blanchard said so well, everyone "has some conception of the difference between right and wrong; he approves of honesty; he responds to love and kindness; he resents it if someone steals his goods or tries to injure him. In other words, he has a conscience which passes judgment on his behavior and the behavior of others, something the Bible calls a law written on his heart."[30] Paul speaks of this law written on human hearts in Romans 2:15.

God has also given witness of Himself in the universe around us. As we view the world and the universe, it is evident that someone made them (see chapter 6 for more on this). Since the creation of the world, God's invisible qualities—His eternal power and divine nature—have been clearly seen and understood from that which He created (Romans 1:20). We know from other Scripture verses that God is an invisible spirit (John 4:24). The physical eye cannot see Him. But His existence is manifest in what He has made—the creation. The creation, which is *visible,* reveals the existence of the Creator, who is *invisible.*

Because all human beings have God's law written on their hearts, and because all can see the revelation of God in creation, all people—*regardless* of whether they have heard about Christ or have read the Bible—are held accountable before God. All are without excuse. Their rightful condemnation, as objects of God's wrath, is justified because their choice to ignore the revelation of God in creation is indefensible (Psalm 19:1-6; Romans 1:20).

The Scriptures indicate that those who respond to the limited light around them (such as God's witness of Himself in the universe) will receive further, more specific light. This is illustrated in the life of Cornelius. This Gentile was obedient to the limited amount of light he had received—that is, he had been obedient to Old Testament revelation (Acts 10:2). But he did not have enough light to believe in Jesus Christ as the Savior. So God sent Peter to Cornelius's house to explain the gospel, after which time Cornelius believed in Jesus and was saved (verses 44-48).

Let us not forget that God desires all to be saved (1 Timothy 2:4) and does not want anyone to perish (2 Peter 3:9). He takes no pleasure in the death of the unsaved (Ezekiel 18:23). Further, God is a fair Judge. "It is unthinkable that God would do wrong, that the Almighty would pervert justice" (Job 34:12). "Will not the Judge of all the earth do right?" (Genesis 18:25).

11

THE EVIDENCE FOR
THE RESURRECTION

Dwight L. Moody, one of the great evangelists of the nineteenth century, once said, "You can't find directions in the New Testament on how to conduct a funeral because Jesus broke up every funeral He attended."[1] He did this by resurrecting people from the dead (for example, John 11:1-44). He also resurrected *Himself* from the dead (John 2:19). Understandably, the resurrection is foundational to the very survival and truth of Christianity. As one scholar stated,

> It should be clear...that the central miracle of NT religion is the resurrection of Christ. Without this miracle

the early church would not have come into being....
Indeed, we would probably never have heard of Jesus
of Nazareth, who would have been forgotten along
with hundreds of other obscure preachers....[2]

Both friends and enemies of Christianity have long recognized that the resurrection of Christ is the foundation stone of the Christian faith. The apostle Paul wrote to the Corinthians: "If Christ has not been raised, your faith is futile; you are still in your sins" (1 Corinthians 15:17).

Paul realized that the most important truths of Christianity stand or fall on the doctrine of Christ's resurrection. If Christ did not rise from the dead, then Christianity is little more than an interesting museum piece.

Atheists, agnostics, and skeptics offer a plethora of objections to the Bible's teaching that Christ rose from the dead. Let's address some of the more notable ones.

Objection: It is unreasonable to believe in the resurrection. "With respect to the resurrection stories in the New Testament, it will be more reasonable for an atheist to believe just about any alternative scenario, no matter how improbable, rather than accept those stories at face value."[3]

Answering the Objection: It is reasonable to believe in the resurrection inasmuch as the historical evidence supports it (Matthew 28:1-15; Mark 16:1-11; Luke 24:1-12; John 20:1-18):

1. *The circumstances at the tomb reveal a missing body.* Following His crucifixion, the body of Jesus was buried in accordance with Jewish burial customs. He was wrapped in a linen cloth, and about 100 pounds of aromatic spices—mixed together to form a gummy substance—were applied to the wrappings of cloth around His body.

After Jesus' body was placed in a solid rock tomb, an extremely large and heavy stone was rolled by means of levers against the entrance. This stone would have weighed in the neighborhood of two tons (4,000 pounds). It is not a stone that would have been easily moved by human beings.

Roman guards were then stationed at the tomb. These strictly disciplined men were highly motivated to succeed in all the responsibilities assigned to them by the Roman government. Fear of cruel punishment produced flawless attention to duty, especially in the night watches. These Roman guards would have affixed on the tomb the Roman seal, a stamp representing Roman power and authority.

All this makes the situation at the tomb following Christ's resurrection highly significant. The Roman seal was broken, which meant automatic crucifixion upside-down for the person responsible. Furthermore, the large stone was moved a good distance from the entrance, as if it had been picked up and carried away. The Roman guards had also fled. The penalty in Rome for a guard leaving his position was death. We can therefore assume they must have had a substantial reason for fleeing!

2. *The biblical account has Jesus appearing first to a woman, Mary Magdalene (John 20:1), a fact that is a highly significant indicator of the authenticity and reliability of the resurrection account.* If the resurrection story were a fabrication, made up by the disciples, no one in a first-century Jewish culture would have invented it this way. According to Jewish law, a woman's testimony was unacceptable in any court of law except in a very few circumstances. A fabricator would have been much more likely to portray Peter or one of the other male disciples at the tomb. Our biblical text, however, tells us that the Lord appeared first to Mary because, in fact, that is what actually happened. After this

appearance, Mary promptly told the disciples the glorious news. That evening, the disciples gathered together in a room with the doors shut for fear of the Jews (John 20:19). This fear was well founded, for after Jesus had been arrested, Annas the high priest specifically asked Jesus about the disciples (John 18:19). Jesus had also warned the disciples, shortly before His crucifixion, "If they persecuted me, they will persecute you also" (John 15:20). These facts no doubt lingered in the disciples' minds when they were together in this locked room.

The disciples' gloom soon turned to joy, for the risen Christ appeared in their midst and said to them, "Peace be with you" (John 20:19). This phrase was a common Hebrew greeting (1 Samuel 25:6). On this occasion, however, there was added significance to Jesus' words. After their conduct on Good Friday (the disciples had all scattered like a bunch of spineless cowards after Jesus' arrest), they may well have expected a rebuke from Jesus. Instead, He displayed compassion by pronouncing peace upon them.

Jesus immediately showed the disciples His hands and His side (John 20:20). The risen Lord wanted them to see that it was truly He. The wounds showed that He did not have another body, but the same body. He was once dead, but now was alive.

3. By all accounts, the disciples came away from the crucifixion frightened and full of doubt, and yet, following Jesus' resurrection appearance to the disciples, their lives were virtually transformed. As Michael Green said, "How have [these early followers] turned, almost overnight, into the indomitable band of enthusiasts who braved opposition, cynicism, ridicule, hardship, prison, and death on three continents, as they preached everywhere Jesus and the resurrection?"[4]

As Jews, these followers would have been predisposed to

believe that no one would rise from the dead before the general resurrection at the end of time. They were not expecting a physical resurrection of Jesus. The only thing that could account for the disciples' sudden incredible transformation into powerful witnesses for Jesus was His resurrection. Only this can explain why they were even willing to die for their beliefs. Christian theologian Barry Leventhal put it this way:

> When Yeshua [Jesus] died, all of his followers, in despair and fear, went into hiding. They thought that Yeshua's entire messianic movement was over. Even though they knew that the Hebrew Scriptures had prophesied that the Messiah would not see bodily corruption in the grave and that Yeshua had even predicted his own resurrection on at least three different occasions, they thought his messianic program had collapsed in utter defeat. And yet in a short time, these very same disciples appeared on the historical scene boldly proclaiming the good news of the gospel, that this Jesus who had been crucified, dead, and buried was now alive from the dead and the Lord of life and the sole determiner of men's eternal destinies.
>
> And what did they get for such an open and bold proclamation? They endured some of the worst abuse and punishment known in their own day. In fact, many of them were tortured and even martyred for their faith in this resurrected Messiah. Men may live for a lie, but to think that thousands will die for that same lie requires a stretch of the imagination.[5]

The apostles defended their belief in Jesus and His resurrection before the Jewish Sanhedrin and the high priest, an intimidating audience to say the least. The high priest said to them, "We gave you strict orders not to teach in this name. Yet you have filled Jerusalem with your teaching and are determined to make us guilty of this man's blood" (Acts 5:28). Peter and the other apostles replied, "We must obey God rather than men! The God of our fathers raised Jesus from the dead—whom you had killed by hanging him on a tree. God exalted him to his own right hand as Prince and Savior that he might give repentance and forgiveness of sins to Israel" (Acts 5:29-31).

These witnesses were convinced beyond any doubt about the reality of Jesus' resurrection:

- "God has raised this Jesus to life, and we are all witnesses of the fact" (Acts 2:32).

- "You killed the author of life, but God raised him from the dead. We are witnesses of this" (Acts 3:15).

- "Then [the rulers, elders, and teachers of the law] called them in again and commanded them not to speak or teach at all in the name of Jesus. But Peter and John replied, 'Judge for yourselves whether it is right in God's sight to obey you rather than God. For we cannot help speaking about what we have seen and heard'" (Acts 4:18-20).

- "We are witnesses of everything he did in the country of the Jews and in Jerusalem. They killed him by hanging him on a tree, but God raised him from the dead on the third day and caused him to be seen" (Acts 10:39-40).

- Paul passed on the truth "that Christ died for our sins according to the Scriptures, that he was buried, that he was raised on the third day according to the Scriptures, and that he appeared to Peter, and then to the Twelve. After that, he appeared to more than five hundred of the brothers at the same time, most of whom are still living, though some have fallen asleep. Then he appeared to James, then to all the apostles, and last of all he appeared to me also, as to one abnormally born" (1 Corinthians 15:3-8).

- "We did not follow cleverly invented stories when we told you about the power and coming of our Lord Jesus Christ, but we were eyewitnesses of his majesty" (2 Peter 1:16).

- "Now Thomas (called Didymus), one of the Twelve, was not with the disciples when Jesus came. So the other disciples told him, 'We have seen the Lord!' But he said to them, 'Unless I see the nail marks in his hands and put my finger where the nails were, and put my hand into his side, I will not believe it.' A week later his disciples were in the house again, and Thomas was with them. Though the doors were locked, Jesus came and stood among them and said, 'Peace be with you!' Then he said to Thomas, 'Put your finger here; see my hands. Reach out your hand and put it into my side. Stop doubting and believe.' Thomas said to him, 'My Lord and my God!' Then Jesus told him, 'Because you have seen me, you have believed; blessed are those who have not seen and yet have believed'" (John 20:24-29).

- "That which was from the beginning, which we have heard, which we have seen with our eyes, which we have looked at and our hands have touched—this we proclaim concerning the Word of life. The life appeared; we have seen it and testify to it, and we proclaim to you the eternal life, which was with the Father and has appeared to us" (1 John 1:1-2).

4. The many thousands of Jews who became unflinching fol-
lowers of Jesus necessarily had to abandon many of their long-held
sacred beliefs and practices that they formerly cherished. The only
way to explain this radical change is the resurrection of Christ.
Norman Geisler and Frank Turek summarize some of the beliefs
and practices these Jews gave up (an abandonment of Jewish doctrine which, according to Judaism, could lead to an eternity in hell)
in order to follow Jesus:

- *The animal sacrifice system*—they replaced it forever by
  the one perfect sacrifice of Christ.

- *The binding supremacy of the Law of Moses*—they say it
  is powerless because of the sinless life of Christ.

- *Strict monotheism*—they now worship Jesus, the God-
  man, despite the fact that 1) their most cherished belief
  has been, "Hear, O Israel: The LORD our God, the LORD
  is one" (Deut. 6:4); and 2) man-worship has always been
  considered blasphemy and punishable by death.

- *The Sabbath*—they no longer observe it even though
  they've always believed that breaking the Sabbath was
  punishable by death (Ex. 31:14).

- *Belief in a conquering Messiah*—Jesus is the opposite of a
  conquering Messiah. He is a sacrificial lamb (at least on his
  first visit!).[6]

In keeping with this, Christian apologist J.P. Moreland argues
that the resurrection explains

> how a large generation of Jewish people (remember,
> most of the early Christians were Jewish) would
> have been willing to risk the damnation of their own

souls to hell and reject what had been sociologically embedded in their community for centuries; namely, the Law must be kept for salvation, sacrifices must be kept for salvation, the Sabbath must be kept, non-trinitarian monotheism, and there is only a political Messiah, not a dying and rising one. How does a group of people in a short time span, a society, disenfranchise themselves from that into which they had been culturally indoctrinated for centuries and risk the damnation of their own souls to hell to follow a carpenter from Nazareth? The most reasonable explanation is there was something about that man that caused this change. He was a miracle worker who rose from the dead.[7]

5. *Only the resurrection of Jesus Christ could explain the conversion of hardcore skeptics in New Testament times.* The apostle Paul is an example. Saul, as he was known formerly, delighted in breathing out "murderous threats against the Lord's disciples" (Acts 9:1). We are told that he "went to the high priest and asked him for letters to the synagogues in Damascus, so that if he found any there who belonged to the Way, whether men or women, he might take them as prisoners to Jerusalem" (verses 1-2). Clearly, Saul was not open to following Jesus Christ, for he hated the disciples of Jesus Christ. Yet as the rest of Acts 9 reveals, Saul had an encounter with the living, resurrected Jesus, and not only became His follower, but became the most explosive preacher and promoter of Jesus to have ever appeared on planet earth. Only the existence of a truly resurrected and living Christ could explain the radical conversion of a hardcore skeptic like Paul.

Another example is James, the half-brother of Jesus. Initially, James was not a believer in Jesus. He was a skeptic. Yet later he not only became a follower of Jesus, but became the prominent leader of the church in Jerusalem. The Jewish historian Josephus tells us that James ended up being stoned to death because of his belief in Jesus. What brought about the radical change in the heart of this skeptic? It was the resurrection of Jesus (John 7:1-5; Acts 1:14; 1 Corinthians 15:7).

Yet another example is doubting Thomas. Thomas, who had not been with the other disciples when Jesus appeared to them, refused to take their word about Jesus' resurrection from the dead. He said, "Unless I see the nail marks in his hands and put my finger where the nails were, and put my hand into his side, I will not believe it" (John 20:25). *Doubting* Thomas soon became *believing* Thomas, for the resurrected Lord appeared to him and invited him to touch His wounds (verses 26-27). Thomas' response to Jesus was, "My Lord and my God!" (verse 28).

6. *Only the resurrection of Jesus could explain the growth and survival of the Christian church.* Vast numbers of people—Jews and Gentiles—became believers in Jesus, and *remained* believers in Jesus, despite the fact that the Roman sword was against the throat of Christianity. Many of these people died for their testimony and commitment to Jesus. The only way to explain such widespread commitment is the reality of a resurrected Jesus who promised eternal life to those who followed Him.

7. *There were too many appearances over too many days to too many people for the resurrection to be easily dismissed.* Acts 1:3 says, "He showed himself to these men and gave many convincing proofs that he was alive. He appeared to them over a period of forty days and spoke about the kingdom of God." Moreover, "He appeared to more than five hundred of the brothers at the same time, most of whom are still living, though some have fallen asleep" (1 Corinthians 15:6). Paul mentions that many of these were "still

living" because if Paul had uttered any falsehood, there were plenty of people who could have stepped forward to call Paul a liar. They did not do this, however, because the post-cross appearances of Christ were well attested to.

8. *The apostle Paul in 1 Corinthians 15:1-4 speaks of Christ's resurrection as part of a public confession that had been handed down for years.* First Corinthians was written around A.D. 55, a mere 20 years after Christ's resurrection. But Bible scholars believe the confession in 1 Corinthians 15:1-4 was formulated within a few years of Jesus' death and resurrection. Christian theologian Gary Habermas says, "We know that Paul wrote 1 Corinthians between A.D. 55 and 57. He indicates in 1 Corinthians 15:1-4 that he has already passed on this creed to the church at Corinth, which would mean it must predate his visit there in A.D. 51. Therefore the creed was being used within twenty years of the Resurrection, which is quite early."[8] Some scholars trace the confession back to within *two years* of the Lord's resurrection.

Objection: Jesus was not physically resurrected, but rather His essence—some part of him—lived on among the disciples. Jackson Carroll, a professor of religion and skeptic regarding the physical resurrection of Jesus, said the four Gospels "were talking not about the resurrection of the flesh but about the resurrection of Christ's selfhood, his essence." Carroll added, "The authors of the New Testament had experiences with an extra-ordinary person and extraordinary events, and they were trying to find ways to talk about all that. They weren't writing scientific history; they were writing faith history."[9]

Answering the Objection: This seems a rather preposterous interpretation. It amounts to saying that even though it was only Christ's "essence" that somehow lived on in the midst of the disciples, the disciples nevertheless went on to claim (dishonestly) that Christ had *physically* risen from the dead. Further, these New Testament witnesses all chose to defend their false claims of Christ's physical resurrection by laying down their lives. They also suffered greatly during their lifetimes for their beliefs (2 Corinthians 11:24-27)—something that is unimaginable if only Jesus' "essence" (whatever that is!) somehow lived on.

Scripture is emphatic that Christ's resurrection was physical in nature. It is noteworthy that the Greek word for "body" (*soma*), when used of a human being, always means physical body in the New Testament. There are no exceptions to this. Greek scholar Robert Gundry, in his authoritative book *Soma in Biblical Theology*, published by Cambridge University Press, speaks of "Paul's exceptionless use of *soma* for a physical body."[10] Hence, all references to Jesus' resurrection "body" (*soma*) in the New Testament must be taken to mean a resurrected *physical* body.

In further support of Christ's physical resurrection is the fact that Christ Himself said to the disciples, "See My hands and My feet, that it is I Myself; touch Me and see, for a spirit does not have flesh and bones as you see that I have" (Luke 24:39 NASB). There are three points worth observing here: 1) The resurrected Christ indicates in this verse that He is not a spirit (nor is He just an "essence"); 2) the resurrected Christ indicates that His resurrection body is made up of flesh and bones; and 3) Christ's physical hands and feet represent physical proof of the materiality of His resurrection from the dead.

Moreover, consider the verbal exchange that took place between Jesus and some Jewish leaders in John 2:19-21: "Jesus answered them, 'Destroy this temple, and I will raise it again in three days.' The Jews replied, 'It has taken forty-six years to build this temple, and you are going to raise it in three days?' But the temple he had spoken of was his body." Jesus here indicated that He would be *bodily raised* from the dead.

We should also note that the resurrected Christ ate physical food on four different occasions. He did this as a means of proving He had a real physical body (Luke 24:30; 24:42-43; John 21:12-13; Acts 1:4).

In addition, the physical body of the resurrected Christ was touched and handled by different people. For example, He was touched by Mary (John 20:17) and by some women (Matthew 28:9). He also challenged the disciples to physically touch Him so they could rest assured that His body was material in nature (Luke 24:39).

Finally, we note the teaching of the apostle Paul that the body that is "sown" in death is the *very same* body that is raised in life (1 Corinthians 15:35-44). That which goes into the grave is raised to life (see verse 42).

Objection: Jesus was not physically resurrected, but rather was *seen* by His followers in a spiritual sense. Skeptic Keith Parson alleges, "The 'appearances' of the risen Jesus mentioned by Paul in his famous formula from 1 Corinthians 15:5-7 are characterized by the verb *ophthe*, which has a meaning that is indeterminate between seeing with the physical eye and 'seeing' with the eye of the mind or spirit. In other words, it is not at all clear whether Paul is claiming that the risen Jesus was literally seen or whether he was 'seen' in some spiritual sense."[11] In view of this, the Bible cannot be used to support a physical resurrection of Jesus.

Answering the Objection: A.T. Robertson, one of the world's greatest New Testament Greek scholars, says that in 1 Corinthians 15:5-7, "Paul means not a mere 'vision,' but actual appearance."[12] The resurrection appearances of Christ are never called "visions" in the New Testament:

The resurrection experiences, including Paul's, are never called "visions" (*optasia*) anywhere in the Gospels or Epistles. During the appearance to Paul, Jesus was both seen and heard. The Gospels do speak of a "vision" of angels (Luke 24:23), and Acts refers to Paul's "heavenly vision" (Acts 26:19) which may be a reference to the vision(s) he and Ananias received later (Acts 9:11-12; cf. 22:8; 26:19). As for the actual appearance to Paul, Christ was both *seen* and *heard* with the physical senses of those present. In 1 Corinthians 15 Paul said Jesus "*appeared* to me also" (vs. 8). In the detailed account of it in Acts 26, Paul said "I *saw* a light from heaven" (vs. 13). That Paul is referring to a physical light is clear from the fact that it was so bright that it blinded the physical eyes (Acts 22:6,8). Paul not only saw the light but he saw Jesus.

Paul also *heard* the voice of Jesus speaking distinctly to him "in Aramaic" (Acts 26:14). The physical voice Paul heard said, "Saul, Saul, why do you persecute me?" (Acts 9:4). Paul carried on a conversation with Jesus (vss. 5-6) and was obedient to the command to go into the city of Damascus (9:6). Paul's miraculous conversion, his tireless efforts for Christ, and his strong emphasis on the physical resurrection of Christ (Romans 4:25; 10:9; 1 Corinthians 15) all show what an indelible impression the physical resurrection made upon him.[13]

Objection: The disciples or other people stole the body of Jesus, and the disciples assumed He had risen from the dead. One atheist argues that "we have tons of evidence that bodies do not disappear and rise into heaven," and therefore the idea that Jesus' body was stolen makes good sense. "Any reasonable person who looks at the evidence without prejudice would conclude that either the tomb was not empty or someone took the body."[14]

Answering the Objection: It is highly unlikely that Jesus' dead body could have been stolen. The tomb had a huge stone that weighed several tons blocking it. It bore the protective seal of the Roman government. It was guarded by elite Roman soldiers trained in the art of defense and killing—soldiers who would have sought to carry out their task even if it meant giving up their own lives. It would not have been easy for anyone to attempt a tomb robbery. Besides, the biblical text indicates that the disciples were scared, discouraged, and disheartened (see Mark 16:10). They were therefore in no frame of mind or spirit to attack the Roman guards and steal the body.

Certainly neither the Romans nor the Jews would have stolen the body. When Christians began claiming Christ had risen from the dead, the Romans and Jews would have loved to be able to parade the dead body around town in order to silence the Christians. But they were unable to do so because they did not have the body.

Also, why would Christians steal the body and then, instead of recanting their false claim of resurrection to save their lives, become imprisoned and go to their deaths (often after being tortured) defending the resurrection? Why engage in such a mad, self-defeating, futile endeavor? If they had stolen the body, why would they go around preaching Christ's resurrection not only to strangers but to their friends and family members—indeed, even to their own children? Why try to pull off such a massive hoax? That wouldn't make sense at all.

As previously noted, one must also consider the noble character of these men. Christ's disciples had been raised from early childhood to give heed to the Ten Commandments, including the commandment against bearing false witness (Exodus 20:16). It stretches credulity to say that *all* these men stepped outside of their normal character to commit such an act.

Besides, there was insufficient time to pull off such a stunt. As William Lane Craig points out,

> The time was too short for such a plot to be hatched and executed. Jesus was unexpectedly given an honorable burial late Friday afternoon; by dawn on Sunday the body was gone. The window of opportunity for coming up with such an idea, assembling the people required, and carrying out the theft is so narrow as to militate against such an explanation.[15]

Objection: The followers of Jesus hallucinated that Jesus rose from the dead.[16]

Answering the Objection: By their nature, hallucinations are individual experiences. They generally happen to individuals. First Corinthians 15:6, by contrast, indicates that the resurrected Jesus was seen by 500 people at a single time. There is no way it can be argued that all 500 people were hallucinating—seeing the *same* hallucination—at the same time. Moreover, Jesus appeared to too many people (many *different kinds* of people) on too many occasions (literally dozens) over too long a time (40 days) for this objection to be feasible. Further, the resurrected Jesus was seen doing a number of different activities—walking with people, eating with people, speaking with people, and being touched by people. The hallucination theory cannot explain this wide diversity of personal interactions.

If Jesus' resurrection involved merely a hallucination, the Roman and Jewish authorities could have easily put an end to the claims of His resurrection by parading Jesus' dead body around town for all to see. The Roman and Jewish leaders would have loved to have this option, but this option was not available because Jesus' body was missing from the tomb.

One must also wonder how it would be possible for so many Jewish people to hallucinate about something that is completely foreign to the their mind-set and expectations. These Jewish people had been conditioned to believe there would be only a single resurrection *at the end of time*—a general resurrection. The resurrection of a single individual prior to this general resurrection was completely foreign to their eschatology. For countless Jews to experience the same hallucination of a single individual rising from the dead when, as Jews, they had been conditioned to believe in a general resurrection at the end of time, stretches all credulity.

Objection: The resurrection can be explained in terms of the distorted memories of the disciples and Jesus' other followers. Atheist Walter Sinnott-Armstrong says the New Testament witnesses "were likely subjected to tremendous social pressures. Their emotions undoubtedly ran high. They probably had neither the training nor the opportunity nor the inclination to do a careful, impartial investigation." Moreover, "most people at that time were gullible, as shown by the plethora of cults. These are exactly the kinds of factors that psychologists have found to distort memory and eyewitness testimony in many cases."[17]

Answering the Objection: Sinnott-Armstrong raises an argument without providing even a shred of historical evidence to support its applicability to the New Testament witnesses. One could easily make this same kind of argument against *any* event in ancient history. In fact, if we were consistent in applying this argument, we could know very little if anything about ancient history. Craig is right when he says, "If one could really refute the specific evidence for putatively historical accounts so summarily…one might as well just close the history department at the university. In fact, most historical scholars who have examined the accounts of the empty tomb of Jesus have concluded that distorting influences have not expunged the historical core of the accounts."[18]

Further, one must challenge Sinnott-Armstrong's claim that people in Bible times were gullible. As C.S. Lewis said,

> When St. Joseph discovered that his bride was pregnant, he was "minded to put her away." He knew enough biology for that. Otherwise, of course, he would not have regarded pregnancy as a proof of infidelity. When he accepted the Christian explanation, he regarded it as a miracle precisely because he knew enough of the laws of nature to know that this was a suspension of them.[19]

Moreover, Lewis observed,

> When the disciples saw Christ walking on the water they were frightened: they would not have been frightened unless they had known the laws of nature and known that this was an exception. If a man had no conception of a regular order in nature, then of course he could not notice departures from that order.[20]

Nothing can be viewed as *abnormal* until one has first grasped the *norm*. People in Bible times knew enough of the norm not to be gullible.

Still further, would Sinnott-Armstrong have us believe that

multitudes of Jews left Judaism, joined the cause of Christ, and ended up being tortured and even brutally killed for their faith in Christ all because of distorted memories? Are we to believe that the 500 who saw the resurrected Jesus at the same time (1 Corinthians 15:6) were *all* suffering from memory problems? Such a possibility is very difficult to imagine.

AN UNBELIEVER'S CONVERSION

The attack on Christianity by its enemies has most often concentrated on the resurrection of Christ because it has been correctly seen that this event is the foundation of the Christian faith. An extraordinary attack was launched in the 1930s by a young British journalist. He was convinced that the resurrection of Christ was sheer fantasy and fable. Perceiving that this doctrine was the keystone of the Christian faith, he decided to gather the available evidence and expose this fraud once and for all.

Since he was a journalist, he was confident he had the necessary mental equipment to rigorously sift through all the evidence. He was determined not to admit anything into evidence that did not meet the same stiff criteria for admission that modern law courts demand.

While doing his research, however, the unexpected happened. He discovered that the case against Christ's resurrection was not nearly so airtight as he had presumed. As a result, the first chapter of his book ended up being entitled, "The Book that Refused to Be Written." In it he describes how, after examining the indisputable evidence, he became persuaded against his will that Christ really did rise bodily from the dead. The book is called *Who Moved the Stone?* and its author is Frank Morison.

Morison made the same discovery that countless others have

made down through the centuries. He discovered that the factual evidence in support of Christ's resurrection is truly staggering. Canon Westcott, a brilliant scholar at Cambridge University, said it well: "Taking all the evidence together, it is not too much to say that there is no historic incident better or more variously supported than the resurrection of Christ."[21]

Sir Edward Clarke similarly said, "As a lawyer, I have made a prolonged study of the evidences for the events of the first Easter Day. To me, the evidence is conclusive, and over and over again in the High Court I have secured the verdict on evidence not nearly so compelling."[22]

Professor Thomas Arnold, the author of the famous three-volume *History of Rome,* was the Chair of Modern History at Oxford University and was well acquainted with the value of evidence in determining historical facts. After examining all the data on Christ's resurrection, he concluded, "I know of no one fact in the history of mankind which is proved by better and fuller evidence of every sort, to the understanding of a fair inquiry, than the great sign which God has given us that Christ died and rose again from the dead."[23]

12

GOD AND THE
PROBLEM OF EVIL

The problem of evil has traditionally been viewed in simple form as a conflict involving three concepts: God's power, God's goodness, and the presence of evil in the world. Common sense seems to tell us that not all three can be true at the same time. Solutions to the problem of evil typically involve modifying one or more of these three concepts in the following ways: limit God's power, limit God's goodness, or modify the existence of evil (such as calling it an illusion).

Today we face the reality of both *moral evil* (evil committed by free moral agents, involving such things as war, crime, cruelty, class struggles, discrimination, slavery, ethnic cleansing, suicide bombings, and various injustices) and *natural evil* (involving such things as hurricanes, floods, earthquakes, and the like). Because both moral and natural evil exist, and because this evil seemingly cannot be reconciled with the presence of a good and all-powerful God, atheists have chosen to jettison belief in God altogether. Agnostics and skeptics remain unsure on the issue. The Christian, however, believes there is a coherent explanation for the problem of evil that is consistent with the existence of an all-good, all-powerful God. Let's now consider the Christian response to the more notable objections that atheists, agnostics, and skeptics voice in regard to evil. Those who desire a more comprehensive treatment of this subject are invited to consult my book *Why Do Bad Things Happen If God Is Good?* (Harvest House Publishers).

Objection: The notion that evil is merely a privation of good is false. Atheist Walter Sinnott-Armstrong says "it would be a sick joke to try to comfort parents whose child just died by saying that their child is not really dead but merely deprived of life."[1]

Answering the Objection: From a philosophical perspective, evil is not something that has an existence *all its own*; rather, it is a corruption of that which already exists. Evil is indeed the absence or privation of something good. Rot, for example, can only exist as long as the tree exists. Tooth decay can only exist as long as the tooth exists. Rust on a car, a decaying carcass, blind eyes, and deaf ears illustrate the same point. Evil exists as a corruption of something good; it is a privation and does not have essence by itself.[2] Norman Geisler tells us, "Evil is like a wound in an arm or moth-holes in a garment. It exists only in another but not in itself."[3] Intelligent design theorist William Dembski explained evil in this way:

> Evil always parasitizes good. Indeed all our words
> for evil presuppose a good that has been perverted.

Impurities presuppose purity, unrighteousness presupposes righteousness, deviation presupposes a way
(i.e., a via) from which we've departed, sin...presup-
poses a target that was missed, and so on.[4]

Actually, we can be a little more precise: Evil involves the
absence of something good that ought to be there. When good
that should be in something is *not* in that something, that is evil.
For example, health ought to be in a human body, but sometimes
people get cancer. That is evil. Hearing ought to be in an ear, but
sometimes people go deaf. That is evil. Sight ought to be in an
eye, but sometimes people go blind. That is evil. Notice, by contrast, that the tree in my front lawn cannot see, but that is not evil
because my tree was never supposed to see. Likewise, if my nose is
missing a wart, that is not evil, because a wart was never supposed
to be on my nose to begin with. To repeat, then, evil involves the
absence of something good that ought to be there, like sight in an
eye, hearing in an ear, or health in a body.[5]

As for Sinnott-Armstrong's jab that "it would be a sick joke to
try to comfort parents whose child just died by saying that their
child is not really dead but merely deprived of life," that is rather
silly, for no one would ever stoop to making such a statement. I
suspect Sinnott-Armstrong knows he has set up a straw-man argument here, for if a child has died, Christians would not, under
any circumstance, deny that the child is dead. But that does not
change the fact that this death involves a *deprivation of life* in the
child's body. When speaking to the child's parents, the Christian
would point the parents to the hope of eternal life in Jesus Christ,
whereas all the atheist could say is, "You child is gone *for good*,
and you'll *never* see him again, for there is *no God* and there is
no afterlife."

Objection: The existence of evil in the universe proves there is no all-good, all-powerful God.[6]

Answering the Objection: If one is going to claim there is no God because there is so much evil in the world, one must first ask, By what criteria is something judged evil in the first place?[7] This is a philosophical dilemma for the atheist. How does one judge some things to be evil and not others? What is the moral measuring stick by which people and events are morally appraised? Robert Morey put it this way:

> How do you know evil when you see it? By what process do you identify evil?...My point is that, as Socrates demonstrated a long time ago, to make a distinction between particulars in which one is good and one is evil, you must have a universal or absolute [standard] to do it. Once you see this, then the ultimate result is that without an infinite reference point for "good," no one can identify what is good or evil. God alone can exhaust the meaning of an infinite good. Thus without the existence of God, there is no "evil" or "good" in an absolute sense but everything is relative. The problem of evil does not negate the existence of God. It actually requires it.[8]

The point is, then, that it is impossible to distinguish evil from good unless one has an infinite reference point that is absolutely good. Otherwise we would be like a person on a boat at sea on a cloudy night without a compass—that is, there would be no way to distinguish north from south without the absolute reference point of the compass needle (pointing north). God is our reference point for distinguishing good from evil.

There is another reason I do not believe the reality of evil disproves the existence of God. When God originally created the universe, it was perfectly good in every way. Genesis 1:31 tells us, "God saw all that he had made, and it was very good." There was no evil. There was nothing in the universe of which it could be said that something good ought to be there but was missing. *Everything* was good.

Today, however, not everything is good. A great deal of evil now exists in the universe that was once entirely good. That can mean only one thing. Something dreadful happened between *then* and *now* to cause the change. A colossal perversion of the good has occurred. To borrow a metaphor, there has been a massive termite invasion into the universe—or, more to the point, an invasion of sin.

Jimmy H. Davis and Harry L. Poe, in their book *Designer Universe: Intelligent Design and the Existence of God*, suggest that the existence of evil in our universe does not disprove the existence of God any more than termites in a house disprove the existence of an architect:

> The fact that ugliness, thorns, death, pain, suffering, and chaos are present in the world does not disprove design. *Infestation by termites* does not prove the house did not have an architect. *Vandalism* does not prove the house did not have an architect. *Arson* does not prove the house did not have an architect. *Sloppy homeowners* who do not paint or carry out the garbage do not prove the house did not have an architect. These matters simply raise questions about the situation of the house since it was built.[9]

Theologically, the Bible is clear that God exists and that He created the universe in a perfectly good state. The Bible is also clear that things have changed dramatically since God created the world. Because of human sin, things are not as they were created to be (Genesis 3). God's original design has been corrupted by an intruder—the intruder of sin. God's "good universe" is no longer good. (Reasons for God's allowance of evil into the world will become clearer later in the chapter.)

Objection: If there is an all-good, all-powerful God, He should get rid of all evil now.[10]

Answering the Objection: One would be wise to rethink the idea that God should simply get rid of all evil immediately. Choosing this option would have definite and fatal implications for each of us. As Paul Little said,

> If God were to stamp out evil today, he would do a complete job. His action would have to include our lies and personal impurities, our lack of love, and our failure to do good. Suppose God were to decree that at midnight tonight all evil would be removed from the universe—who of us would still be here after midnight?[11]

Let us be clear on this: Desiring a universe in which God brings about instant justice has the definite downside of yielding a people-less universe. Absent the cross, you and I and everyone else would be absolute "goners." *Show over!* God would be the only one left! After all, each of us has committed some evil, whether it is by commission or by omission, by word, deed, or thought.[12] In the interest of self-preservation, I am glad God does not wipe out all evil immediately!

Christian theists believe it is important to remember that God is not finished yet. It is simply wrong to conclude that God is not dealing with the problem of evil because He has not dealt with it once-for-all *in the present moment.* God's definitive dealing with evil is yet future. Christian philosopher Peter Kreeft suggests that "since the solution is future, it is not yet. We are in a story, and only the end of the story explains the rest of it, just as only the conclusion of an argument explains why the premises are selected as they are."[13] When we read a good novel, we often do not understand everything that has taken place in the story until the very end of the book. That is when our perspective on the story becomes complete. That is when we say, "Oh, I get it now!" Likewise, one day in the future we will come to the last chapter in the "human story," and all will become clear. Kreeft explains:

> On this day, the mystery of suffering and the deeper and more original mysteries of sin and death will be solved, not just in theory but in practice; not just explained but removed. God will tie up the loose ends of the torn tapestry of history, and the story which now seems to be a tortured tangle will appear as a masterpiece of wisdom and beauty.[14]

Meanwhile, we can rest in the assurance that God has put boundaries on the spread of evil. God has even now taken steps to ensure that evil does not run utterly amok:

- God has given us human government to withstand lawlessness (Romans 13:1-7).

- God founded the church to be a light in the midst of the darkness, to strengthen God's people, and even to help restrain the growth of wickedness in the world through the power of the Holy Spirit (see, for example, 1 Timothy 3:15; Acts 16:5).

- God has given us the family unit to bring stability to society (see, for example, Proverbs 22:15; 23:13).

- God has, in His Word, given us a moral standard to guide us and keep us on the right path (Psalm 119).[15]

- God has promised a future day of accounting in which all human beings will face the divine Judge (Hebrews 9:27). For Christians, an awareness of this future day serves as a deterrent to committing evil acts.

Objection: If there were an all-good and all-powerful God, surely He could have arranged things so that human beings would never sin.[16]

Answering the Objection: A scenario in which people never had the possibility of sinning would necessitate that these people no longer be truly human. They would no longer have the capacity to make choices and to freely love. This scenario would require that God create robots who act only in programmed ways—like one of those chatty dolls where you pull a string on its back and it says, "I love you." Paul Little notes that with such a doll,

> there would never be any hot words, never any conflict, never anything said or done that would make you sad! But who would want that? There would never be any love, either. Love is voluntary. God could have made us like robots, but we would have ceased to be men. God apparently thought it worth the risk of creating us as we are.[17]

In a similar vein, Kreeft observes that love is the highest value in the universe, and in a world of robots, such love would be entirely absent. "Real love—our love of God and our love of each other—

must involve a choice. But with the granting of that choice comes the possibility that people would choose instead to hate."[18]

Love cannot be programmed in a coercive way; it must be freely expressed. Unless human beings can freely choose *not to* love, they cannot freely choose *to* love. The possibility of the one necessitates the possibility of the other.[19]

God wanted Adam, Eve, and all humanity to show love by freely choosing obedience. That is why God gave human beings a free will. One Christian thinker notes that "forced love is rape; and God is not a divine rapist. He will not do anything to coerce their decision."[20] Yet a free choice, as noted above, always leaves the possibility of a wrong choice. In other words, "Evil is inherent in the risky gift of free will."[21]

It is wise to consider the fact that there are certain things God simply cannot do.[22] For example, God cannot make square circles. Nor can He make round squares. It is impossible for God to lie, since such an act would violate His holy nature. It is impossible for God to eliminate all evil without eliminating free choice. It is logically impossible to *make* someone *freely* do something. Because free choice is necessary to the existence of a moral universe—a universe that includes the free expression of love—God cannot eliminate evil without also eliminating this good moral universe.[23]

The only way God could guarantee that His free creatures would never choose wrongly would be to tamper with their freedom in some way. God could so involve Himself in the world that every time someone was about to commit a crime, He supernaturally distracts that person away from the crime just in the nick of time so that no evil results. If this were the case, however, God would be in the business of full-time distraction, setting forth virtually billions of distractions per hour all over the world to prevent evil from happening.

Such a scenario does not allow for true freedom on our part. Further, God's distraction of humans about to commit evil does not take care of the evil in the human heart that was about to give birth to the evil act. In reality, then, the distraction has not prevented evil, it has only stopped the outward manifestation of evil that was already inwardly present in the human heart.

It comes down to this: either God gives free will to humans or He does not. If He gives them freedom, then they must maintain the capacity to actually *use* that freedom, rightly or wrongly. Judy Salisbury is right when she says,

> He cannot give human beings free choice sometimes and not other times. He cannot create beings as free moral agents, then snap His fingers and make them robots whenever they stray from His will. God cannot create beings with free choice and then force them to make right choices. If that were the case, they would not be free moral agents who have the responsibility and capacity to choose to bless or curse Him.[24]

At this juncture, the atheist may object that if evil is due to human free will, then God Himself is ultimately responsible for evil since He is the one who gave humans a free will. However, simply because God gave us the gift of free will does not mean He is responsible for how we *use* that free will.

From a scriptural perspective, it seems clear that God's plan—from the very beginning—allowed for the possibility of evil when He bestowed upon humans the freedom of choice. The actual origin of evil, however, came as a result of a man who directed his will away from God and toward his own selfish desires.[25] "Whereas God created the *fact* of freedom, humans perform the *acts* of freedom. God made evil *possible*; creatures make it *actual*."[26] Ever since Adam and Eve made evil actual on that tragic day in the Garden of Eden, a sin nature has been passed on to every man and woman (Romans 5:12; 1 Corinthians 15:22), and it is out of the sin nature that we today continue to use our free wills to make evil actual (Mark 7:20-23). Yet again, God is not responsible for the evil humans commit.

Theologians Gordon R. Lewis and Bruce A. Demarest give us an illustration in the person of Henry Ford: "Henry Ford is the final cause of all Ford cars, for there would not be any if he had not invented them to provide transportation. But Henry Ford, who could well have envisioned misuses of his automobiles, apparently felt it wiser, in a kind of benefit-evil analysis, to invent them than not."[27] However, when a person who has had one too many drinks gets in a Ford car and ends up in a head-on collision that kills innocent people, Henry Ford does not thereby become guilty of a crime. By analogy, we cannot blame the evil in the world on God simply because God gave humans a free will, for it was the creatures' wrong use of free will that has caused such evil. Lewis and Demarest conclude:

> Although God has not told us specifically why he chose to create, we suggest that in infinite wisdom, taking into account all the data of omniscient foreknowledge in a kind of foreseen benefits-evils analysis, he concluded that it was better to create than not to create. Analogously, although some married couples may hesitate to bring children into a fallen world with all the known risks or evils, most do have children. Apparently they conclude that the evils are far outweighed by the inestimable value of enduring loving relationships with children (and possibly grandchildren) throughout their lives.[28]

Objection: Natural disasters cannot be blamed on human free will and sin. Since horrible natural disasters occur regularly in our world, it is impossible that an all-good, all-powerful God exists. Atheist Walter Sinnott-Armstrong wrote, "Even if the value of free will did explain why God allows evil that is caused by humans, it still would not explain why God allows natural evil. Natural evil is evil that arises independently of human actions. It includes most of the pain, anguish, and loss of life that is caused by lightning and earthquakes and diseases and so on."[29]

Answering the Objection: Contrary to the claims of atheists, even natural evils such as earthquakes, tornados, and floods have their origin in the wrong use of human free choice. We must not forget that we are living in a fallen world, and because of that, we are subject to disasters in the world of nature that would not have occurred had man not rebelled against God in the beginning.

Scripture indicates that when Adam fell, one of the consequences was that the earth was cursed (Genesis 3:17). Romans 8:20 tells us that the entire creation was subjected to futility and the bondage of corruption. Conditions began to deteriorate on planet earth. Human paradise was no longer a paradise. The environment of this world changed dramatically.

As time went on, the world only got worse. Human sin continued to spread to the point that it eventually became necessary for God to destroy humankind by the flood of Noah's day (Genesis 6–8). Today we know that even local floods can cause tremendous damage. In recent history it has been found that floodwaters can carry granite stones weighing 350 tons more than 100 yards. Boulders weighing 210 tons have been moved 15 to 20 feet. That being the case, we can imagine the damage that would be done to the earth by a universal flood that covered even the highest mountains (Genesis 7:19).

For the first time in human history, over 70 percent of the earth's surface was now covered by water. In addition, due to the catastrophic effects of the flood, no doubt including some shifting of the earth's plates, there were now higher mountains and lower valleys. These changes led to the emergence of new and destructive weather patterns on earth. Clearly, then, one result of the wrong use of free will by the people of Noah's day is that natural disasters now occur with more frequency.

One must also keep in mind that some natural disasters occur due to the laws of nature that God has put in place in our universe. For example, gravity is good because it keeps our feet planted on earth, but this same gravity can cause an avalanche of boulders to come crashing down on us. Fire is good because it enables us to cook our food, but if we get too close to the fire, we will get burned. Water is good because it quenches our thirst, but if we fall into deep water, we may end up drowning.

Objection: The Christian "free will" explanation of the problem of evil fails because it would not be possible for a finite being to make choices contrary to what an omnipotent being wants. Atheist George Smith argues that "to speak of frustrating or acting contrary to the wishes of an omnipotent being makes no sense whatsoever. There can be no barriers to divine omnipotence, no obstacles to thwart his desires, so we must assume that the present state of the world is precisely as God desires it to be."[30] Since it is unthinkable that God would will the horrible suffering that now exists in our world, He must not exist.

Answering the Objection: Scripture portrays God as being absolutely sovereign (Psalm 135:6; Ephesians 1:11). Scripture also portrays human beings as having a free will (Genesis 3:1-7). It is inscrutable to humanity's finite understanding how both divine sovereignty and human free will can both be true, but both doctrines are taught in Scripture.

The atheistic objection does not give proper appreciation to human free will. When Adam sinned in the Garden of Eden, God said to him, "What is this you have done?" (Genesis 3:13). Adam could not respond, "You sovereignly made me do this, and I had no choice." Likewise, Jesus in the New Testament stated to some Jews, "O Jerusalem, Jerusalem, you who kill the prophets and stone those sent to you, how often I have longed to gather your children together, as a hen gathers her chicks under her wings, *but you were not willing*" (Matthew 23:37, emphasis added). Here is an example of God (Jesus) willing something, but *humans willed something entirely different.*

Hence, the atheistic position that "acting contrary to the wishes of an omnipotent being makes no sense whatsoever" displays great ignorance. Man can and does act contrary to God. This is why Scripture so often exhorts Christians to be obedient to the Word of God. People do have the freedom to make choices.

Objection: If there were an all-powerful and all-good God, there would not be evil unless there was an adequate compensating good. In other words, there would be no gratuitous evil.[31]

Answering the Objection: The Christian agrees that there is much evil in our world, but the Christian disagrees that *gratuitous* suffering exists. It is certainly true that from our limited, finite perspective we are unaware of why certain bad things have happened to us. More often than not, we simply cannot assess why God is allowing something to happen to us. This does not mean, however, that the evil is gratuitous. A Christian philosopher explains it this way:

In chaos theory, it's been shown that even the flutter

of a butterfly's wings could set in motion forces that would result in a hurricane over the Atlantic, and yet no one observing that butterfly would be able to predict that outcome. Similarly, when we see, say, the murder of an innocent man, we have no idea of what ripple effect that might send through history, how God's morally sufficient reason for permitting that might not emerge until later. We're simply not in a good position to assess that kind of probability.[32]

When speaking publicly on this issue, I sometimes compare each of our lives to a single thread in the tapestry of life. As single threads, we cannot see the entire tapestry, and are therefore ignorant of the overall scheme of things. God, however, is the master-craftsman, weaving each thread just as He sees fit, bringing about an eventual masterpiece. In this scenario, "the transcendent and sovereign God sees the end of history from its beginning and providentially orders history so that His purposes are ultimately achieved through human free decisions."[33] We, as finite human beings, however, are completely ignorant of the vast complexities involved in God working among free agents to sovereignly bring history to its ordained end. One day, when we are in heaven, I believe we will see that tapestry. Then, and only then, will we say, "Ahhh, I get it now!"

As God weaves the circumstances in our lives that will eventually yield a masterpiece in heaven, He sometimes purposefully allows us to experience short-range pains because of the long-range benefits that can eventually come about. Biblically, there are a number of "goods" that God may bring about through His allowance of suffering:

Faith Muscles Strengthened. Great Christian thinkers have often compared faith to a muscle. A muscle has to be repeatedly stretched to its limit of endurance in order to build more strength. Without increased stress in training, the muscle simply will not grow.

In the same way, faith must be repeatedly tested to the limit of its endurance in order to expand and develop. I believe God allows His children to go through trying experiences in order to develop their faith muscles (1 Peter 1:7). This learning process takes place in the school of real life—with all of its difficult trials and tribulations.

Consider Israel's sojourn in the book of Exodus as an example. Following Israel's deliverance from Egypt, God first led the people to Marah, a place where they would be forced to trust God to transform the water and make it drinkable. It is significant that God led the people to Marah *before* leading them to Elim, a gorgeous oasis with plenty of good water (Exodus 15:22-27). God could have bypassed Marah altogether and brought the Israelites directly to Elim if He had wanted to. But, as is characteristic of God, He purposefully led them through the route that would yield maximum conditioning of their faith muscles, where they would be forced to trust in His promises of sustenance. God does this to us as well. He often governs our circumstances so as to yield maximum conditioning of our faith muscles (1 Peter 1:7). God takes us through the "school of hard knocks" to teach us that He is reliable.

We see this illustrated in the life of Joseph, who was sold into slavery by his own brothers (see Genesis 38–39). While Joseph's situation seemed hopeless, God was still in control. God ended up using a long sequence of negative circumstances over the course of several years to take Joseph from slavery to a position of great authority in Egypt (Genesis 41). What we have to realize is that during the years of suffering, Joseph had no idea what God's intentions were. He did not know that God was using his dire circumstances to bring him to a position of prominence. That is why it is so important to trust God, no matter what the circumstances. In Joseph's case, God truly did bring about a greater good through the pain he suffered. Joseph summarized this truth when he later told his brothers, "You meant evil against me, but God meant it for good" (Genesis 50:20). Our faith in God must ever rest upon the belief that God can bring a greater good out of any evil that befalls us.

We see this in the life of the apostle Paul, who trusted God as few others have. Paul was thrown into prison repeatedly during his work of ministry (see, for example, Acts 16:23-37; Ephesians 3:1; Philippians 1:7; Colossians 4:10; Philemon 9). While this must have been painful to Paul, we need to keep in mind that Paul wrote Ephesians, Philippians, Colossians, and Philemon (four important New Testament books) while he was in prison. Truly, God did bring about a greater good through Paul's suffering. No wonder Paul wrote, "We know that God causes all things to work together for good to those who love God" (Romans 8:28 NASB).

And what about the death of Jesus on the cross of Calvary? An eyewitness observing the occurrence of this event would likely see no good in the horrible scene that transpired. Yet all the while, God was unfolding His wonderful plan of redemption, in which the greater good of human salvation would be brought about by this death on the cross (2 Corinthians 5:21; 1 Peter 2:24; 1 John 2:2). What appeared to be the worst tragedy of all turned out to be the greatest blessing of all.

Saving Faith. God often uses suffering to bring people to saving faith in God. The hard reality is that people often do not turn to God until they feel their need for Him. Interestingly, studies have proven that it is the nations that endure intense suffering that experience the most rapid growth in evangelical Christianity.[34] One must wonder whether there would be *any* growth in Christianity if suffering simply did not exist. If a world of suffering is necessary in order to bring people to eternal life in Jesus Christ, then such suffering is worth it, for the glories of the afterlife are far beyond what any human can fathom.

Christian scholar Os Guinness said this about Auschwitz and saving faith:

> It is often said that after Auschwitz there cannot be a God—evil is so overwhelming that it is the "rock of atheism." But as Viktor Frankl pointed out, those who say that [about evil] were not in Auschwitz themselves. Far more people deepened or discovered faith in Auschwitz than lost it. He then gave a beautiful picture of faith in the face of evil. A small and inadequate faith, he said, is like a small fire; it can be blown out by a small breeze. True faith, by contrast, is like a strong fire. When it is hit by a strong wind, it is fanned into an inextinguishable blaze.[35]

Character Development. We humans often tend to interpret events in our lives from an earthly perspective. Evil often feels devastating to us because of our assumption that God's purpose for us is happiness. *If our well-being is God's purpose,* we ask, *then why is this horrible thing happening to me?*

We must come to understand that God is operating in our lives from the perspective of eternity. He cares more about *holiness* than He does about *happiness.*[36] Christian author Paul Powell suggests that "God's goal is not primarily to make us comfortable but to conform us to the image of His Son, Jesus Christ. And in the pursuit of that goal He can and does use all of life's experiences."[37]

God may therefore allow us to go through a season of hurt that has no apparent earthly benefit, but has immense benefit in terms of our eternal future with God. God is involved in our character development (James 1:2-4; 1 Peter 1:6-7). Miles Stanford wrote that "God does not hurry in His development of our Christian life. He is working from and for eternity."[38] God is infinitely wise in allowing events to come into our lives that will mold us in ways that will optimize our future life in heaven. He has an agenda, and He is working in our lives to fulfill that agenda.

Objection: Because Christianity has been used throughout church history as an excuse for brutal, heartless, and senseless atrocities, Christianity cannot be true. A prime example of Christian cruelty is the Crusades, which began in A.D. 1163 when Pope Alexander III instructed church bishops to uncover evidence of heresy and then take action against the heretics. In what followed, there was no "due process" for the accused, and "Christian" armies beheaded enemies, tortured them, cast them alive into fire, and worse. Charles Templeton charges that the church during the Middle Ages was "a terrorist organization."[39] "Why, then, would one want to believe in the God of Christians?" atheists ask.

Answering the Objection: It is sad but true that "Christians" have been guilty of committing some atrocities in church history. A proper response must involve not a *denial* but *confession* that wrongs have been committed on certain occasions. Certainly what occurred during the Crusades, in particular, went against the "love your enemy" philosophy of He whom those armies claimed to serve—Jesus Christ. These campaigns of terror were travesties of unparalleled proportions. Christians should make it clear they do not endorse the atrocities that took place supposedly in the name of Jesus Christ.

When atheists or skeptics point to the darker periods of church history, we need to point out that these occurrences of violence were isolated, and were not a pattern. These incidents were the exception and not the rule in terms of the philosophy of Christians throughout most of church history. If one examines the historical record, one will find that much of church history has been characterized by God-honoring love, benevolence, compassion, and generosity. One would do well to study the history of missionaries and the enormously positive influence they have had on various peoples around the world. One would also do well to study the many ways the church has taken care of the poor and needy throughout church history.

Further, in the interest of fairness, not all who call themselves "Christians" are indeed Christians (Matthew 7:22-23). Some people are authentic Christians, and others are cultural Christians. In like manner, when we refer to "the church," there is a difference between the true church (made up of only true believers in Jesus Christ) and institutional churches (and even state churches). Hence, when people make a general statement and say "the church is guilty of this or that," they usually lump together authentic Christians with cultural Christians, and the true church with the institutional church. This is neither fair nor accurate.

Yet despite this distinction, one must concede that some authentic Christians are guilty of having participated in atrocities. This illustrates one of the primary planks of Christianity—that is, *all human beings are deeply engulfed in sin* (Romans 3:23). When a person becomes a Christian, he retains the sin nature. He is forgiven by virtue of Christ's sacrifice on the cross, but he can still violate God's will and commit sinful acts.

C.S. Lewis once said that Christians are at the same time the best argument *for* and the best argument *against* Christianity. In other words, some Christians live in a way that makes it hard to believe that Christianity is true. Yet other Christians live such virtuous lives that they give powerful evidence for the truth of Christianity.

Of course, it was never God's intention that Christians alone be the "measuring stick" as to whether or not Christianity is true. One's evaluation of Christianity should focus on the life and teachings of Jesus Christ alone. He is the *only* one who is without sin and duplicity.

THE CHARACTER ASSASSINATION OF GOD

One strategy atheists and skeptics sometimes use to argue against Christians is to make God look bad, and then proceed to argue that He thus cannot possibly exist. For example, some argue that the God of the Old Testament is cruel and vindictive, and either participated in or condoned many atrocities. He is therefore unworthy of belief. Others point out what they perceive to be a contradiction between a loving God and the reality of hell, and then proceed to argue against both God and hell. In this concluding chapter, I will answer these two pivotal objections.

Objection: The God of the Old Testament is cruel and vindictive, and either participated in or condoned many atrocities. He is therefore unworthy of belief. Thomas Jefferson described God as "cruel, vindictive, capricious and unjust."[1] George Smith cites a number of Old Testament passages which he thinks prove that the God of the Old Testament is evil. For example, in Isaiah 45:7 God says, "I form the light and create darkness, I bring prosperity and create disaster; I, the Lord, do all these things." Smith alleges that God sanctioned human sacrifices, such as that of Jephthah's daughter (Judges 11:30-39). God is said to have sanctioned slavery (Exodus 21.2-6; Leviticus 25:44-46), commanded Abraham to sacrifice his son (Genesis 22:2), hardened Pharaoh's heart (Exodus 4:21), and caused prophets to lie (2 Chronicles 18:20-21). God works everything toward His own ends, "even the wicked for a day of disaster" (Proverbs 16:4). The Old Testament also credits the Israelites, acting under orders from God Himself, with killing men, women, and children through conquest (Joshua 6:21).[2]

Answering the Objection: Foundationally, it is important to correct the misconception that the God of the Old Testament is different from the God of the New Testament. The Old and New Testaments point to the same God—a God of both love *and* judgment. On the one hand, God did judge people in Old Testament times when the circumstances called for it. This was the case when He sent ten horrible plagues against the Egyptians (Exodus 7–11). However, He is also seen displaying love and grace throughout the Old Testament. Following Adam and Eve's sin, for example, God's promise of a coming redeemer was an act of love and grace (Genesis 3:15). God's provision of an ark for Noah and his family was an act of love and grace (Genesis 6:9-22). God's provision of the covenants was an act of love and grace (Genesis 12:1-3; 2 Samuel 7:12-16). God's sending of the prophets to give special revelation to Israel was an act of love and grace. Interestingly, Norman Geisler did a word study on the word "mercy" and found that 72 percent of the occurrences of the word are found in the Old Testament.[3]

In the New Testament, the love of God was continually manifested to people through the person of Jesus Christ. In fact, we might even say that Jesus is "love incarnate." It is also true, however, that some of the most scathing denouncements from God—especially in regard to the Jewish leaders—came from the mouth of Jesus (see Matthew 23:27-28,33). Further, the New Testament speaks a great deal about eternal punishment. We can conclude, then, that the God of the Old and New Testaments is a God of love *and* judgment. God Himself affirmed, "I the Lord do not change" (Malachi 3:6).

Does God create disaster (Isaiah 45:7)? In this verse, God said, "I form the light and create darkness, I bring prosperity and create disaster. I, the LORD, do all these things." In this verse, the Hebrew word for "disaster" does not mean "moral evil." In fact, Hebrew linguists tell us that the word need not have any moral connotations at all.[4] This word would be perfectly fitting for the plagues that God inflicted on the Egyptians through Moses. These plagues involved not moral evil but rather calamitous events engineered to bring the Egyptians to repentance. God as the Judge of the earth can rightly inflict such plagues on sinful human beings without having His character impugned with accusations of evil. Certainly such plagues may *seem* evil to those experiencing them, but the reality is that these people were experiencing due justice. "The Bible is clear that God is morally perfect (cf. Deut. 32:4; Matt. 5:48), and it is impossible for Him to sin (Heb. 6:18). At the same time, His absolute justice demands that He punish sin."[5] In the case of the Egyptians, God was merely bringing just judgment on unrepentant sinners. God's good end—the deliverance of the Israelites from Egyptian bondage—was the result of this judgment.

Did God command Jephthah to sacrifice his daughter (Judges 11:30-39)? Christian scholars have dealt with this difficult passage in several different ways. One view is that Jephthah actually did offer his daughter as a burnt sacrifice to the Lord. If this is the case, this does not in any way mean that God endorsed what Jephthah did. He was certainly not under orders from God to do this. God had earlier revealed that human sacrifice was absolutely forbidden (Leviticus 18:21; 20:2-5; Deuteronomy 12:31; 18:10).

We must keep in mind that simply because a human action is recorded in the Bible does not mean that God agrees with it. God certainly does not agree with the words or actions of Satan, but the Bible nevertheless accurately reports on his words and actions. In the case of Jephthah, the author of the book of Judges may have simply provided an objective account of the event without passing judgment.

One must also remember that the book of Judges chronicles for us a period in human history when everyone was doing what was right in his or her own eyes. Judges 21:25 says, "In those days Israel had no king; everyone did as he saw fit." It is very possible that Jephthah was simply doing what was right in his own eyes, thereby victimizing his daughter. If Jephthah actually sacrificed her, we can only conclude that he was acting in great folly and was going against the will of God, despite his good motives and apparent desire to please the Lord.

Another way to interpret this passage is that Jephthah offered up his daughter in the sense of consecrating her for service at the tabernacle for the rest of her life and devoting her to celibacy. This would involve offering up his daughter in a spiritual way instead of physically giving her up as a burnt offering. As the apostle Paul said in Romans 12:1, people can be offered to God as "a living sacrifice."

If Jephthah's daughter was indeed offered as a living sacrifice, this would mean she was consecrated to a life of perpetual virginity, which, from a Jewish perspective, was a tremendous sacrifice. She would not be able to bring up children to continue her father's lineage.

This may explain why his daughter responded by saying, "'Grant me this one request,' she said. 'Give me two months to roam the hills and weep with my friends, because I will never marry'" (Judges 11:37). Note that she did not weep because of an impending death. She wept because she would never marry and hence would remain a virgin.

Did God sanction slavery (Exodus 21:2-6)? Earlier in this book we noted that God has never condoned slavery. From the very beginning, God declared that all humans are created in His image (Genesis 1:27). The apostle Paul also declared that "we are the offspring of God" (Acts 17:29 NKJV), and that God "has made from one blood every nation of men to dwell on all the face of the earth" (verse 26 NKJV). Moreover, despite the fact that slavery was countenanced in the Semitic cultures of the day, the law in the Bible demanded that slaves eventually be set free (Exodus 21:2; Leviticus 25:40). Likewise, servants had to be treated with respect (Exodus 21:20,26). Israel, itself in slavery in Egypt for a prolonged time, was constantly reminded by God of this (Deuteronomy 5:15), and their emancipation became the model for the liberation of all slaves (Leviticus 25:40).

Further, in the New Testament, Paul declared that in Christianity "there is neither Jew nor Greek, there is neither slave nor free, there is neither male nor female; for you are all one in Christ Jesus" (Galatians 3:28). All social classes are broken down in Christ; we are all equal before God. Though the apostle Paul urges, "Slaves, be obedient to those who are your masters" (Ephesians 6:5 NASB;

see also Colossians 3:22), he is not thereby approving of the institution of slavery, but simply alluding to the *de facto* situation in
his day. He is simply instructing servants to be good workers, just
as believers should be today, but he was not thereby commending
slavery.

Did God intend for Abraham to kill his own son (Genesis 22:2)?
The context of Genesis 22 makes it clear that God never intended
for this command to be fulfilled. God restrained Abraham's hand
just in the nick of time: "'Do not lay a hand on the boy,' he said. 'Do
not do anything to him. Now I know that you fear God, because
you have not withheld from me your son, your only son'" (Genesis
22:12). Scholars agree that God was only testing Abraham's faith.
The test served to show that Abraham loved God more than he
loved his own son.

Did God harden Pharaoh's heart (Exodus 4:21)? In this verse
we are informed that God hardened the heart of the Pharaoh of
Egypt. More broadly, ten times in the text of Scripture it is said
that the Pharaoh hardened *his own* heart (Exodus 7:13,14,22;
8:15,19,32; 9:7,34,35; 13:15), and ten times that God hardened
Pharaoh's heart (4:21; 7:3; 9:12; 10:1,20,27; 11:10; 14:4,8,17).
The Pharaoh hardened *his own* heart seven times before God first
hardened it, though the *prediction* that God would do it preceded
all.

It would seem, from the whole of Scripture, that God
hardens on the same grounds as showing mercy. If men will
accept mercy, He will give it to them. If they will not, thus
hardening themselves, He is only just and righteous in judging
them. *Mercy* is the effect of a right attitude; *hardening* is the
effect of stubbornness or a wrong attitude toward God. It is
like clay and wax in the heat of the sun. The same sunshine
hardens one and softens the other. The responsibility is with

the materials, not with the sun. Scholars have suggested that the danger of resisting God is that He will eventually give us over to our own choices (see Romans 1:24-28).

Did God cause prophets to lie (2 Chronicles 18:20-21)? Scripture forbids lying (Exodus 20:16). Lying is viewed as a sin (Psalm 59:12) and is considered an abomination to God (Proverbs 12:22). Further, Numbers 23:19 explicitly tells us that "God is not a man, that he should lie."

It is true that in 2 Chronicles 18:20-21 God *permits* the activity of a "lying spirit." We must make a distinction, however, between what God *causes* and what He *allows*. For example, God allowed Adam's sin in the Garden of Eden, but He did not cause it. God allowed Lucifer's rebellion against Him, but He did not cause it. God allowed Ananias and Sapphira to lie to Peter, but He did not cause them to do so. Likewise, God *permitted* the activity of a lying spirit, but He did not *cause* it. Therefore, God's character cannot be impugned.

Did God create the wicked so He could bring disaster upon them (Proverbs 16:4)? In Proverbs 16:4, we read, "The LORD works out everything for his own ends—even the wicked for a day of disaster." This verse does not mean that God specifically created certain wicked people for the sole purpose of destroying them or sending them to hell. Scripture assures us that God is not willing that *any* should perish (2 Peter 3:9), and that God loves the whole world of humanity (John 3:16). God "wants all men to be saved and to come to the knowledge of the truth" (1 Timothy 2:4). The price of redemption that Christ paid at the cross is made available to *all* people (1 John 2:2). These verses provide an important backdrop to the proper interpretation of Proverbs 16:4, for if we learn anything from such verses, it is that God cares for and loves all people.

I believe *The Expositor's Bible Commentary* is correct in noting that the primary thrust of the passage is that, in the end, there will be commensurate justice corresponding to human actions:

> God in his sovereignty ensures that everything in life receives its appropriate retribution....The point is that God ensures that everyone's actions and their consequences correspond—certainly the wicked for the day of calamity. In God's order there is just retribution for every act, for every act includes its answer or consequence.[6]

Why did God order the extermination of whole peoples (Joshua 6:21)? It is true that God commanded His people, the Israelites, to exterminate "whole peoples"—the Canaanites being a primary example. God's command was issued not because God is cruel and vindictive, but because the Canaanites were so horrible, so evil, so oppressive, and so cancerous to society that—like a human cancer—the only option was complete removal. Old Testament scholar Walter Kaiser comments on why the Canaanites were dealt with so severely: "They were cut off to prevent Israel and the rest of the world from being corrupted (Deut. 20:16-18). When a people starts to burn their children in honor of their gods (Lev. 18:21), practice sodomy, bestiality [having sex with animals], and all sorts of loathsome vices (Lev. 18:23,24; 20:3), the land itself begins to 'vomit' them out as the body heaves under the load of internal poisons (Lev. 18:25,27-30)."[7] In other words, human society itself would have been poisoned without the utter removal of the cancerous Canaanites. God would have been showing utter disregard for the righteous if He had not acted to stop this gangrenous nation from taking over all society.

We must keep in mind that the Canaanites had had plenty of

time to repent. The biblical pattern is that when nations repent, God withholds judgment. In Jeremiah 18:7-8, we read God's own words regarding this: "If at any time I announce that a nation or kingdom is to be uprooted, torn down and destroyed, and if that nation I warned repents of its evil, then I will relent and not inflict on it the disaster I had planned." This principle is clearly illustrated for us in the case of Nineveh. God had prophesied judgment, but Nineveh repented and God withheld that judgment (see Jonah 3). It is noteworthy that God is often seen showing mercy where repentance is evident (Exodus 32:14; 2 Samuel 24:6; Amos 7:3,7).

Kaiser notes that "Canaan had, as it were, a final forty-year countdown as they heard of the events in Egypt, at the crossing of the Red Sea, and what happened to the kings who opposed Israel along the way." Hence, "God waited for the 'cup of iniquity' to fill up—and fill up it did without any signs of change in spite of the marvelous signs given so that the nations, along with Pharaoh and the Egyptians, 'might know that He was the Lord.'"[8] The Canaanites were not acting blindly. They had heard of the God of the Israelites, and knew what was expected of them, but they defied Him and continued in their sinful ways. Hence, they were ripe for judgment.

Further, let us not forget that God is absolutely sovereign over the affairs of life and death. God is the One who creates life, and He maintains the right to take life when circumstances call for it. You and I do not have the right to take another's life because we did not create that life. God, however, is the Creator, and as the Creator, He sovereignly rules over the creation. When people rebel against Him, God as the divine Judge retains the right to end their lives.

The foundation of all this is the absolute holiness of God.

Because He is absolutely holy, He can do none other than to punish sin and rebellion against Him. Too often today, people like to talk only about the love of God. While God is a God of love (Psalm 33:5; 86:5; Jeremiah 31:3; 1 John 4:8), He is also a holy God (Psalm 99:9; Isaiah 6:3) who shows wrath against sin (Revelation 20:11-15). We must maintain a balanced, biblical view of God's nature.

Objection: The idea of a loving God cannot possibly be reconciled with the existence of hell, in which unbelievers are said to suffer for all eternity. One atheist charged that "Jesus repeatedly threatened disbelievers with eternal torment, and we must wonder how the doctrine of hell can be reconciled with the notion of an all-merciful God."[9] The doctrine of hell "undoubtedly ranks as the most vicious and reprehensible doctrine of classical Christianity."[10]

Some atheists compare God to Adolf Hitler (1889–1945), only Hitler is considered the better of the two because he burned Jews for only five or ten minutes, whereas God burns evil people for all eternity.[11] Atheists also say it is absurd for God to allow serial killer David Berkowitz into heaven just because he prayed a prayer to become a Christian, while Gandhi, who prayed no such prayer, will be barred from heaven and be sent to hell. How is that fair?[12]

Answering the Objection: God does not want to send anyone to hell. God is, by nature, love (1 John 4:8), and He loves every human being (John 3:16). He is "not wanting anyone to perish, but everyone to come to repentance" (2 Peter 3:9). All throughout Scripture, God is portrayed as pleading with people to turn from their sins and turn to Him for salvation.

The fact that God wants people to be saved is evidenced by the fact He sent Jesus to pay the penalty for our sins by dying on the cross (John 3:16-17). Sadly, however, not all people are willing to admit that they sin and are in need of forgiveness. They do not accept Jesus' death on their behalf. God therefore allows them to experience the results of their choice (see Luke 16:19-31).

C.S. Lewis once said that in the end, there are two groups of people. One group of people says to God, "Thy will be done." These are those who have placed their faith in Jesus Christ and will live forever with God in heaven. The second group of people are those to whom God says, sadly, "Thy will be done!" These are those who have rejected Jesus Christ and will spend eternity apart from Him. God does not force anyone to be saved against his or her will.

In arguing against hell, atheists often appeal to unfair comparisons that generate more heat than light. The atheists' comparison of Hitler and God is an example. Yet the comparison is faulty because the victims of Hitler's death camps were innocent, but those who will suffer in hell *are not* innocent. "They are there because they have deliberately chosen to reject God and because they have failed to live up to the demands of his moral law. Therefore, their condemnation is just."[13] Those in Hitler's death camps *did not* deserve to be there. Those who will be in hell *do* deserve to be there. Therefore, for atheists to compare Hitler and God is wrong.

The atheists' complaint about David Berkowitz going to heaven and Gandhi going to hell is also misguided. We may think of Berkowitz as especially evil and Gandhi as especially good, but we are using the wrong measuring stick—comparing one human being against another human being. The proper measuring stick is the absolutely holy God of the universe. By that comparison, *all* human beings are fallen in sin and deserving of eternal punishment in hell. Ravi Zacharias gives us an interesting observation regarding our tendency to compare ourselves to others:

> David Berkowitz can say, "Wait a minute; I'm not Hitler! I didn't kill millions, I just killed a few." Or

"I wasn't Jeffrey Dahmer; I didn't eat my victims."
We tend to do the kind of comparisons by which we
always emerge better than someone else, and so we
think we're good. But by the perfect moral standard
of God, we all fail.[14]

Romans 3:23 flatly asserts, "All have sinned and fall short of
the glory of God." "The wages of sin is death" (Romans 6:23).
Hence, *all* are deserving of death—no exceptions.

For those, like David Berkowitz, who commit horrendous
crimes before becoming Christians, they may be saved, but now
they face the difficult task of living with their conscience for the
rest of their lives. A person can truly suffer "hell on earth" because
of his or her past actions.

One truth that has always helped me with this difficult dilemma
is that our God of perfect justice, based on peoples' actions, assigns
levels of reward for those who end up in heaven as well as *levels of
punishment* for those who end up in hell. In support of the idea that
there will be degrees of punishment in hell, Luke 12:47-48 tells us,
"That servant who knows his master's will and does not get ready
or does not do what his master wants will be beaten with *many*
blows. But the one who does not know and does things deserving
punishment will be beaten with *few* blows. From everyone who
has been given much, *much will be demanded;* and from the one
who has been entrusted with much, *much more will be asked*"
(emphasis added). (Other verses that indicate levels of punishment in hell include Matthew 10:15; 16:27; Revelation 20:12-13;
22:12.) Likewise, the idea that there will be levels of reward in
heaven is clear from Psalm 62:12, Jeremiah 17:10, Matthew 16:27,
1 Corinthians 4:5, Ephesians 6:7–8, and other verses. *There will be
perfect justice in the end.*

CONCLUSION

We have seen in this chapter that atheists have engaged in a character assassination of God, arguing that He is cruel and vindictive, condones human sacrifice and slavery, creates disaster, hardens hearts, causes prophets to lie, orders the extermination of certain people, and sends certain people to hell. Such a God, they say, is unworthy of belief.

As I've demonstrated, however, the God described by atheists is nothing but a false and demeaning caricature of the God of the Bible. I urge the reader to keep in mind something that Solomon, the wisest man who ever lived, once said: "The first to present his case seems right, till another comes forward and questions him" (Proverbs 18:17). The atheist caricature of God may seem convincing to a person unschooled in biblical truths, but when the biblical data about God is consulted in its proper context, the *authentic* God comes into clear focus and *He truly* is worthy of belief. He is eternal (1 Timothy 1:17), all-powerful (Psalm 147:5), all-knowing (Psalm 139:11-12), everywhere-present (Psalm 139:7-8), holy (Leviticus 11:44), just (Genesis 18:25), righteous (Deuteronomy 32:4), good (Psalm 25:8), kind (Isaiah 54:8), merciful (2 Corinthians 1:3), loving (1 John 4:8), and patient (2 Peter 3:9), and He offers *everyone* the free and wonderful gift of salvation. Atheists would do well to follow the advice of the psalmist, who urged, "Taste and see that the Lord is good" (Psalm 34:8).

POSTSCRIPT

A CALL TO COURTESY

As I close, I think it is appropriate to reflect for a brief moment on Peter's advice in 1 Peter 3:15: "Always be prepared to give an answer to everyone who asks you to give the reason for the hope that you have. *But do this with gentleness and respect*" (emphasis added). These two qualities—"gentleness" and "respect"—should govern the way we interact with atheists, agnostics, and skeptics. I have always found that a strong biblical answer combined with courteous communication is a highly effective *modus operandi*.

It is highly revealing to observe how different translators render the latter portion of 1 Peter 3:15. The New American Standard Version says we are to be prepared to give answers with "gentleness and reverence." The New English Bible says we are to do so "with modesty and respect." The Amplified Bible says we are to do so "courteously and respectfully." The New Testament in Modern Speech says we are to "argue gently and respectfully."

The word *gentleness* means "considerate or kindly in disposition," and involves mannerisms that are "not harsh or severe." The word *respect* refers to "the state of being regarded with honor or esteem."[1] Such words indicate that it's not just *what* we say that is important, it is also *how we say it* that is important.

Don't get me wrong. We must do all we can to give firmly convincing evidences regarding why we believe in God and why we believe Christianity is true. We must not back up one inch in our defense of the truth. At the same time, however, our defense *must* be in the context of courtesy and respect.

Granted, showing courtesy and respect may be precisely the opposite of how an atheist may treat a Christian, but Christians are called by God to overlook discourteous treatment and handle themselves virtuously in all encounters (see Matthew 5:40-44). Believe me when I tell you that how you handle yourself will speak volumes about the faith you profess. Further, your gentleness will go a long way toward preventing communication barriers that inevitably emerge when *discussions* deteriorate into *arguments*.

Someone once said, "Gentle words fall lightly, but they have great weight." There is much wisdom in those words. Let us therefore resolve to set forth powerful arguments in our defense of the Christian God, but let us also resolve to keep those arguments gentle and respectful.

An Invitation to Believe

Receiving Jesus Christ as your Savior is the most important decision you could ever make in your life. Entering into a personal relationship with Him affects your eternal destiny. If you go into eternity without this relationship, you will spend eternity apart from Him.

If you will allow me, I would like to tell you how you can come into a personal relationship with Jesus.

First you need to recognize that...

GOD DESIRES A PERSONAL RELATIONSHIP WITH YOU

God created you (Genesis 1:27). And He did not just create you to exist all alone and apart from Him. He created you with a view to coming into a personal relationship with Him.

God had face-to-face encounters and fellowship with Adam

and Eve, the first couple (Genesis 3:8-19). Just as God fellowshiped with them, so He desires to fellowship with you (1 John 1:5-7). God loves you (John 3:16). Never forget that fact.

The problem is...

HUMANITY HAS A SIN PROBLEM THAT PREVENTS A RELATIONSHIP WITH GOD

When Adam and Eve chose to sin against God in the Garden of Eden, they catapulted the entire human race—to which they gave birth—into sin. Since that time, every human being has been born into the world with a sin nature.

The apostle Paul affirmed that "sin entered the world through one man, and death through sin" (Romans 5:12). We are told that "through the disobedience of the one man the many were made sinners" (Romans 5:19). Ultimately this means that "death came through a man...in Adam all die" (1 Corinthians 15:21-22).

Jesus often spoke of sin in metaphors that illustrate the havoc sin can wreak in one's life. He described sin as blindness (Matthew 23:16-26), sickness (Matthew 9:12), being enslaved in bondage (John 8:34), and living in darkness (John 8:12; 12:35-46). Moreover, Jesus taught that sin is a universal condition and that all people are guilty before God (Luke 7:37-48).

Jesus also taught that both inner thoughts and external acts render a person guilty (Matthew 5:28). He taught that from within the human heart come evil thoughts, sexual immorality, theft, murder, adultery, greed, malice, deceit, envy, slander, arrogance, and folly (Mark 7:21-23). Moreover, He affirmed that God is fully aware of every person's sins, both external acts and inner thoughts. Nothing escapes His notice (Matthew 22:18; Luke 6:8; John 4:17-19).

Of course, some people are more morally upright than others. However, we all fall short of God's infinite standards (Romans

3:23). In a contest to see who can throw a rock to the moon, I am sure a muscular athlete would be able to throw the rock much further than I could. But ultimately, all human beings would fall short in accomplishing this task. Similarly, all of us fall short of measuring up to God's perfect holy standards.

Though the sin problem is a serious one, God has graciously provided a solution:

JESUS DIED FOR OUR SINS AND MADE SALVATION POSSIBLE

God's absolute holiness demands that sin be punished. The good news of the gospel, however, is that Jesus has taken this punishment on Himself. God loves us so much that He sent Jesus to bear the penalty for our sins!

Jesus affirmed that it was for the very purpose of dying that He came into the world (John 12:27). Moreover, He perceived His death as being a sacrificial offering for the sins of humanity (Matthew 26:26-28). Jesus took His sacrificial mission with utmost seriousness, for He knew that without Him, humanity would certainly perish (Matthew 16:25; John 3:16) and spend eternity apart from God in a place of great suffering (Matthew 10:28; 11:23; 23:33; 25:41; Luke 16:22-28).

Jesus therefore described His mission this way: "The Son of Man did not come to be served, but to serve, and to give his life as a ransom for many" (Matthew 20:28). "The Son of Man came to seek and to save what was lost" (Luke 19:10). "God did not send his Son into the world to condemn the world, but to save the world through him" (John 3:17).

Please be aware that the benefits of Christ's death on the cross are not automatically applied to your life. To receive the gift of salvation, you must...

BELIEVE IN JESUS CHRIST THE SAVIOR

By His sacrificial death on the cross, Jesus took the sins of the entire world on Himself and made salvation available for everyone (1 John 2:2). But this salvation is not automatic. Only those who personally choose to believe in Christ are saved. This is the consistent testimony of the biblical Jesus. Listen to His words:

- "For God so loved the world that he gave his one and only Son, that whoever believes in him shall not perish but have eternal life" (John 3:16).

- "For my Father's will is that everyone who looks to the Son and believes in him shall have eternal life, and I will raise him up at the last day" (John 6:40).

- "I am the resurrection and the life. He who believes in me will live, even though he dies" (John 11:25).

Choosing *not* to believe in Jesus, by contrast, leads to eternal condemnation: "Whoever believes in him is not condemned, but whoever does not believe stands condemned already because he has not believed in the name of God's one and only Son" (John 3:18).

FREE AT LAST: FORGIVEN OF ALL SINS

When you believe in Christ the Savior, a wonderful thing happens. God forgives you of all your sins. *All of them!* He puts them completely out of His sight. Ponder for a few minutes the following verses, which speak of the forgiveness of those who have placed their belief in Christ:

- "In him we have redemption through his blood, the forgiveness of sins, in accordance with the riches of God's grace" (Ephesians 1:7).

- God said, "Their sins and lawless acts I will remember no more" (Hebrews 10:17-18).

- "Blessed is he whose transgressions are forgiven, whose sins are covered. Blessed is the man whose sin the LORD does not count against him and in whose spirit is no deceit" (Psalm 32:1-2).

- "For as high as the heavens are above the earth, so great is his love for those who fear him; as far as the east is from the west, so far has he removed our transgressions from us" (Psalm 103:11-12).

Such forgiveness is wonderful indeed, for none of us can possibly work our way into heaven, or be good enough to warrant God's good favor. Because of what Jesus has done for us, we can freely receive the gift of salvation. It is a gift provided solely through the grace of God (Ephesians 2:8-9). It becomes ours by placing our faith in Jesus.

DON'T PUT IT OFF

It is highly dangerous to put off turning to Christ for salvation, for you do not know the day of your death. What if it happens this evening? "Death is the destiny of every man; the living should take this to heart" (Ecclesiastes 7:2).

If God is speaking to your heart now, then now is your door of opportunity to believe. "Seek the LORD while he may be found; call on him while he is near" (Isaiah 55:6).

FOLLOW ME IN PRAYER

Would you like to place your faith in Jesus for the forgiveness of sins, thereby guaranteeing your eternal place in heaven along His side? If so, pray the following prayer with me.

Keep in mind that it is not the prayer itself that saves you. It is the faith in your heart that saves you. So, let the following prayer be a simple expression of the faith that is in your heart:

> *Dear Jesus:*
> *I want to have a relationship with You. I know I cannot save myself, because I know I am a sinner. Thank You for dying on the cross on my behalf. I believe You died for me, and I accept Your free gift of salvation.*
> *Thank You, Jesus. Amen.*

WELCOME TO GOD'S FOREVER FAMILY

On the authority of the Word of God, I can now assure you that you are a part of God's forever family. If you prayed the above prayer with a heart of faith, you will spend all eternity by the side of Jesus in heaven. Welcome to God's family!

WHAT TO DO NEXT

1. Purchase a Bible and read from it daily. Read at least one chapter a day, followed by a time of prayer. I recommend starting with the Gospel of John.

2. Join a Bible-believing church immediately. Get involved in it. Join a Bible study group at the church so you will have regular fellowship with other Christians.

3. *Please write to me:* Ron Rhodes, P.O. Box 2526, Frisco, TX, 75034. I would love to hear from you if you have made a decision for Christ.

NOTES

Introduction: What You Believe Matters

1. William Provine, cited in William A. Dembski and James M. Jushiner, eds., *Signs of Intelligence: Understanding Intelligent Design* (Grand Rapids: Brazos Press, 2001), p. 45.
2. William Lane Craig and Walter Sinnott-Armstrong, *God? A Debate Between a Christian and an Atheist* (Oxford: Oxford University Press, 2004), p. ix.
3. Norman Geisler and Frank Turek, *I Don't Have Enough Faith to Be an Atheist* (Wheaton, IL: Crossway Books, 2004), p. 20.
4. Geisler and Turek, p. 40.
5. Elliot Miller, "Breaking Through the 'Relativity Barrier,'" *Christian Research Journal*, Winter/Spring 1988, p. 7.
6. Geisler and Turek, p. 58.
7. Geisler and Turek, p. 35.
8. Elliot Miller, "The 1993 Parliament of the World's Religions: The Fundamentalism of Tolerance," *Christian Research Journal*, Winter 1994; CRI Web site, www.equip.org.

Chapter 1: Understanding Atheism, Agnosticism, and Skepticism

1. Michael Martin, "Atheism," *Microsoft Encarta Online Encyclopedia 2005*, Microsoft Corporation; Internet, www.encarta.msn.com.
2. Scott Simon, "Analysis: Atheism in America," *Weekend Edition*, January 10, 2004; Internet, http://www.highbeam.com.
3. Uwe Siemon-Netto, "Analysis: Atheism Worldwide in Decline," United Press International, copyright 2005; Internet, http://www.washtimes.com.
4. "Atheism Becoming Less Popular," *CBN News*, March 7, 2005; Internet, http://www.cbn.com/cbnnews.

269

5. Robert A. Morey, *The New Atheism and the Erosion of Freedom* (Minneapolis, MN: Bethany House Publishers, 1986), p. 38.

6. Martin, "Atheism," *Encarta*.

7. See Norman Geisler and Ron Brooks, *When Skeptics Ask* (Wheaton, IL: Victor Books, 1990), p. 38.

8. David Eller, *Natural Atheism* (Cranford, NJ: American Atheist Press, 2004), quoted in a review in *American Atheist*, Spring 2004; Internet, http://www.atheists.org.

9. Eller, *Natural Atheism*.

10. George H. Smith, *Atheism: The Case Against God* (Amherst, NY: Prometheus Books, 1989), p. 7.

11. Richard S. Russell, "Letter to the Editor," *Church & State*, July 1, 2004; Internet.

12. Cliff Walker, "Introduction to Activistic Atheism," *Positive Atheism*, Internet, www.positiveatheism.org.

13. Isaac Asimov; cited in Dan Story, *Defending Your Faith: How to Answer the Tough Questions* (Nashville, TN: Thomas Nelson Publishers, 1992), p. 21.

14. American Atheists home page, www.atheists.org.

15. Carl Sagan, *Cosmos* (New York: Ballantine Books, 1985), p. 4.

16. See, for example, eds. William A. Dembski and James M. Kushiner, *Signs of Intelligence* (Grand Rapids: Brazos Press, 2001), p. 46.

17. Dylan Evans and Howard Selina, *Introducing Evolution* (Cambridge: Totem Books, 2001), p. 34.

18. *The Science of Biology* (New York: McGraw-Hill, 1963), p. 39.

19. Alvin C. Plantinga, *God, Freedom, and Evil* (Grand Rapids: Eerdmans, 2002), p. 7.

20. Cited in Millard Erickson, *Introducing Christian Doctrine* (Grand Rapids: Baker Book House, 1996), pp. 138-39.

21. Summarized by Norman Geisler, *Baker Encyclopedia of Christian Apologetics* (Grand Rapids: Baker Books, 1999), p. 57.

22. See Geisler, *Baker Encyclopedia of Christian Apologetics*, p. 57.

23. Alister McGrath, "The Twilight of Atheism," *Christianity Today*, March 2005, vol. 49, no. 3, p. 36.

24. Smith, *Atheism*, p. 9.

25. Norman Geisler and Paul Feinberg, *Introduction to Philosophy: A Christian Perspective* (Grand Rapids, MI: Baker Book House, 1980), p. 296.

26. Norman Geisler, *Christian Apologetics* (Grand Rapids: Baker Books, 1978), p. 13.

27. Geisler, *Baker Encyclopedia of Christian Apologetics*, p. 12.

28. J. Budziszewski, "Why I Am Not an Atheist," in *Why I Am a Christian: Leading Thinkers Explain Why They Believe*, eds. Norman Geisler and Paul Hoffman (Grand Rapids: Baker Books, 2001), p. 54.

29. Josh McDowell and Don Stewart, *Handbook of Today's Religions* (San Bernardino, CA: Here's Life Publishers, 1989), pp. 415-16.

30. J.E. Wood, "Separation of Church and State," in *Dictionary of Christianity in America* (Downers Grove, IL: InterVarsity Press, 1990), p. 268.

31. James Madison; cited by Wood, "Separations," p. 267.

32. U.S. Supreme Court Justice Hugo Black, majority opinion; *Everson v. Board of Education* 330 U.S. 1 (1947) "Supreme Court Cases: Emerson v. Board of Education, 1947," at: http://www.phschool.com/atschool/supreme_court_cases/everson.html.

33. Charles Ryrie, *Ryrie Study Bible*, in Accordance Bible Software, Oaksoft, 2005.

Chapter 2: Why Isn't the Evidence Overtly Clear?

1. Bob and Gretchen Passantino, "Imagine There's No Heaven: Contemporary Atheism Speaks Out in Humanist Manifesto 2000," *Christian Research Journal,* vol. 22 no. 3; Internet version, www.equip.org.

2. Ravi Zacharias, *The Real Face of Atheism* (Grand Rapids: Baker, 2004), p. 36.

3. Robert Morey, *The New Atheism and the Erosion of Freedom* (Minneapolis, MN: Bethany House Publishers, 1986), pp. 143-44.

4. George Smith; quoted in Dan Story, *Defending Your Faith: How to Answer the Tough Questions* (Nashville: Thomas Nelson Publishers, 1992), pp. 19-20.

5. George Smith, *Atheism: The Case Against God* (Amherst, NY: Prometheus Books, 1989), p. 98.

6. Norman Geisler and Frank Turek, *I Don't Have Enough Faith to Be an Atheist* (Wheaton, IL: Crossway Books, 2004), pp. 26-27.

7. Geisler and Turek, *I Don't Have Enough Faith*, pp. 26-27.

8. W.K. Clifford, "The Ethics of Belief," in *Readings in the Philosophy of Religion*, ed. Baruch A. Brody (Englewood Cliffs, NJ: Prentice-Hall, 1974), p. 246.

9. Cliff Walker, "Introduction to Activistic Atheism," 2005, *Positive Atheism Magazine* Web site, http://www.positiveatheism.org.

10. See "Naturalism," *The Columbia Encyclopedia,* 7th ed., online edition.

11. *Contact,* screenplay by James V. Hart and Michael Goldenberg, directed by Robert Zemeckis, produced by Warner Brothers, 1997.

12. William Lane Craig; cited in Geisler and Turek, *I Don't Have Enough Faith*, pp. 126-27.

13. Kenneth Richard Samples, *Without a Doubt: Answering the 20 Toughest Faith Questions* (Grand Rapids: Baker Books, 2004), pp. 36-37.

14. C.S. Lewis as cited in John A. Witmer, "The Doctrine of Miracles," *Bibliotheca Sacra*, Logos Bible Software, electronic media.

15. *Evangelical Dictionary of Biblical Theology,* Logos Bible Software, electronic media.

16. Kenneth Boa and Larry Moody, *I'm Glad You Asked* (Wheaton, IL: Victor, 1994), p. 52.

17. Douglas Connelly, *Miracles: What the Bible Says* (Downers Grove, IL: InterVarsity Press, 1997), p. 29.

18. James Oliver Buswell, *A Systematic Theology of the Christian Religion* (Grand Rapids: Zondervan Publishing House, 1979), p. 180.

19. "WE ARE ATHEISTS Because . . . ," posted at the American Atheists Web site, http://www.atheists.org/visitors/center/because.html.

20. J.I. Packer, *Knowing Christianity* (Wheaton, IL: Harold Shaw Publishers, 1995), p. 16.

21. Geisler and Turek, *I Don't Have Enough Faith,* p. 24.

Chapter 3: Why There Is *Something* Rather than *Nothing*

1. Based on A.K. Morrison, cited in John MacArthur, *The Superiority of Christ* (Chicago, IL: Moody, 1986), pp. 33-34.

2. Martin Bard, "The Impossibility of Deity," *The American Atheist,* vol. 37, no. 1, posted at the American Atheist Web site, http://www.americanatheist.org/.

3. Kenneth Richard Samples, *Without a Doubt: Answering the 20 Toughest Faith Questions* (Grand Rapids: Baker Books, 2004), p. 23.

4. Dan Story, *Defending Your Faith* (Nashville: Thomas Nelson, 1992), p. 24.

5. Norman Geisler and Ron Brooks, *When Skeptics Ask* (Wheaton, IL: Victor Books, 1990), pp. 18-19.

6. David Hume to John Stewart, February 1754, in *The Letters of David Hume,* ed. J.Y.T. Greig (Oxford: Clarendon Press, 1932), 1:187.

7. Norman Geisler and Frank Turek, *I Don't Have Enough Faith to Be an Atheist* (Wheaton, IL: Crossway Books, 2004), p. 75.

8. Jimmy Williams, "A (Not So) Brief Defense of Christianity," Probe Ministries Web site, http://www.probe.org.

9. "God and the Scientists: A New Debate, An Old Question," posted at the American Atheists Web site, http://www.americanatheists.org/.

10. See Geisler and Turek, *I Don't Have Enough Faith,* p. 91.

11. Isaac Asimov, "In the Game of Energy and Thermodynamics, You Can't Even Break Even," *Smithsonian,* June 1970, p. 6.

12. Asimov, "In the Game," p. 10.

13. Henry Morris, "Seven Reasons for Opposing Evolution," *Bibliotheca Sacra* (Dallas, TX: Dallas Theological Seminary [Electronic edition by Galaxie Software]), 1999.

14. Del Ratzsch, *The Battle of Beginnings: Why Neither Side Is Winning the Creation-Evolution Debate* (Downers Grove, IL: InterVarsity Press, 1996), p. 91.

15. Lincoln Barnett, *The Universe and Dr. Einstein* (New York: Amereon Ltd., 1950), pp. 102-3, insert added.

16. Robert Jastrow, *God and the Astronomers* (New York: W.W. Norton & Company, Inc., 1992), p. 33.

17. J.W.N. Sullivan, *The Limitations of Science* (New York: Augustus M. Kelley Publishers, 1930), p. 24.

18. Stephen Hawking and Roger Penrose, *The Nature of Space and Time* (Princeton, NJ: Princeton University Press, 1996), p. 20.

19. Hugh Ross, *The Creator and the Cosmos* (Colorado Springs, CO: NavPress, 2001), p. 32.

20. Among competing scientific theories that have been suggested as replacements for the big bang theory by various scientists are the Plasma Theory, the Steady State Theory, String Theory, the Multiple-Universe Theory, and a number of variations of the Inflation Theory (over 50 variations). The fact that some of the scientific community has voiced doubt about the big bang theory should give one pause in accepting it. As a young-earth creationist myself, I personally have doubts about it—but because so many scientists as well as reliable Christian apologists believe in its validity, it is included in this chapter as a possible support for the second premise of the kalam cosmological argument. Even without the support of the big bang theory, the second premise of the kalam cosmological argument finds more than adequate support from the second law of thermodynamics.

21. Understandably, many Christians—more specifically, old-earth creationists—believe the big bang theory relates directly to how God brought the universe into being in the beginning (Genesis 1:1).

22. Jastrow, *God and the Astronomers*, p. 12; see also pp. 28-29.

23. Jastrow, *God and the Astronomers*, p. 12.

24. Norman L. Geisler and Ronald Brooks, *When Skeptics Ask*, The Norman Geisler CD-ROM Library (Grand Rapids: Baker Book House, 2002).

25. Paul Recer, "Universe Found 13 Billion Years Old," AP Online, April 25, 2002; see also Jimmy H. Davis and Harry L. Poe, *Designer Universe: Intelligent Design and the Existence of God* (Nashville: Broadman & Holman Publishers, 2002), pp. 80-81.

26. Jastrow, *God and the Astronomers*, p. 13.

27. Jastrow, *God and the Astronomers*, p. 55.

28. Michael Behe, *Darwin's Black Box: The Biochemical Challenge to Evolution* (New York: The Free Press, 1996), p. 244.

29. Ralph Muncaster, *Dismantling Evolution* (Eugene, OR: Harvest House Publishers, 2003), pp. 202-3.

30. British cosmologist Sir Arthur Eddington said the very idea was repugnant to him. See Ross, *The Creator and the Cosmos*, p. 77.

31. William A. Dembski, *Intelligent Design: The Bridge Between Science and Theology* (Downers Grove, IL: InterVarsity Press, 1999), pp. 204-5; Muncaster, *Dismantling Evolution*, p. 201.

32. Jastrow, *God and the Astronomers*, p. 119.

33. "Scientists and Theologians Discover a Common Ground," *U.S. News and World Report*, July 20, 1998, p. 52.

34. Ross, *The Creator and the Cosmos*, p. 32.
35. George Smith, *Atheism: The Case Against God* (Amherst, NY: Prometheus Books, 1989), pp. 239-40.
36. William Lane Craig and Walter Sinnott-Armstrong, *God? A Debate Between a Christian and an Atheist* (Oxford: Oxford University Press, 2004), p. 131.
37. See Geisler and Turek, *I Don't Have Enough Faith*, p. 93.

Chapter 4: Naturalism Versus the Possibility of Miracles
1. Paul B. Weisz, *The Science of Biology* (New York: McGraw-Hill, 1963), p. 39.
2. William A. Dembski, *Intelligent Design: The Bridge Between Science and Theology* (Downers Grove, IL: InterVarsity Press, 1999), p. 103.
3. Phillip Johnson, *Reason in the Balance: The Case Against Naturalism in Science, Law & Education* (Downers Grove, IL: InterVarsity Press, 1995), p. 38.
4. Benedict Spinoza, in George Smith, *Atheism: The Case Against God* (Amherst, NY: Prometheus Books, 1989), p. 199.
5. Del Ratzsch, *The Battle of Beginnings: Why Neither Side Is Winning the Creation-Evolution Debate* (Downers Grove, IL: InterVarsity Press, 1996), p. 14.
6. Michael Behe, "Huxley: From Devil's Disciple to Evolution's High Priest," Book Review, *National Review*, vol. 50, February 9, 1998, p. 54.
7. See Dembski, *Intelligent Design*, p. 100.
8. Phillip E. Johnson, *Defeating Darwinism by Opening Minds* (Downers Grove, IL: InterVarsity Press, 1997), pp. 92, 114-15.
9. Michael Martin, "Atheism," *Microsoft Encarta Online Encyclopedia 2005*, http://encarta.msn.com © 1997-2005 Microsoft Corporation.
10. Norman Geisler, "Miracles, Arguments Against," in *Baker Encyclopedia of Christian Apologetics* (Grand Rapids: Baker Book House, 1999), pp. 457-68.
11. "Religious Doctrines and Dogmas: In the 18th and early 19th centuries," *Encyclopædia Britannica*, online edition.
12. David Hume, "An Enquiry Concerning Human Understanding" (1777), entire essay reproduced in R. Douglas Geivett and Gary R. Habermas, *In Defense of Miracles: A Comprehensive Case for God's Action in History* (Downers Grove, IL: InterVarsity Press, 1997), p. 33.
13. Smith, *Atheism*, pp. 216-17.
14. C.S. Lewis, cited in Jodie Berndt, *Celebration of Miracles* (Nashville: Thomas Nelson Publishers, 1995), p. 20.
15. John Witmer, "The Doctrine of Miracles," *Bibliotheca Sacra*, Logos Bible Software, electronic media.
16. Louis Berkhof, *Systematic Theology* (Grand Rapids: William B. Eerdmans Publishing Co., 1982), p. 177.
17. William Lane Craig, cited in Lee Strobel, *The Case for Faith* (Grand Rapids: Zondervan, 2000), p. 63.
18. Charles Ryrie, *Survey of Bible Doctrine*, QuickVerse Library, electronic media.

19. Berkhof, *Systematic Theology*, p. 177.
20. Quoted in Norman Geisler and Ronald Brooks, *When Skeptics Ask* (Wheaton, IL: Victor Press, 1989), p. 76.
21. Geisler and Brooks, *When Skeptics Ask*, p. 76.
22. Kenneth Boa and Larry Moody, *I'm Glad You Asked* (Wheaton, IL: Victor Books, 1994), pp. 50-51.
23. Norman Geisler, cited in Geivett and Habermas, *In Defense of Miracles*, p. 78. See also Henry Clarence Thiessen, *Lectures in Systematic Theology* (Grand Rapids: Eerdmans, 1979), p. 12.
24. Thiessen, *Lectures in Systematic Theology*, p. 12, emphasis added.
25. Geisler and Brooks, *When Skeptics Ask*, pp. 79-80.
26. Atheistic philosopher Michael Martin often makes this point.
27. Peter Kreeft and Ronald Tacelli, *Handbook of Christian Apologetics* (Downers Grove, IL: InterVarsity Press, 1994), p. 109.
28. See, for example, Frank R. Zindler, "Reversing Science," *The Probing Mind*, April 1990, posted at the American Atheists Web site, http://www.atheists.org/evolution/reversing.html.
29. Henry Morris, "Seven Reasons for Opposing Evolution," *Bibliotheca Sacra* (Dallas, TX: Dallas Theological Seminary [Electronic edition by Galaxie Software]), 1999.
30. Lincoln Barnett, *The Universe and Dr. Einstein* (New York: Amereon Ltd., 1950), pp. 102-3, insert added.
31. Dembski, *Intelligent Design*, pp. 17, 128.
32. The *Merriam-Webster's Online Dictionary* defines archaeology as "The *scientific* study of material remains (as fossil, relics, artifacts, and monuments) of past human life and activities" (emphasis added): http://www.m-w/com/.
33. James Oliver Buswell, *A Systematic Theology of the Christian Religion* (Grand Rapids: Zondervan Publishing House, 1979), p. 176.
34. C.S. Lewis, *God in the Dock* (Grand Rapids: Eerdmans, 1972), p. 26.
35. Lewis, *God in the Dock*, p. 26.
36. Ron Rhodes, *The Complete Book of Bible Answers* (Eugene, OR: Harvest House Publishers, 1999), p. 304.
37. Josh McDowell and Don Stewart, *Answers to Tough Questions* (Nashville: Thomas Nelson Publishers, 1993), p. 84.
38. Gerhard Nehls, *Christians Ask Muslims*, in *The World of Islam* CD-ROM, electronic media.
39. Paul Little, *Know Why You Believe* (Downers Grove, IL: InterVarsity Press, 1975), p. 59.
40. Charles Hodge, *Systematic Theology*, Logos Software, electronic media.
41. Geisler, *Baker Encyclopedia of Christian Apologetics*, p. 450.
42. Isaac Asimov admitted he could not prove that God did not exist. Isaac Asimov

interview by Paul Kurtz, "An Interview with Isaac Asimov on Science and the Bible," *Free Inquiry,* vol. 2, Spring 1982, p. 9.

Chapter 5: Evolution: A Flawed Theory

1. Huston Smith, "Evolution and Evolutionism," *Christian Century,* July 7–14, 1982, p. 755.
2. Daniel Dennett, as cited in Dylan Evans and Howard Selina, *Introducing Evolution* (Cambridge: Totem Books, 2001), p. 6.
3. Evans and Selina, *Introducing Evolution,* p. 6.
4. Richard Dawkins, cited in eds. William A. Dembski and James M. Kushiner, *Signs of Intelligence* (Grand Rapids: Brazos Press, 2001), p. 44.
5. *Humanist Manifesto II,* American Humanist Association, 1973.
6. James Hitchcock, *What Is Secular Humanism?* (Ann Arbor, MI: Servant Books, 1982), Introduction.
7. Isaac Asimov, *Isaac Asimov's Book of Science and Nature Quotations* (New York: Weidenfeld & Nicolson, 1988), p. xvi.
8. Frederick Edwords, "The Humanist Philosophy in Perspective," *The Humanist,* January/February 1984, n.p.
9. Jay Gould, as cited in Rachel Ramer, "In Debate with Evolutionists," Statement DC742, Christian Research Institute, Rancho Santa Margarita, CA.
10. William Nowers, "Darwinism in Denial," *The Washington Times,* November 25, 2001, Electric Library.
11. Phillip Johnson, *Darwin on Trial* (Downers Grove, IL: InterVarsity Press, 1993), p. 87.
12. Hank Hanegraaff, *The Face that Demonstrates the Farce of Evolution* (Nashville: W Publishing Group, 1998), p. 172.
13. Chris Colby, "Evolution," *The World and I,* vol. 11, January 1, 1996, p. 294, electric library.
14. David Lane, "Special Creation or Evolution: No Middle Ground," *Bibliotheca Sacra* (Dallas, TX: Dallas Theological Seminary, 1999), electronic edition by Galaxie Software.
15. See Johnson, *Darwin on Trial,* p. 69.
16. Jonathan Wells, "Issues in the Creation-Evolution Controversies," *The World and I,* vol. 11, January 1, 1996, p. 294, electric library.
17. Frank Zindler, "'Creation Science' and the Fact of Evolution," *The Probing Mind,* October 1987, posted at the American Atheists Web site, http://www.atheists.org/evolution/creationscience.html.
18. *The American Heritage Dictionary of the English Language* (Houghton Mifflin Company, 2000), online edition.
19. Rod Caird, *Ape Man: The Story of Human Evolution* (New York: MacMillan, 1994), p. 112.
20. Millard Erickson, *Christian Theology* (Grand Rapids: Baker Book House, 1985), p. 479.

21. John Morris, "Do Peppered Moths Prove Evolution?" *Back to Genesis,* no. 64b, April 1994, online edition.

22. Richard Milton, *Shattering the Myths of Darwinism* (Rochester, VT: Park Street Press, 1997), pp. 141-42, emphasis added.

23. Lane Lester, "Genetics: Enemy of Evolution," *Creation Research Society Quarterly,* vol. 31, no. 4, 1995, online edition.

24. Gary Parker, "Creation, Mutation, and Variation," *Impact,* no. 89, November 1980, Institute for Creation Research, online edition.

25. Gleason Archer, *Encyclopedia of Bible Difficulties* (Grand Rapids: Zondervan, 1982), p. 56. See also Jerry Bergman, "Some Biological Problems with the Natural Selection Theory," *Creation Research Society Quarterly,* vol. 29, no. 3, December 1992, online edition.

26. Phillip Johnson, *Reason in the Balance: The Case Against Naturalism in Science, Law & Education* (Downers Grove, IL: InterVarsity Press, 1995), p. 81.

27. H.J. Muller, "Radiation Damage to the Genetic Material," *American Scientist,* vol. 38, January 1950, p. 35.

28. Evolutionists themselves admit this. See Evans and Selina, *Introducing Evolution,* p. 61.

29. *Science: Order and Reality,* eds. Laurel Hicks, Delores Shimmin, Gregory Rickard, Ed Rickard, Julie Rickard, Barbara Porcher, Cindy Froman (Pensacola, FL: A Beka Book, 1993), p. 392.

30. See Steve Jones, *Darwin's Ghost: The Origin of Species Updated* (New York: Random House, 2000), p. 111.

31. Milton, *Shattering the Myths,* p. 155.

32. See Johnson, *Darwin on Trial,* p. 32.

33. Austin Cline, "Is Evolution Science? Anatomical Homologies," at About.com Web site, http://atheism.about.com/library/FAQs/evolution/blfaq_evolution_evidence07.htm, insert added.

34. See George Howe, "Homology and Origins," *Creation Matters,* vol. 4, no. 5, September-October 1999, pp. 1, 3-5.

35. Austin Cline, "Is Evolution Science? Vestigial Organs," at About.com Web site, http://atheism.about.com/library/FAQs/evolution/blfaq_evolution_evidence08.htm.

36. See Michael Behe, *Darwin's Black Box: The Biochemical Challenge to Evolution* (New York: The Free Press, 1996), p. 226.

37. Henry Morris, *Scientific Creationism* (Green Forest, AR: Master Books, 2001), p. 76.

38. Norman Geisler, *Baker Encyclopedia of Christian Apologetics,* in The Norman Geisler CD-ROM Library (Grand Rapids: Baker Book House, 2002).

39. Geisler, *Baker Encyclopedia of Christian Apologetics.*

40. J.P. Moreland, *The Creation Hypothesis: Scientific Evidence for an Intelligent Designer* (Downers Grove, IL: InterVarsity Press, 1994), pp. 222-23.

41. Frank Zindler, "Reversing Science," *The Probing Mind,* April, 1990, posted at the American Atheists Web site, http://www.atheists.org/evolution/reversing.html.

42. H.L. Willmington, *Willmington's Guide to the Bible* (Wheaton, IL: Tyndale House Publishers, 1984), p. 28.

43. Stephen Jay Gould, *I Have Landed: The End of a Beginning in Natural History* (New York: Harmony Books, 2002), p. 251. See also Richard Fortey, *Life: A Natural History of the First Four Billion Years of Life on Earth* (New York: Alfred A. Knopf, 1999), pp. 100-6.

44. Dembski and Kushiner, eds., *Signs of Intelligence,* p. 149.

45. Johnson, *Darwin on Trial,* p. 24.

46. Duane Gish, *Evolution: The Fossils Still Say No!* (El Cajon, CA: Institute for Creation Research, 1995), p. 27.

47. Ernst Mayr, *What Evolution Is* (New York: Basic Books, 2001), p. 60.

48. Bryn Nelson, "Find May Give Clue to Cambrian 'Explosion,'" *Newsday,* July 20, 2001, p. A28.

49. See Henry Morris, *The Biblical Basis for Modern Science* (Grand Rapids: Baker Book House, 1984), p. 339.

50. Frank Zindler, "Half a Wing and No Prayer," *The Probing Mind,* April 1986, posted at the American Atheists Web site, http://www.atheists.org/evolution/half awing.html.

51. Morris, *Scientific Creationism,* p. 341.

52. John Noble Wilford, "An Early Bird Mars Theory on Dinosaurs," in *The Science Times Book of Fossils and Evolution,* ed. Nicholas Wade (New York: The Lyons Press, 1998), pp. 65-66. See also "A New Flap Over Birds' Evolutionary Path," *Newsday,* November 19, 1996; Dinshaw K. Dadachanjim, "Origins of Life Reconsidered," *The World and I,* September 1, 1997; James Vicini, "Bird's Descent from Dinosaurs In Doubt," Reuters, November 14, 1996.

53. Hank Hanegraaff, "FACE the Facts about Evolution," Statement DF803, Christian Research Institute, Rancho Santa Margarita, CA.

54. Stephen Jay Gould, "The Return of Hopeful Monsters," *Natural History* 76 (June-July 1977):24.

55. Stephen Jay Gould, "Evolution's Erratic Pace," *Natural History* 86 (May 1977):14-15.

56. Stephen Jay Gould, "Is a New and General Theory of Evolution Emerging?" *Paleobiology* 6 (1980):40.

57. Austin Cline, "Punctuated Equilibrium," at About.com Web site, http://atheism.about.com/library/glossary/evolution/bldef_punctuatedequil.htm.

58. Gish, *Evolution,* p. 34.

Chapter 6: The Intelligent Design of the Universe

1. "God and the Scientists: A New Debate, An Old Question," posted at American Atheists Web site, August 26, 1999, http://www.atheists.org/flash.line/atheism6.htm.

2. "The Craig-Jesseph Debate: Does God Exist?" Dr. Craig's Opening Arguments, transcript posted at www.leaderu.com, Internet.

3. Norman Geisler and Ron Brooks, *When Skeptics Ask* (Wheaton, IL: Victor Books, 1990), p. 20.

4. William Dembski, *Intelligent Design: The Bridge Between Science and Theology* (Downers Grove, IL: InterVarsity Press, 1999), p. 126.

5. Michael Behe, William Dembski, and Stephen Meyer, *Science and Evidence for Design in the Universe* (San Francisco, CA: Ignatius Press, 2002), p. 53.

6. William Dembski and James Kushiner, eds., *Signs of Intelligence* (Grand Rapids, MI: Brazos Press, 2001), p. 48.

7. Phillip E. Johnson, *Defeating Darwinism by Opening Minds* (Downers Grove, IL: InterVarsity Press, 1997), p. 23.

8. Dembski, *Intelligent Design*, p. 127.

9. For example, Robert Jastrow, *God and the Astronomers* (New York: W.W. Norton & Company, Inc., 1992).

10. Frank Zindler, "Half a Wing and No Prayer," *The Probing Mind*, April, 1986, posted at the American Atheists Web site, http://www.atheists.org/evolution/half awing.html.

11. Behe, Dembski, and Meyer, *Science and Evidence*, p. 119.

12. Helen Fryman, "The Intelligent Design Movement," *Creation Matters*, vol. 5, no. 2, March-April 2000, p. 4.

13. Michael Behe, "A Mousetrap Defended: Response to Critics," Discovery Institute, July 31, 2003; Michael Behe, "Blind Evolution or Intelligent Design: Address to the American Museum of Natural History," April 23, 2002, Discovery Institute Web site (www.discovery.org).

14. Behe, Dembski, and Meyer, *Science and Evidence*, p. 119.

15. Dembski and Kushiner, eds., *Signs of Intelligence*, p. 94.

16. Joseph Paturi, "The Human Body—God's Masterpiece," *Creation Ex Nihilo*, vol. 20, no. 4, September-November 1998, pp. 54-55.

17. George Sim Johnston, "Designed for Living," *Wall Street Journal,* October 15, 1999, Discovery Institute Web site (www.discovery.org). See also Tom Wagner, "Darwin vs. the Eye," *Creation Ex Nihilo*, vol. 16, no. 4, September-November 1994, pp. 10-13.

18. Philip E. Johnson, *Darwin on Trial* (Downers Grove, IL: InterVarsity Press, 1993), p. 34.

19. See Johnson, *Darwin on Trial*, p. 35. See also Phillip E. Johnson, *Reason in the Balance: The Case Against Naturalism in Science, Law & Education* (Downers Grove, IL: InterVarsity Press, 1995), pp. 78-79.

20. Johnson, *Reason in the Balance*, p. 81.

21. John Whitcomb, *The Early Earth* (Grand Rapids: Baker Book House, 1979), p. 87.

22. Johnson, *Defeating Darwinism by Opening Minds,* p. 77.

23. For example, Ernst Haeckel.

24. Dembski and Kushiner, eds., *Signs of Intelligence*, p. 93. See also Frank Salisbury, "Doubts about the Modern Synthetic Theory of Evolution," *American Biology Teacher* (September 1971), p. 336. Henry Morris, *Scientific Creationism* (Green Forest, AR: Master Books, 2001), p. 62.

25. Charles Darwin, *On the Origin of Species* (New York: The Modern Library, 1856 ed. reprint), p. 162.

26. J.P. Moreland, *The Creation Hypothesis: Scientific Evidence for an Intelligent Designer* (Downers Grove, IL: InterVarsity Press, 1994), p. 68.

27. Dembski and Kushiner, eds., *Signs of Intelligence*, p. 11.

28. Johnson, *Defeating Darwinism by Opening Minds*, p. 77.

29. Dembski and Kushiner, eds., *Signs of Intelligence*, p. 103.

30. Behe, Dembski, and Meyer, *Science and Evidence*, pp. 67-68.

31. Norman Geisler and Joseph Holden, *Living Loud: Defending Your Faith* (Nashville: Broadman Holman Publishers, 2002), p. 56.

32. Keith Parson, cited in J.P. Moreland and Kai Nielsen, *Does God Exist? The Great Debate* (Nashville: Thomas Nelson Publishers, 1990), pp. 184-85.

33. Richard Dawkins, *The Blind Watchmaker* (New York: W.W. Norton, 1996), p. 115.

34. Russell Grigg, "A Brief History of Design," *Creation Ex Nihilo*, vol. 22, no. 2, March-May 2000, p. 52.

35. Such as Windows 98, for example. Cyrus Farivar, "UC-Berkeley Scholars Weigh In On Challenge to Evolution," *University Wire*, March 11, 2002, electric library.

36. Dembski and Kushiner, eds., *Signs of Intelligence*, p. 115; Jimmy H. Davis and Harry L. Poe, *Designer Universe: Intelligent Design and the Existence of God* (Nashville: Broadman and Holman, 2002), pp. 202-3.

37. Bill Gates, *The Road Ahead* (Boulder, CO: Blue Penguin, 1996), p. 228; in Behe, Dembski, and Meyer, *Science and Evidence*, p. 71. See also Jay Richards, "Intelligent Design Theory: Why It Matters," IntellectualCapital.com, July 25, 1999.

38. Moreland, *The Creation Hypothesis*, p. 82.

39. Holly Morris, "Life's Grand Design," *U.S. News & World Report*, July 29, 2002, p. 52.

40. "Challenging Darwin," *The Washington Times*, September 19, 2002, electric library.

41. David Eller, "Confronting Intelligent Design: A Report from the Studio," *American Atheist Magazine*, Autumn, 2003, posted at the *American Atheist Magazine* Web site, http://www.findarticles.com/p/articles/mi_m0OBB/is_4_41/ai_111268788.

42. Dembski, *Intelligent Design*, p. 257.

43. Davis and Poe, *Designer Universe*, p. 115; Dembski, *Intelligent Design*, pp. 17, 128.

44. Dembski, *Intelligent Design*, p. 17.

45. Davis and Poe, *Designer Universe,* p. 119.
46. Benjamin Wiker, "Does Science Point to God?: The Intelligent Design Revolution," *Crisis,* April 8, 2003, Discovery Institute Web site (www.discovery.org).
47. Robin Collins, "The Fine-Tuning Design Argument: A Scientific Argument for the Existence of God," *Reason for the Hope Within,* September 1, 1998, Discovery Institute Web site (www.discovery.org).
48. Kenneth Richard Samples, *Without a Doubt: Answering the 20 Toughest Faith Questions* (Grand Rapids: Baker Books, 2004), p. 24.
49. Collins, "The Fine-Tuning Design Argument."
50. Hugh Ross, *The Creator and the Cosmos* (Colorado Springs, CO: NavPress, 2001), p. 151.
51. Hank Hanegraaff, "The Failure of Evolution to Account for the Miracle of Life," *Christian Research Journal,* Summer 1998, online edition.
52. Norman Geisler and Frank Turek, *I Don't Have Enough Faith to Be an Atheist* (Wheaton, IL: Crossway Books, 2004), p. 98.
53. Geisler and Turek, *I Don't Have Enough Faith,* p. 105-6.
54. William Lane Craig, "Why I Believe God Exists," in *Why I Am a Christian: Leading Thinkers Explain Why They Believe,* eds. Norman Geisler and Paul Hoffman (Grand Rapids: Baker Books, 2001), p. 68.
55. Eller, "Confronting Intelligent Design: A Report from the Studio."
56. Robert Jastrow, cited in Geisler and Turek, *I Don't Have Enough Faith,* p. 88.
57. Fritjof Capra, *The Turning Point* (New York: Simon and Schuster, 1984), p. 96.

Chapter 7: Morality and the Absolutely Moral Lawgiver

1. B.A. Robinson, "Atheism: Beliefs about Atheism by Some Christians," Ontario Consultants on Religious Tolerance, October 4, 2002, posted at the Religious Tolerance Web site, http://www.religioustolerance.org/atheist2/htm.
2. Flavius Josephus, *Against Apion* (Grand Rapids: Kregel Publications, 1974), p. 622.
3. H.L. Strack and P. Billerbeck, *Kommentar zum Neuen Testament aus Talmud und Midrasch* (Munchen, 1893), 2:495; cited by Werner Neuer, *Man and Woman in Christian Perspective* (Wheaton, IL: Crossway Books, 1990), p. 93.
4. M. Aboth 1.5; cited by Neuer, p. 93.
5. R. Nicole, "Women, Biblical Concept of," *Evangelical Dictionary of Theology,* ed. Walter A. Elwell (Grand Rapids: Baker Book House, 1984), p. 1177.
6. Kenneth Richard Samples, *Without a Doubt: Answering the 20 Toughest Faith Questions* (Grand Rapids: Baker Books, 2004), p. 201.
7. Karl Rahner, quoted in the *Wittenberg Door,* June/July 1988, p. 4.
8. Friedrich Nietzsche, cited in Lee Strobel, *The Case for Faith* (Grand Rapids: Zondervan, 2000), p. 150.

9. Samples, *Without a Doubt*, p. 202.

10. Michael Martin, "Atheism," *Microsoft Encarta Online Encyclopedia 2005;* Internet.

11. Norman Geisler and Frank Turek, *I Don't Have Enough Faith to Be an Atheist* (Wheaton, IL: Crossway Books, 2004), p. 30.

12. Lee Strobel, cited in Geisler and Turek, *I Don't Have Enough Faith,* p. 163.

13. Strobel, *The Case for Faith,* p. 226.

14. Aldous Huxley, cited in Josh McDowell, *The New Evidence that Demands a Verdict* (Nashville: Thomas Nelson Publishers, 1999), p. xli.

15. J. Budziszewski, "Why I Am Not an Atheist," in *Why I Am a Christian,* eds. Norman Geisler and Paul Hoffman (Grand Rapids, MI: Baker, 2003), p. 53.

16. "The Craig-Nielsen Debate: God, Morality and Evil," Dr. Nielsen's Opening Statement, posted at "The Virtual Office of Dr. William Lane Craig," at www.lea deru.com.

17. Samples, *Without a Doubt,* p. 27.

18. Norman Geisler, *Baker Encyclopedia of Christian Apologetics* (Grand Rapids: Baker Books, 1999), p. 58.

19. William Lane Craig and Walter Sinnott-Armstrong, *God? A Debate Between a Christian and an Atheist* (Oxford: Oxford University Press, 2004), p. 33.

20. William Lane Craig, "The Craig-Pigliucci Debate: Does God Exist?" Dr. Craig's Second Rebuttal, posted at "The Virtual Office of Dr. William Lane Craig," at www.leaderu.com.

21. Craig and Sinnott-Armstrong, *God?* p. 17.

22. Wayne Martindale and Jerry Root, eds., *The Quotable C.S. Lewis* (Wheaton, IL: Tyndale House Publishers, 1989), p. 441.

23. See Geisler and Turek, *I Don't have Enough Faith,* p. 187.

24. Ray Cotton, "Morality Apart From God: Is It Possible?" posted at the Probe Ministries Web site, www.probe.org.

25. Martindale and Root, eds., *The Quotable C.S. Lewis,* p. 438.

26. Dan Story, *Defending Your Faith: How to Answer the Tough Questions* (Nashville: Thomas Nelson Publishers, 1992), p. 29.

27. Norman Geisler and Ronald Brooks, *When Skeptics Ask* (Wheaton, IL: Victor Books, 1990), p. 30.

28. See Geisler and Brooks, *When Skeptics Ask,* p. 30.

29. William Lane Craig, "Why I Believe God Exists," in Norman Geisler and Paul Hoffman, *Why I Am a Christian: Leading Thinkers Explain Why They Believe* (Grand Rapids: Baker Books, 1999), p. 75.

Chapter 8: The Reliability of the Bible—Part 1

1. *Faith Under Fire*, Fox Network, June 4, 2005.

2. Norman Geisler and William Nix, *A General Introduction to the Bible* (Chicago, IL: Moody Press, 1978), p. 28.

3. Craig Blomberg, "The Seventy-Four 'Scholars': Who Does the Jesus Seminar Really Speak For?" *Christian Research Journal,* Fall 1994, p. 36.

4. Lee Strobel, *The Case for Christ* (Grand Rapids: Zondervan, 1998), p. 97.

5. Sir William Ramsey, cited in Josh McDowell, *The New Evidence that Demands a Verdict* (Nashville: Thomas Nelson Publishers, 1999), p. 63.

6. Norman Geisler and Frank Turek, *I Don't Have Enough Faith to Be an Atheist* (Wheaton, IL: Crossway Books, 2004), p. 256.

7. Geisler and Turek, *I Don't Have Enough Faith,* p. 261.

8. Farrell Till, "Archaeology and Biblical Accuracy," Infidels Web site, http://www. infidels.org/library/magazines/tsr/1998/2/982front.html.

9. Nelson Glueck, *Rivers in the Desert* (Philadelphia, PA: Jewish Publications Society of America, 1969), p. 31.

10. William Albright, cited in Josh McDowell, *Evidence that Demands a Verdict* (San Bernardino, CA: Campus Crusade for Christ, 1972), p. 68.

11. Skeptic Michael Shermer made a case for this on *Faith Under Fire,* June 4, 2005.

12. Gary Habermas, *Ancient Evidence for the Life of Jesus* (Nashville: Thomas Nelson Publishers, 1984), p. 65.

13. Habermas, *Ancient Evidence,* p. 66.

14. Data on Justin Martyr, the Didache, Polycarp, and Irenaeus is derived from Geisler and Nix, *A General Introduction,* p. 190.

15. Translated by Louis Feldman (Loeb Edition).

16. Strobel, *The Case for Christ,* pp. 79-80.

17. *The Babylonian Talmud,* translated by I. Epstein (London: Soncino, 1935), vol. III, Sanhedrin 43a, p. 281; cited in Gary Habermas, *The Historical Jesus* (Joplin, MO: College Press, 1996), p. 203.

18. Shabbath 104b.

19. Pliny, *Letters,* translated by William Melmoth, revised by W.M.L. Hutchinson (Cambridge: Harvard University Press, 1935), vol. II, X:96; cited in Habermas, *The Historical Jesus,* p. 199.

20. Tacitus, *Annals* 15.44, cited in Strobel, *The Case for Christ,* p. 82.

21. N.D. Anderson, *Christianity: The Witness of History* (London: Tyndale, 1969), p. 19; cited in Habermas, *The Historical Jesus,* pp. 189-90.

22. Julius Africanus, *Chronography,* 18.1, cited in McDowell, *The New Evidence that Demands a Verdict,* pp. 57-58.

23. Geisler and Turek, *I Don't Have Enough Faith,* p. 223.

24. See, for example, Frank Zindler, "The Real Bible: Who's Got It?" May 1986, posted at American Atheists Web site, http://www.atheists.org/christianity/real bible.html.

25. See McDowell, *The New Evidence that Demands a Verdict,* p. 34.

26. Gleason Archer, *A Survey of Old Testament Introduction* (Chicago, IL: Moody Press, 1964), p. 19.

27. Paul Little, *Know Why You Believe* (Downers Grove, IL: InterVarsity Press, 1975), p. 41.

28. Dan Story, *Defending Your Faith: How to Answer the Tough Questions* (Nashville: Thomas Nelson Publishers, 1992), p. 35.

29. Zindler, "The Real Bible: Who's Got It?"

30. Strobel, *The Case for Christ,* pp. 64-65.

31. F.F. Bruce, *The New Testament Documents: Are They Reliable?* (Downers Grove, IL: InterVarsity Press, 1984), p. 19.

32. Bruce Metzger, cited in Strobel, *The Case for Christ,* pp. 64-65.

33. Michael Martin, *The Case Against Christianity* (Philadelphia, PA: Temple University Press, 1993).

34. See Gary Habermas, "Why I Believe the New Testament Is Historically Reliable," in Norman Geisler and Paul Hoffman, *Why I Am a Christian: Leading Thinkers Explain Why They Believe* (Grand Rapids: Baker Books, 2001), p. 148.

35. Norman Geisler, *Christian Apologetics* (Grand Rapids: Baker Book House, 1975), p. 306.

36. Rene Pache, *The Inspiration and Authority of Scripture* (Chicago, IL: Moody Press, 1978), p. 192.

37. Benjamin Warfield, as cited in Pache, *The Inspiration,* p. 193.

38. This chart is adapted from Geisler, *Christian Apologetics,* p. 307.

39. Sir Frederic Kenyon, in Little, *Know Why You Believe,* p. 48.

40. J.P. Moreland and Kai Nielsen, *Does God Exist? The Great Debate* (Nashville: Thomas Nelson Publishers, 1990), p. 39.

41. Zindler, "The Real Bible: Who's Got It?"

Chapter 9: The Reliability of the Bible—Part 2

1. George Smith, *Atheism: The Case Against God* (New York: Prometheus, 1989), p. 207.

2. Norman Geisler and Ron Brooks, *When Skeptics Ask* (Wheaton, IL: Victor Books, 1990), p. 115.

3. John Ankerberg, John Weldon, and Walter C. Kaiser, *The Case for Jesus the Messiah* (Chattanooga, TN: The John Ankerberg Evangelistic Association, 1989), p. 16.

4. Smith, *Atheism,* p. 207.

5. Cited in Ron Rhodes, "Witnessing to Liberals," see "Articles of Interest" at www. ronrhodes.org.

6. Smith, *Atheism,* pp. 209-10.

7. Smith, *Atheism,* p. 207.

8. Kenneth Richard Samples, *Without a Doubt: Answering the 20 Toughest Faith Questions* (Grand Rapids: Baker Books, 2004), p. 35.

9. Samples, *Without a Doubt,* p. 35.

10. Smith, *Atheism,* p. 203.

11. Norman Geisler and Thomas Howe, *When Critics Ask* (Wheaton, IL: Victor Books, 1992), p. 15.
12. Geisler and Howe, *When Critics Ask*, pp. 16-26. Used with permission.
13. Geisler and Howe, *When Critics Ask*, p. 22.

Chapter 10: The Evidence for Jesus

1. Lewis Sperry Chafer, *Systematic Theology*, vol. 2 (Dallas, TX: Dallas Seminary Press, 1978), p. 399.
2. George Smith, *Atheism: The Case Against God* (New York: Prometheus, 1989), p. 215.
3. C.S. Lewis, cited in Josh McDowell, *The New Evidence that Demands a Verdict* (Nashville, TN: Thomas Nelson Publishers, 1999), p. xxxvii.
4. See, for example, Earl Doherty, "An American and Atheist Novelist on the History of Religious Ideas," Part IV, posted at the American Atheists Web site, http://www. atheists.org/Atheism/fisher4.html.
5. Ronald Nash, "Was the New Testament Influenced by Pagan Religions?" Statement DB109, Christian Research Institute, www.equip.org.
6. Bruce Metzger, *Historical and Literary Studies: Pagan, Jewish, and Christian* (Grand Rapids: William B. Eerdmans Publishing Co., 1968), p. 11.
7. Nash, "Was the New Testament Influenced by Pagan Religions?"
8. Nash, "Was the New Testament Influenced by Pagan Religions?"
9. William Lane Craig and Walter Sinnott-Armstrong, *God? A Debate Between a Christian and an Atheist* (Oxford: Oxford University Press, 2004), pp. 70-71.
10. Craig and Sinnott-Armstrong, *God?* p. 71.
11. Frank Zindler, "Blind Faith," Part I, posted at The American Atheist Web site, http://www.AmericanAtheist.org/. See also Stephen VanEck, "All Prophets Were False," posted at the Infidels Web site, http://www.infidels.org/library/magazines/ tsr/1995/3/3proph95.html.
12. This objection sometimes surfaces on atheist and skeptic Web sites on the Internet.
13. See Lee Strobel, *The Case for Christ* (Grand Rapids: Zondervan, 1998), p. 133.
14. See Robert Reymond, *Jesus, Divine Messiah: The New Testament Witness* (Phillipsburg, NJ: Presbyterian and Reformed, 1990), p. 94.
15. See Robert Lightner, *The God of the Bible* (Grand Rapids: Baker Book House, 1978), p. 117.
16. Rob Bowman, *Jehovah's Witnesses, Jesus Christ, and the Gospel of John* (Grand Rapids: Baker Book House, 1989), p. 99.
17. William Barclay, *The Gospel of John*, vol. 2 (Philadelphia, PA: Westminster Press, 1956), pp. 42-3.
18. Millard Erickson, *The Word Became Flesh: A Contemporary Incarnational Christology* (Grand Rapids: Baker Book House, 1991), p. 434.

19. Jon Buell and Quentin Hyder, *Jesus: God, Ghost or Guru?* (Grand Rapids: Zondervan Publishing House, 1978), p. 27.

20. Reymond, *Jesus, Divine Messiah,* pp. 92-94.

21. Erickson, *The Word Became Flesh,* pp. 28-29.

22. David Wells, *The Person of Christ* (Westchester, IL: Crossway Books, 1984), pp. 64-65.

23. This objection sometimes surfaces on atheist and skeptic Web sites.

24. Smith, *Atheism,* p. 215.

25. Review of Ernest Renan, *The Life of Jesus* (London: Watts, n.d.), posted at Infidels Web site, http://www.infidels.org/library/historical/ernest_renan/life_of_jesus.html.

26. Peter Kreeft and Ronald Tacelli, *A Handbook of Christian Apologetics* (Downers Grove, IL: InterVarsity Press, 1994), p. 159.

27. Lee Strobel, *The Case for Faith* (Grand Rapids: Zondervan, 2000), pp. 146-47.

28. Ravi Zacharias, cited in Strobel, *The Case for Faith,* p. 150.

29. Zacharias, in Strobel, *The Case for Faith,* p. 156.

30. John Blanchard, *Whatever Happened to Hell?* (Durham, England: Evangelical Press, 1993), p. 113.

Chapter 11: The Evidence for the Resurrection

1. D.L. Moody, cited in Tim LaHaye, *Jesus: Who Is He?* (Sisters, OR: Multnomah Books, 1996), p. 150.

2. *Evangelical Dictionary of Theology,* ed. Walter A. Elwell (Grand Rapids, MI: Baker Book House, 1984), p. 724.

3. J.P. Moreland and Kai Nielsen, *Does God Exist? The Great Debate* (Nashville: Thomas Nelson Publishers, 1990), p. 192.

4. Michael Green, *Man Alive!* (Downers Grove, IL: InterVarsity Press, 1968), pp. 23-24.

5. Barry Leventhal, "Why I Believe Jesus Is the Promised Messiah," in Norman Geisler and Paul Hoffman, *Why I Am a Christian: Leading Thinkers Explain Why They Believe* (Grand Rapids: Baker Books, 2001), p. 214.

6. Norman Geisler and Frank Turek, *I Don't Have Enough Faith to Be an Atheist* (Wheaton, IL: Crossway Books, 2004), pp. 290-91.

7. Moreland and Nielsen, *Does God Exist?* p. 42.

8. Gary Habermas, in Lee Strobel, *The Case for Christ* (Grand Rapids: Zondervan, 1998), p. 230.

9. Jackson Carroll, as cited in Nancy Gibbs, "The Message of Miracles," *Time,* April 10, 1995, p. 64.

10. Robert Gundry, *Soma in Biblical Theology* (Cambridge, MA: Cambridge University Press, 1976), p. 168.

11. Keith Parson, as cited in Moreland and Nielsen, *Does God Exist?* pp. 190-91.

12. A.T. Robertson, *Word Pictures in the New Testament,* e-Sword Bible software.

13. Norman Geisler, "Evidence for the Resurrection of Jesus Christ from the Dead," Ankerberg Theological Research Institute Web site, www.johnankerberg.com.

14. Walter Sinnott-Armstrong, in William Lane Craig and Walter Sinnott-Armstrong, *God? A Debate Between a Christian and an Atheist* (Oxford: Oxford University Press, 2004), pp. 37-38.

15. Craig and Sinnott-Armstrong, *God?* pp. 72-73.

16. This objection often surfaces at atheist and skeptic Web sites on the Internet.

17. Craig and Sinnott-Armstrong, *God?* p. 37.

18. Craig and Sinnott-Armstrong, *God?* p. 70.

19. C.S. Lewis, cited in Ron Rhodes, "Witnessing to Liberals," *Christian Research Journal,* Winter 1993, p. 30.

20. Lewis, cited in Rhodes, "Witnessing to Liberals."

21. Canon Westcott, *The Gospel of the Resurrection,* Bible Illustrations, Logos Bible Software.

22. Sir Edward Clarke; cited by John Stott, *Basic Christianity* (Downers Grove, IL: InterVarsity Press, 1971), p. 47.

23. Cited by Wilbur Smith, *Sermons on the Christian Life;* cited in Bible Illustrations, Logos Bible Software.

Chapter 12: God and the Problem of Evil

1. William Lane Craig and Walter Sinnott-Armstrong, *God? A Debate Between a Christian and an Atheist* (Oxford: Oxford University Press, 2004), p. 89.

2. Kenneth Boa and Larry Moody, *I'm Glad You Asked* (Wheaton, IL: Victor Books, 1994), p. 129.

3. Norman Geisler, *Baker Encyclopedia of Christian Apologetics* (Grand Rapids: Baker Book House, 1999), p. 220.

4. William Dembski, *Intelligent Design: The Bridge Between Science and Theology* (Downers Grove, IL: InterVarsity Press, 1999), p. 263.

5. Geisler, *Baker Encyclopedia of Christian Apologetics,* p. 220.

6. Charles Templeton said the one thing that caused him to lose faith in God was a photograph in *Life* magazine of a black woman in Africa living in an area that had suffered a drought. She was pictured holding her dead child, looking up to heaven with a bereaved expression on her face. See Lee Strobel, *The Case for Faith* (Grand Rapids: Zondervan, 2000), p. 14.

7. Robert Morey, *The New Atheism and the Erosion of Freedom* (Minneapolis, MN: Bethany House Publishers, 1986), p. 153.

8. Morey, p. 153, insert added.

9. Jimmy Davis and Harry Poe, *Designer Universe: Intelligent Design and the Existence of God* (Nashville: Broadman & Holman Publishers, 2002), p. 221, emphasis added.

10. Annie Besant, "Why I Do Not Believe in God," *The American Atheist,* vol. 35, no. 4, posted at http://www.americanatheist.org/, insert added.

11. Paul Little, *Know Why You Believe* (Downers Grove, IL: InterVarsity Press, 1975), p. 81.

12. Millard Erickson, *Christian Theology* (Grand Rapids, MI: Baker Book House, 1987), p. 425.

13. Peter Kreeft, *Making Sense Out of Suffering* (Ann Arbor, MI: Servant Books, 1986), p. 123.

14. Kreeft, p. 123. Robert Morey, in like manner, suggests that God is dealing with the problem of evil in a progressive way that will not be complete until the future day of judgment. Speaking to an atheist, Morey argues, "You assume that God can solve the problem only in one single act. But why can't He deal with evil in a progressive way? Why does He have to deal with it all at once? Can't He deal with it throughout time as we know it and then bring it to climax on the Day of Judgment? You are assuming that the only way for God to deal with evil is in one single act. This is an erroneous assumption on your part. I am not saying that evil no longer exists. I am saying that God has solved the problem but in a long-term way, in stages" (Morey, pp. 154-55).

15. Dan Story, *Defending Your Faith* (Nashville: Thomas Nelson Publishers, 1992), pp. 176-77.

16. This objection sometimes surfaces at atheist and skeptic Web sites on the Internet.

17. Little, *Know Why You Believe*, p. 81.

18. Peter Kreeft, cited in Strobel, *The Case for Faith*, p. 37.

19. Gregory Boyd, *Is God to Blame? Beyond Pat Answers to the Problem of Suffering* (Downers Grove, IL: InterVarsity Press, 2003), p. 63.

20. Norman Geisler and Ronald Brooks, *When Skeptics Ask* (Wheaton, IL: Victor Books, 1990), p. 73.

21. Little, *Know Why You Believe*, p. 87.

22. William Lane Craig, *No Easy Answers* (Chicago, IL: Moody Press, 1990), p. 80.

23. Geisler, *Baker Encyclopedia of Christian Apologetics.*

24. Judy Salisbury, *A Christian Woman's Guide to Reasons for Faith* (Eugene, OR: Harvest House Publishers, 2003), pp. 119-20.

25. Boa and Moody, *I'm Glad You Asked*, p. 131.

26. Norman Geisler and Jeff Amanu, "Evil," in *New Dictionary of Theology*, eds. Sinclair Ferguson and David Wright (Downers Grove, IL: InterVarsity Press, 1988), p. 242.

27. Gordon R. Lewis and Bruce A. Demarest, *Integrative Theology* (Grand Rapids: Zondervan, 1996), I:322.

28. Lewis and Demarest, *Integrative Theology*, I:323.

29. Craig and Sinnott-Armstrong, *God?* pp. 92-93. Likewise, George Smith asks, "Why, in a world for which God is ultimately responsible, are there natural disasters that kill millions? Why are there diseases that cause suffering and cripple

innocent men, women and children?" George Smith, *Atheism: The Case Against God* (Amherst, NY: Prometheus Books, 1989), p. 80.

30. Smith, *Atheism*, pp. 82–83.
31. Craig and Sinnott-Armstrong, *God?* p. 85.
32. "The Craig-Washington Debate Does God Exist?" Dr. Craig's Third Rebuttal, Internet.
33. Craig and Sinnott-Armstrong, *God?*, pp. 116-17.
34. "The Craig-Jesseph Debate Does God Exist?" Dr. Craig's Second Rebuttal, Internet.
35. "Os Guinness Looks Evil in the Eye," interview with Os Guinness by Stan Guthrie, *Christianity Today*, March 10, 2005, Internet.
36. Craig, *No Easy Answers*, p. 90.
37. Paul Powell, *When the Hurt Won't Go Away* (Wheaton, IL: Victor Books, 1986), p. 62.
38. Miles Stanford, *Principles of Spiritual Growth* (Lincoln, NE: Back to the Bible, 1976), p. 11.
39. Cited in Strobel, *The Case for Faith*, p. 198.

Chapter 13: The Character Assassination of God

1. Thomas Jefferson, cited in George Smith, *Atheism: The Case Against God* (Amherst, NY: Prometheus Books, 1989), pp. 76-78.
2. Smith, *Atheism*, pp. 76-78.
3. Norman Geisler, cited in Lee Strobel, *The Case for Faith* (Grand Rapids: Zondervan, 2000), pp. 117-18.
4. See Norman Geisler, "God, Evil, and Dispensations," *Walvoord: A Tribute*, ed. Donald K. Campbell (Chicago, IL: Moody Press, 1982), p. 98.
5. Norman Geisler and Thomas Howe, *When Critics Ask: A Popular Handbook on Bible Difficulties* (Wheaton, IL: Victor Books, 1992), p. 271.
6. *The Expositor's Bible Commentary*, ed. Frank E. Gaebelein, in Accordance Bible Software, Oaksoft, 2003.
7. Walter C. Kaiser, Jr., *Toward Old Testament Ethics* (Grand Rapids: Zondervan, 1983), pp. 267-68, insert added.
8. Kaiser, *Toward Old Testament Ethics*, p. 268.
9. Smith, *Atheism*, p. 78.
10. Smith, *Atheism*, p. 299.
11. "The Craig-Bradley Debate: Can a Loving God Send People to Hell?" Internet.
12. Strobel, *The Case for Faith*, p. 158.
13. "The Craig-Bradley Debate: Can a Loving God Send People to Hell?" Internet.
14. Ravi Zacharias, cited in Strobel, *The Case for Faith*, p. 158.

Postscript: A Call to Courtesy

1. These definitions are derived from www.dictionary.com.

BIBLIOGRAPHY

Behe, Michael. *Darwin's Black Box.* New York: The Free Press, 1996.

Behe, Michael, William A. Dembski, and Stephen C. Meyer. *Science and Evidence for Design in the Universe.* Fort Collins, CO: Ignatius Press, 2002.

Berkhof, Louis. *Manual of Christian Doctrine.* Grand Rapids: Wm. B. Eerdmans Publishing Co., 1983.

———. *Systematic Theology.* Grand Rapids: Wm. B. Eerdmans Publishing Co., 1982.

Buswell, James O. *A Systematic Theology of the Christian Religion.* Grand Rapids: Zondervan Publishing House, 1979.

Craig, William Lane. *The Existence of God and the Beginning of the Universe.* San Bernardino, CA: Here's Life Publishers, 1979.

———. *No Easy Answers: Finding Hope in Doubt, Failure, and Unanswered Prayer.* Chicago, IL: Moody Press, 1990.

Craig, William Lane, and Walter Sinnott-Armstrong. *God? A Debate Between a Christian and an Atheist.* Oxford: Oxford University Press, 2004.

Davis, Jimmy H., and Harry L. Poe. *Designer Universe: Intelligent Design and the Existence of God.* Nashville, TN: Broadman & Holman, 2002.

Dawkins, Richard. *The Blind Watchmaker: Why the Evidence of Evolution Reveals a Universe Without Design.* New York: W.W. Norton, 1996.

Dembski, William A. *The Design Inference: Eliminating Chance Through Small Probabilities.* Cambridge: Cambridge University Press, 1998.

———. *Intelligent Design: The Bridge Between Science and Theology.* Downers Grove, IL: InterVarsity Press, 1999.

Dembski, William A., ed. *Mere Creation: Science, Faith and Intelligent Design.* Downers Grove, IL: InterVarsity Press, 1998.

Dembski, William A., and James M. Kushiner, eds. *Signs of Intelligence: Understanding Intelligent Design.* Grand Rapids: Brazos Press, 2001.

Denton, Michael. *Evolution: A Theory in Crisis.* Bethesda, MD: Adler and Adler, 1985.

Erickson, Millard J. *Christian Theology,* unabridged, one-volume edition. Grand Rapids: Baker Book House, 1987.

Evangelical Dictionary of Theology. Edited by Walter Elwell. Grand Rapids: Baker Book House, 1984.

Evans, Dylan, and Howard Selina. *Introducing Evolution.* Cambridge: Totem Books, 2001.

Feinberg, John S. *The Many Faces of Evil: Theological Systems and the Problem of Evil.* Grand Rapids: Zondervan, 1994.

Fortey, Richard. *Life: A Natural History of the First Four Billion Years of Life on Earth.* New York: Alfred A. Knopf, 1997.

Geisler, Norman. *Baker Encyclopedia of Christian Apologetics.* Grand Rapids: Baker Books, 1999.

———. *Christian Apologetics.* Grand Rapids: Baker Books, 1976.

Geisler, Norman, and Frank Turek. *I Don't Have Enough Faith to Be an Atheist.* Wheaton, IL: Crossway Books, 2004.

Geisler, Norman, and Paul Feinberg. *Introduction to Philosophy: A Christian Perspective.* Grand Rapids: Baker Books, 1980.

Geisler, Norman, and Paul Hoffman. *Why I Am a Christian: Leading Thinkers Explain Why They Believe.* Grand Rapids: Baker Books, 2001.

Geisler, Norman, and Ronald Brooks. *When Skeptics Ask.* Grand Rapids: Baker Books, 1989.

Geisler, Norman, and Thomas Howe. *When Critics Ask: A Popular Handbook on Bible Difficulties.* Grand Rapids: Baker Books, 1992.

Geivett, R. Douglas. *Evil and the Evidence for God: The Challenge of John Hick's Theodicy.* Philadelphia, PA: Temple University Press, 1993.

Gordon, Lewis, and Bruce Demarest. *Integrative Theology.* Grand Rapids: Zondervan, 1996.

Gould, Stephen Jay. *I Have Landed: The End of a Beginning in Natural History.* New York: Harmony Books, 2002.

Grudem, Wayne. *Systematic Theology: An Introduction to Biblical Doctrine.* Grand Rapids: Zondervan, 1994.

Guinness, Os. *Unspeakable: Facing Up to Evil in an Age of Genocide and Terror.* San Francisco: HarperSanFrancisco, 2005.

Hodge, Charles. *Systematic Theology,* abridged edition. Edited by Edward N. Gross. Grand Rapids: Baker Book House, 1988.

Jastrow, Robert. *God and the Astronomers.* New York, Norton, 1992.

Johnson, Phillip E. *Reason in the Balance: The Case Against Naturalism in Science, Law and Education.* Downers Grove, IL: InterVarsity Press, 1995.

———. *Darwin on Trial.* Downers Grove, IL: InterVarsity Press, 1993.

———. *Defeating Darwinism by Opening Minds.* Downers Grove, IL: InterVarsity Press, 1997.

Kreeft, Peter. *Making Sense Out of Suffering.* Ann Arbor, MI: Servant Books, 1986.

Kreeft, Peter, and Ronald Tacelli. *Handbook of Christian Apologetics.* Downers Grove, IL: InterVarsity Press, 1994.

Little, Paul. *Know Why You Believe.* Downers Grove: InterVarsity Press, 1975.

Lubenow, Marvin L. *Bones of Contention: A Creationist Assessment of Human Fossils.* Grand Rapids: Baker Book House, 1992.

McDowell, Josh. *The New Evidence that Demands a Verdict.* Nashville: Thomas Nelson Publishers, 1999.

McDowell, Josh, and Don Stewart. *Handbook of Today's Religions.* San Bernardino, CA: Here's Life Publishers, 1989.

Moreland, J.P., and Kai Nielsen. *Does God Exist? The Great Debate.* Nashville: Thomas Nelson Publishers, 1990.

Morey, Robert. *The New Atheism and the Erosion of Freedom.* Minneapolis: Bethany House Publishers, 1986.

Muncaster, Ralph. *A Skeptic's Search for God: Convincing Evidence for His Existence.* Eugene, OR: Harvest House Publishers, 2002.

Packer, J.I. *Knowing God.* Downers Grove, IL: InterVarsity Press, 1979.

Plantinga, Alvin C. *God, Freedom, and Evil.* Grand Rapids: William B. Eerdmans Publishing Co., 1974.

Ratzsch, Del. *The Battle of Beginnings.* Downers Grove, IL: InterVarsity Press,1996.

Rhodes, Ron. *The 10 Things You Should Know About the Creation-Evolution Debate.* Eugene, OR: Harvest House Publishers, 2004.

————. *Christ Before the Manger: The Life and Times of the Preincarnate Christ.* Grand Rapids: Baker Book House, 1992.

————. *The Complete Book of Bible Answers.* Eugene, OR: Harvest House Publishers, 1997.

————. *The Heart of Christianity: What It Means to Believe in Jesus.* Eugene, OR: Harvest House Publishers, 1996.

————. *Heaven: The Undiscovered Country—Exploring the Wonder of the Afterlife.* Eugene, OR: Harvest House Publishers, 1996.

————. *What Did Jesus Mean?* Eugene, OR: Harvest House Publishers, 1998.

————. *Why Do Bad Things Happen if God Is Good?* Eugene, OR: Harvest House Publishers, 2004.

Ross, Hugh. *The Creator and the Cosmos.* Colorado Springs, CO: NavPress, 2001.

Ryrie, Charles C. *Basic Theology.* Wheaton, IL: Victor Books, 1986.

Samples, Kenneth Richard. *Without a Doubt: Answering the 20 Toughest Faith Questions.* Grand Rapids: Baker Books, 2004.

Smith, George. *Atheism: The Case Against God.* New York: Prometheus Books, 1989.

Story, Dan. *Defending Your Faith: How to Answer the Tough Questions.* Nashville: Thomas Nelson Publishers, 1992.

Strobel, Lee. *The Case for Christ.* Grand Rapids: Zondervan Books, 1998.

————. *The Case for Faith.* Grand Rapids: Zondervan Books, 2000.

Zacharias, Ravi. *The Real Face of Atheism.* Grand Rapids: Baker Books, 2004.

About the Author

Dr. Ron Rhodes
Reasoning from the Scripture Ministries
P.O. Box 2526
Frisco, TX 75034

Web site: www.ronrhodes.org

E-mail: ronrhodes@earthlink.net

Free newsletter available upon request.

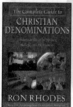